American & Soviet Aid

:

A Comparative Analysis

Robert S. Walters

University of Pittsburgh Press

American and Soviet Aid

To Linda

Contents

Tables and Figures

Preface

‡ This work was conceived five years ago, at a time when most of the literature on Soviet and American economic aid stressed fundamental differences in the goals, the methods of execution, and the results (economic and political) of the two programs. Moreover, among Western analysts of American and Soviet aid there was a tendency to conclude that the USSR was having much greater success with the aid instrument than was the United States. A major reason for this interpretation of relative aid performance was the fact that U.S. aid practices and problems throughout the fifties were analyzed and compared implicitly with a newly initiated Soviet aid effort which was only at the commitment stage and for which there was very little information on actual performance in the field. Soviet economic aid disbursements began in earnest at sustained levels only in 1961.

Now, after a decade of Soviet aid activities, there is enough evidence available to undertake a meaningful comparative analysis of the American and Soviet programs in practice. It is only through a comparison of aid efforts that we will be able to determine those aspects of economic assistance programs which are peculiar to one donor or the other, and those which seem to be characteristic features of any large aid program.

The focus of this work is upon the use of aid by the donors rather than the utility of aid to the recipients. Thus, the analysis is concerned with specific aid projects and programs in the field only insofar as they are illustrative of more general policies followed by the United States and the USSR in their aid efforts. Soviet and American aid will be described and compared in terms of what the donors expect from distributing aid (that is, why they are in the aid business), the evolution of doctrine as to the nature of the development process in less developed countries and aid's role in it, the magnitude, scope, and direction of aid disbursements, the programming practices used to distribute aid, the operational emphases of the programs, the terms accompanying aid, the problems the donors have faced in their efforts, and the results derived from aid.

Most of the research and the initial draft of this manuscript were completed during my tenure as a research fellow at The Brookings Institution in 1966–67. The following academic year I was afforded the rare opportunity to rethink and entirely rewrite the manuscript under a Horace H. Rackham postdoctoral research fellowship at the University of Michigan. I am most grateful to these institutions for their support. Moreover, I wish to express my thanks to the Center for Russian and East European Studies at the University of Michigan and its director Morris Bornstein for providing me with working space and secretarial assistance during the 1967–68 academic year.

Many individuals helped me in this effort. There are a number of persons in Washington, inside and outside of government service, who were indispensable in the gathering of facts on both aid programs, but who for understandable reasons would probably prefer to remain anonymous. More specifically, I wish to thank Robert Asher, Michel Hervé, and Karl Mathiason of The Brookings Institution for their insights on various aspects of American economic assistance. Philip Mosely of Columbia University generously made available research materials he has collected for a work on Soviet policies in the third world. William Ballis, Morris Bornstein, and Inis Claude read the manuscript at various points in its development and I owe them all a substantial intellectual debt for their various suggestions. Above all, I wish to thank Harold Jacobson whose advice, sustained interest, and substantive contributions at every stage of the evolution of the study are largely responsible for its appearance in book form. Of course, any errors of fact or inadequacies of interpretation are the responsibility of the author alone.

Finally, I wish to thank Beverly Reifert for her thoroughly professional job in typing the manuscript.

My wife has had to share the burdens in addition to the joys which accompany a publication effort. Because of her unbounded tolerance and usual good humor in the face of my various moods throughout this enterprise, the book is dedicated to her.

American and Soviet Aid

1

Introduction

‡ In 1966 the less developed countries[1] had a population of 1.6 billion—approximately one-half of the world's population. They comprise approximately one-half of the total land area of the world and number over ninety (a statistic particularly significant in the context of the United Nations, which is composed of 126 members). Even taking into account the fact that these figures do not accurately reflect the limitations in the political and economic power, influence, and significance of the LDCs in the world arena, they are, nevertheless, impressive enough to demonstrate convincingly the folly of any major power which would neglect to regard them as a crucial factor in international relations.

The United States and the Soviet Union have, indeed, recognized the importance of these countries, and nowhere is this manifested more clearly than in their distribution of substantial amounts of economic assistance to the less developed countries. The emergence of economic aid as an important instrument in the overall foreign policies of these great powers is evidenced by the length of time over which both countries have conducted aid programs, by the magnitude of cumulative aid commitments, and by the number and diversity of less developed countries which have been aid recipients. More specifically, economic assistance has become a primary means by which the United States and the

Soviet Union have sought to establish ties and exert influence in the third world.[2]

The reason for the importance attached to economic aid as an instrument of foreign policy lies largely in the LDCs themselves. Almost all of these nations were once subjects of colonial rule, and they emerged from colonialism and remain today at what they consider to be an intolerable level of economic development. The average per capita gross national product of less developed countries in 1968 was $196. The significance of this figure can be more fully appreciated when it is compared to the 1968 per capita GNP of the United States which was $4,000, approximately twenty times larger.[3] This difference in economic productivity has been firmly grasped by the leadership of the third world, and it has provided the foundation for their increasingly vocal political demand for the extraction of economic aid from the United States, the USSR, and other advanced countries.

The commitment to the goal of economic development is universal among leaders of all political philosophies in the third world. Max Millikan notes in this regard that "a half century ago the notion that to remain in power a ruling group in an Asian or African country had to demonstrate that it had positive plans for raising standards of living would have been laughable. Today it is accepted as obvious by politicians in all less developed countries."[4] Regardless of the probability of generating self-sustained economic growth in the LDCs, the fact is that these peoples are committed to that goal and give high priority to it.

Given this low level of economic development and the saliency of the political demand for economic growth in the less developed countries, it is no surprise that economic assistance should become a primary instrument in Soviet and American relations with the LDCs.

In addition to the positive demands for economic aid emanating from the third world, the political and military climate of the international arena since World War II has made economic assistance an instrument attractive to donors as well as recipients. It would appear, for example, that the reliance upon economic instruments by the United States and the USSR is based in part upon the fear of the consequences of competition on the military plane in a nuclear age. With increasing frequency economic means have come to be used as alternatives, if not substitutes, for tasks which used to be accomplished through military means. There seems to be a tacit understanding by both the United States and the Soviet Union that the dollar and the ruble—and not the display of military prowess—should pave the way to power in the less developed countries.

The carrot has increasingly come to replace the stick in relations between the great powers and the LDCs. If the United States were seeking to open up Japan today instead of in the mid-nineteenth century, it would send an undersecretary of state for economic affairs with a trade-and-aid package, not Commodore Perry and the fleet.

Finally, the emergence of a well-articulated opposition to colonialism, particularly in its overt forms, has prompted the leading powers to rely more on trade, aid, and other more subtle means of influence with less developed countries. It is the manner in which one of these economic instruments—aid—has been used and the expectations associated with the distribution of aid by the United States and the USSR which we wish to examine here.

Due to the emphasis on economic aid in Soviet and American relations with the LDCs it seems appropriate that an inquiry be made comparing the two programs on a more systematic basis than has heretofore appeared in the literature. As a result of the complexity of the aid instrument there are many basic approaches which one could take in such a comparative analysis: (1) the role of economic assistance in the economic and political development of the recipient; (2) the role of economic aid in the array of commercial and financial mechanisms used in the transfer of resources to the less developed countries; (3) the role of domestic political forces within and outside of the government of the donor nations in affecting the nature and amount of aid extended to the LDCs; and (4) the role of economic aid in the foreign policies of the donors. While a comprehensive study of economic assistance would require a detailed examination of all these and other facets of the problem, our basic concern will be with the last of the approaches mentioned above: economic aid as an instrument of foreign policy.

Whereas there are different reasons for initiating and continuing aid donations, it is indisputable that a common characteristic of all aid programs of Communist and non-Communist states alike is their function as an instrument of foreign policy. Thus, Taiwan may give aid to Africa to seek support for its position on the China question in the United Nations, France may give aid to her former colonies and other LDCs to maintain cultural influence in the third world, Yugoslavia and West Germany may give aid to promote and secure their positions in commercial markets, the United States may give aid to exert influence and to promote the economic and political development of the LDCs, and the Soviet Union may give aid to secure political and economic influence in less developed countries. But the essence of all these programs is their role in the foreign policy of the donor nations.

The irony in taking this position is that while most aid observers and participants in the United States agree readily to the proposition that all other countries, particularly the USSR, use aid for purposes of promoting their political interests abroad, many seem reluctant to view the American program in that context. Averell Harriman, a former U.S. aid administrator and by no means an unsophisticated thinker on questions of economic assistance, illustrated in testimony before the House Committee on Foreign Affairs this asymmetry in viewing the nature of Soviet and American aid:

I think our attitude [on economic assistance] is one quite different from the Soviets. The Soviet is going in there to try to get some political benefit, I think, from what they do. Whereas, ours is the most earnest and sincere and honest attempt to help the countries [LDCs] achieve the objective of improving the standard of living.[5]

In spite of this statement and the sentiment it represents, it would seem indisputable that the American aid effort, like that of the USSR and other aid donors, is fundamentally a foreign policy instrument. Many scholars, including John Montgomery, Edward Mason, Herbert Feis, and Hans Morgenthau,[6] have come to this conclusion. But one need only look at the presentation of the aid program to Congress every year, the testimony of aid administrators, and the aid legislation itself to be convinced. Take, for example, Section 2 of the Mutual Security Act of 1951, an early legislative act providing the framework for the United States economic aid program:

The Congress declares it to be the purpose of this act to maintain the security and to promote the foreign policy of the United States by authorizing military, economic, and technical assistance to friendly countries to strengthen the mutual security and individual and collective defenses of the free world, to develop their resources in the interest of their security and independence and the national interest of the United States and to facilitate the effective participation of those countries in the United Nations system of collective security. The purposes of the Mutual Defense Assistance Act of 1949 . . . the Economic Cooperation Act of 1948 . . . and the Act for International Development [other legislation covering all aspects of the U.S. aid program, economic and military] shall hereafter be deemed to include this purpose.[7]

An obvious consequence of the acceptance of the proposition that aid is basically an instrument of foreign policy—and the facts indicate that this is indeed the case—is to focus on the aid donor rather than the recipient. The approach itself thus explains why relatively little will be said about the less developed countries in comparison to the United States and the USSR, their foreign policies, and the nature of their aid programs.

2

Motivations for American Economic Aid

‡ Why do the United States and the Soviet Union give economic assistance? What results do they expect as a consequence? In what ways have they used aid in attempts to achieve these results? This and the following chapter seek answers to these questions. By addressing them we can begin to understand the nature of Soviet and American economic assistance. It would be virtually impossible to evaluate the achievements and to understand the difficulties of the programs without first attempting to understand the desires and expectations of the donors regarding their economic assistance.

U.S. Policy Toward the LDCs

At the end of World War II the United States adhered to a policy of condemnation of colonialism and of favoring independence for colonial peoples, with the reservation that the grant of independence should not be too hurried and should be given only to those peoples who desire it and are capable of assuming the responsibilities involved.[1] Consistent with this policy, the Philippines were granted independence on July 4, 1946. The United States also gave prompt recognition to the new states as they emerged in South and Southeast Asia—Burma, India, Pakistan, and Ceylon. The United States played its most active role through bilateral and multilateral means in helping to bring to an end the Dutch-Indonesian hostilities and supporting the Indonesian demand for independence.[2]

But in spite of American support for independence movements among the colonies, United States policy from 1945 to 1949 was characterized by the recognition of the European metropoles as primary agents in colonial states. Thus, until the outbreak of the Korean War the United States followed its traditional policy of deference to colonial powers in Southeast Asia[3] and other colonial areas.

This relatively passive role vis-à-vis the colonial states was accompanied by, and was partially a result of, an American preoccupation with the Communist threat in Europe. The priority of Europe in American foreign policy during the immediate postwar period was most clearly manifested in the substantial commitment of U.S. economic and military resources through the creation of the Marshall Plan and the North Atlantic Treaty Organization (NATO).

Several factors combined, however, to shift American interest toward the less developed countries in Asia. In Europe the success of the West in breaking the Berlin blockade and the effectiveness of NATO and the Marshall Plan evidenced a significant increase in the military, economic, and political stability of the area; consequently, the danger of Communist inroads in Europe seemed greatly diminished. In Asia, on the other hand, numerous countries were faced with armed Communist insurrection after 1948, China had fallen into the hands of Mao Tse-tung during 1949, and in 1950 the invasion of South Korea by North Korea had locked those two countries in a war. These events, along with the increasing inability of the European metropoles to maintain their influence in Asia, resulted in the abandonment of the traditional passive role played by the United States in its relations with less developed countries of South and Southeast Asia.

Economic and military assistance became the primary mechanisms through which the United States executed this policy shift and forged direct relations with most of the less developed countries. During the period between 1951 and 1956 the dominating circumstance determining the nature of American aid to the less developed countries was the Communist threat. Emphasis was placed on military aid to the LDCs designed to enable local forces to deter and/or meet overt Communist aggression of the Korean type. The largest amounts of economic assistance were distributed through a funding category the purpose of which was to assist less developed countries in the maintenance of a larger military establishment than could be provided for locally.

During the early and mid-fifties American foreign policy in general, as reflected in the economic aid program, tolerated neutralists but did not suffer them gladly. Secretary of State Dulles defended U.S. aid to India and Yugoslavia in the face of congressional attacks on these programs. However, his well-known strictures concerning the immorality and irresponsibility of neutralism as a foreign policy for LDCs and the policy of constructing an alliance system including less developed countries to ring the Communist world serve to demonstrate the primary interest of the United States in bringing the LDCs into commitment with the Western camp. It was not until 1957—at which time, incidentally, economic development replaced anticommunism as the dominant theme in American aid presentations—that the United States came to accept neutralism as a legitimate policy not fundamentally at odds with American interests in the third world.

Particularly by the early 1960s, the emergence of many African states with neutralist foreign policies provided irrefutable proof that neutralism was a numerically impressive movement in international politics which had to be accommodated in U.S. foreign policy. In addition, as the Afro-Asian neutralist camp grew in size and maturity, it revealed itself as an extremely diverse and heterogeneous phenomenon on most issues—thus rendering obsolete the Dulles concept of a relatively clearcut, bipolarized world (a Western analogue to Stalin's two-camp theory). Increased American understanding of neutralism as a manifestation of intense Afro-Asian nationalism and the awareness that these states were as jealous of their independence vis-à-vis the Communist countries as they were in their relations with the West enabled the United States to support neutralists more completely in their desire for economic development and independence from the West as well as the East.[4]

This shift in United States policy towards neutralism and economic aid for development was facilitated and subsequently accelerated by a gradual change in the Soviet-American confrontation from hostility to what has been called in the 1960s a "mixed-adversity" relationship.[5] By the late 1950s the relative thaw in the cold war enabled the United States to liberate itself from an almost exclusive preoccupation with anticommunism and to seek a new, more durable approach to relations with the less developed countries on grounds of mutual interest rather than of Western defense.

With this brief survey of U.S. policy in mind, economic assistance can be seen as a basic instrument through which the United States has implemented its foreign policy in the third world. This assumption necessarily involves an attempt to identify the major expectations and motivations underlying the aid program.

A note of caution should be introduced at this point regarding the attribution of traits such as expectations and motivations to a state or to a complex political program of a state. This practice invites the tendency to reify the state. Notwithstanding this danger, however, it is convenient to talk of such things as motivations underlying a nation's behavior when the state-as-actor approach is adopted for purposes of analysis.[6] Hopefully, an explicit recognition of this tendency toward reification can minimize the analytical dangers involved in the approach while still allowing the use of a verbal shorthand to discuss the question of what the United States hopes to accomplish through the extension of economic aid to the less developed countries.

The analysis which follows rests on the assumption that it is possible to identify most of the major factors motivating U.S. economic assistance through statements made about the program by decision-makers and scholars, combined with observations of actual behavior by the donor in the implementation of aid. All of the factors mentioned can be viewed as forces within the United States which serve to generate aid funds.

Economic assistance is used in different ways depending on the reasons for which it is extended. Therefore, some illustrative examples of the types of aid characteristic of the various factors prompting aid will be presented in addition to the expectations and motivations underlying the program.

Short-Term Political Influence

Several expectations of a short-term political nature are readily observable in U.S. aid rhetoric and behavior. One such expectation is that the United States can demonstrate its good intentions toward the less developed countries through the distribution of economic assistance. This gesture, in turn, is expected to elicit from the aid recipients goodwill and lasting friendship toward the United States. Henry G. Bennett, head of the technical assistance program in 1951, enunciated the friendship function of aid as follows: "We hope both the people and the governments [of aid recipient nations] will feel proud of the fact that they have been able to advance themselves through American assistance, and their friendship and understanding for the United States will be much greater."[7]

A second short-term political use of economic aid is prompted by the desire to gain greater access to decision-makers in the less developed countries. In this context economic assistance performs the function of a lubricant facilitating or making possible the conduct of diplomacy. The clearest manifestation of aid for such purposes is what is often called *presence aid* to newly independent countries of Africa. Since presence aid so vividly exemplifies certain of the political motivations underlying the American economic aid program, it is appropriate to quote at some length a description of its nature from a memorandum prepared by the Agency for International Development (AID) for the Senate Foreign Relations Committee in 1965:

The U.S. Government carefully considers whether diplomatic, aid and cultural relations between the new nation and its former metropole will adequately maintain a Western orientation within the country, or whether the United States wishes to establish more extensive ties with the new nation than diplomatic relations alone permit, in order to bolster the country's Western orientation and/or to promote more specific U.S. interests. . . .

In several of the east and southeast African countries which have become independent since 1960, U.S. economic aid programs were initiated before independence in an effort to establish working relations and begin building influence with the emerging leaders and groups. . . .

. . . Total reliance on the former colonial power is often politically unacceptable in the newly independent state. Moreover, the U.S. position on, for example, issues before the U.N. may differ from that of the former metropole. In such cases a modest U.S. assistance program may "sweeten" and thereby make possible continued primary reliance on the formed [*sic*] metropole, and/or may demonstrate U.S. concern and interest and thereby increase receptivity to U.S. views on international issues.[8]

Presence aid is found in its purest form in certain African countries with small programs, such as Niger, but it constitutes in one form or another at least a portion of virtually every program offered by the United States. This is not to suggest that the American program is different in its political characteristics from economic aid programs operated by other countries; indeed, in Niger, for example, in 1967 every country which maintained an embassy (France, the United States, West Germany, Israel, and Taiwan) gave aid in some form virtually as a prerequisite for access to the local government officials.

American economic assistance has been used in an attempt to influence the foreign policies of less developed countries. In its most salient form this has involved making aid extensions conditional upon the recipient's adoption of the American position on a specific foreign policy issue. The program of U.S. food shipments to India under the Food-For-Peace Act (which went into effect January 1, 1967) affords a good example of this use of aid. Congressional amendments to this act "prevent the United States from supplying food to countries that trade in any fashion with North Vietnam or that sell anything but medicine or nonstrategic food and agricultural commodities to Cuba."[9] This prerequisite was clearly designed to influence the position of India and other recipients on a matter of some importance in the foreign policy calculus of the United States. India's prime minister accepted aid with these stipulations at significant domestic political cost since the opposition accused the government of subordinating India's interests to American demands.[10]

Economic aid has also been utilized to influence domestic political development in the less developed countries. The evidence suggests there is little real understanding in any quarter of the political development process, much less a systematic method for guiding, by means of aid, political development of the less developed countries in a manner consistent with U.S. interests.[11] These interests would include the promotion of a pluralistic society, strong local government institutions, and democracy. However, the termination (though often temporary) of American economic assistance to dictatorial regimes coming to power through a coup d'etat is a minimal effort to use aid as a means of discouraging political behavior deemed by the United States to be inappropriate to the interests of a less developed country. Regardless of the efficacy of U.S. aid in influencing domestic political development of the less developed countries, the desire to use aid for this purpose is a motivating factor in the American aid effort.[12]

Thus, there are at least several types of direct, short-term political influence the desire for which serves as a motivation for American economic assistance. The expectation of amity, access to decision-makers, and influence over foreign and domestic policies of less developed countries are all important factors prompting the U.S. aid effort.

Anticommunism and Western Security

Due to the advent of the cold war following World War II, it is not surprising that, in addition to the political motivations outlined above, anticommunism and, more specifically, security vis-à-vis the Communist camp have played a dominant role among the motivations underlying the U.S. economic assistance program.

As to the more general proposition that anticommunism provides a significant motivating factor for U.S. economic assistance there can be little doubt. The conclusions of almost all students of

economic aid, the geographical distribution of U.S. economic
assistance, and American aid rhetoric all support this proposition.
One is especially impressed by the saliency of anticommunism as
a driving force in the American economic assistance program
when he looks through the congressional hearings of the last two
decades. Congressmen and aid administrators alike assert anticommunism as a basic tenet of aid.

This thrust in American aid has been played upon by the
Soviet leadership in its communications with the third world.
Khrushchev has suggested that the anti-Communist motivation
for U.S. and Western economic assistance is so pervasive that the
LDCs should give the USSR credit for whatever Western aid
they receive:

This aid which the capitalist countries are planning to extend to the states
which have recently won their independence should also be viewed as a
particular kind of Soviet aid to these states. If the Soviet Union [and the
Communist camp] did not exist, is it likely that the monopolies of the
imperialist powers would aid the underdeveloped countries? Of course not.
This has never happened in the past.[13]

As an instrument directed against communism, economic assistance has been used in various ways. It has been used as a
carrot to entice less developed countries into, or to reward them
for, joining the Western camp. Of the total economic aid distributed by AID and its predecessor agencies to the less developed
countries through fiscal year 1968, almost half went to nine LDCs
in the U.S. alliance system.[14] Aid has also been used in conjunction with other means to shore up unstable regimes in less developed countries against an actual or perceived Communist challenge during periods of economic and political crisis. American
economic assistance to the Dominican Republic subsequent to
the events in 1965 and to Greece in the late forties provides
examples of this type of aid.

Anticommunism as a motivation for American economic assistance is also manifested in the use of aid as a counterweight or
alternative to Communist aid programs in certain less developed
countries where it is felt that Communist aid may result in exces-

sive dependence on the Communist states, or where this aid is felt to conflict with vital U.S. interests.[15] American aid to Guinea after 1962 is a case in point.

On a more general plane, anticommunism can be considered as the basic underpinning of U.S. economic assistance to the extent that American interest in, and aid to, the less developed countries has been generated by the fear that such countries are most vulnerable to Communist inroads. The question raised here is whether or not the United States would show this interest and give aid were it not for the Communist threat. The answer is undoubtedly yes—as there are other motivating factors for economic assistance—but the interest would have been less, and the aid amounts smaller.

The military security of the less developed countries and of the United States—a factor closely related to anticommunism—has also prompted economic assistance. From 1951 to 1956 U.S. economic aid was viewed primarily in terms of supplementing the military assistance program. Military aid in the form of equipment, training, and advice was to provide security in the less developed countries from the external threat of Communist aggression (for which Korea after 1950 was the prototype) as well as from the internal threat of Communist-led armed insurrection. Economic aid in the form of capital equipment, technical assistance, and budgetary support was given for the purpose of maintaining domestic stability by subsidizing the military burden and providing the stimulus for at least modest economic progress.

The presence of military security as a significant motivation for U.S. economic aid, particularly during the early and mid-fifties, is exemplified in this statement by Secretary of State Dean Acheson: "Economic and technical assistance must be sufficient to support the military programs and to deal with some of the fundamental problems of weakness where weapons alone are no defense."[16] Also it should be noted that the preponderance of American economic assistance at this time was in the form of Defense Support which was defined as "economic aid to help . . . less developed countries receiving U.S. military aid to meet some of the economic and political burdens incurred by expanding the local defense establishment. The primary purpose therefore is military security, but some economic development may result as a byproduct."[17] Thus, economic aid has often followed and supplemented military assistance. South Korea, Taiwan, and Pakistan are the most striking examples of this facet of the American program.

Economic Benefits for the United States

The use of economic assistance to secure economic advantages for the United States has also been considered a motivation underlying the American aid program. It is argued that through aid which promotes economic development in less developed countries the United States can ensure adequate supplies of strategic raw materials, promote a favorable climate for private foreign investment in the LDCs, and create a larger demand for U.S. exports as a result of increased prosperity in these nations.

As a motivation for aid this argument acquires more significance when presented in its negative form. If the U.S. precipitates the universal hostility of the LDCs by denying them economic assistance and otherwise ignoring their demands, the long-range economic consequences could be a shortage of strategic raw materials, a dearth of opportunity for private foreign investment, and the lack of an adequate market for U.S. exports. When stated in this manner the economic benefit factor approximates the question of long-range influence and system maintenance, a motivation for U.S. aid discussed below.

In reality it would appear that the countries of the West have but a modest economic stake in the less developed countries. Only about one-fifth of Western exports go to the LDCs and this proportion has been falling since World War II. Intra-Western exchange is the fastest expanding and largest component of trade in the advanced market economies.[18] It is this trade which dominates the attention of policy-makers in the United States and Europe as evidenced by the emphasis accorded the Kennedy Round relative to that of the United Nations Conference on Trade and Development.

The distinctly secondary economic importance of the less developed countries to the West and the United States makes it unlikely that economic benefit for the donor is a strong motivating factor in the aid program. Practices which are frequently pointed to in confirmation of aid's contribution to the American economy are more often attempts to minimize the costs of aid to the United States than they are attempts to use aid for American economic benefit. For example, the practice of tying aid to purchases in the United States was designed primarily to lessen the negative impact of economic assistance on the overall U.S. balance-of-payments position, rather than to secure markets for American enterprises.

In the final analysis, it is unquestionably the fact that attempts have been made to maximize the economic benefits of the aid program accruing to the United States. Export-Import Bank long-term loans to the LDCs promote American exports, one-third of American steel exports are financed through AID,[19] and the U.S. merchant marine benefits from requirements that recipients use American bottoms to ship aid-financed goods whenever possible. But these practices do not mean that economic benefit for the United States is the driving force behind the aid effort.

Humanitarianism

Though it is difficult to point to specific cases other than emergency relief following natural disasters and contributions to some United Nations programs like UNICEF, humanitarianism must be considered an element motivating U.S. economic assistance. Humanitarianism is expressed in two distinct, but related, forms in this context—as a manifestation of Christian moral traditions and as an emergent secular commitment to international social welfare. Congressman Chester E. Merrow of New Hampshire provides us with a good sample of the religious commitment as an incentive for giving aid:

I cannot see for the life of me how we as a Christian nation can turn our back on giving economic assistance to these various countries, realizing the conditions in which they find themselves, and so I make the point that even if security were not involved, we would have the moral obligation.

As I have thought of these problems, . . . my mind always reverts to a statement in the story of the Last Judgment: "Inasmuch as you have done it unto one of the least of these my brethren, you have done it unto Me."[20]

The secular analogue to the religious reasons prompting aid is the extension of the national welfare state concept to the international community. The basis of this concept is an assertion of respect for the inherent value and dignity of the individual and the commitment to guarantee certain minimum living conditions consistent with the maintenance of that dignity. Many different national policies exist in an attempt to realize this commitment, but at the core of all of them is the transfer of resources from the rich to the poor in the nation. When the welfare state concept is extended to the international plane, economic assistance to the less developed countries becomes a mechanism through which wealth is transferred from the rich (states) to the poor (states) in the world. This feeling of obligation which triggers the transfer of wealth is certainly infinitely greater in a national community than in the international community, since there is some question as to the very existence of the latter in a meaningful sense. On the other hand, even if an international community does not yet exist in a form strong enough to internationalize welfare statism, many insist upon the need for the development of such a community, and economic assistance plays a central role in thought along this line.[21]

Underlying both the religious and the welfare state motivations for donating economic assistance is the moral dilemma facing the United States as a nation of immense abundance in a world where over half the population lives in poverty. Whereas humanitarianism is not always clearly visible in the calculus of the United States economic aid program, it nevertheless does constitute a factor in the generation of aid funds in America. It helps explain why aid is given even if it does not help much to explain how United States aid is implemented.

Cultural Influence and System Maintenance

Cultural influence and system maintenance provides a convenient rubric under which to discuss the long-term indirect motivations and expectations underlying United States economic assistance. By culture we mean simply the general attitudes, patterns of thought, and behavior (social, economic, and political) of a community. System maintenance is used in a loose sense to mean the preservation of the basic international order now existing for which the United States feels responsible and provides leadership.

Through economic assistance to the less developed countries, in conjunction with all other aspects of its foreign policy, the United States hopes to promote the acceptance of basic Western values in the third world. The nature of the cultural influence desired includes such things as the acceptance of private enterprise and private foreign investment as legitimate and desired aspects of economic growth in the LDCs. In addition, the United States seeks to promote the acceptance of basic Western values as to the structure of society and the legitimate forms of government. It is hoped that the less developed countries can realize their aspirations for political and economic development with the recognition that their achievements were supported and facilitated by the developed countries of the West, and the United States in particular.

Like economic benefits as a motivation for American economic assistance, the offering of aid because of the desire for cultural influence takes on more significance when viewed in a negative sense. United States economic assistance for this purpose is fundamentally preventive in nature. A most serious danger could face the United States in the long run (in fifty years or so) if the less developed countries of today grow to maturity through a process which results in hostility toward American and Western values in general. We have noted before that the ninety or so less developed countries comprise approximately one half of the world's population and land area. If, in addition, through economic development they come to control anywhere near the proportion of the world's industrial resources as that of their population, the international economic and political influence of these countries will be enormous. If the basic orientation of these countries is anti-American and anti-Western, the consequences for United States economic well-being, international political influence, and military security are obvious.

The possibility of such developments is not absurd when it is recognized that strong anti-Western feelings already exist because of the colonial past and that the inevitable frustrations which lie ahead for the less developed countries in their search for prosperity and influence may magnify the intensity of these feelings. Through economic assistance, as one of several coordinated instruments (cultural diplomacy, trade, etc.), the United States hopes to prevent the occurrence of just such a process.[22]

Economic assistance has several uses as an instrument facilitating maintenance of the international system for which the United States accepts responsibility and provides leadership. One important desire of the United States in this context is the minimization of violent conflict anywhere in the non-Communist world which would lead to disruption of the existing order. There is a conviction held in the United States that the improvement of economic well-being in the less developed countries is crucial to permit these states to establish stable domestic and international relationships with a minimum of violence.

This conviction that economic backwardness and violence are highly correlated was forcefully illustrated in a speech by Secretary of Defense Robert McNamara, in which he divided the countries of the world into rich, middle-income, poor, and very poor, with a rich country defined as one with a per capita income of $750 a year or more. He stated that of the twenty-seven countries in the rich category there was only one major upheaval in domestic territory since 1958. On the other hand, 48 percent of the middle-income countries, 69 percent of the poor countries, and 87 percent of the very poor countries have suffered serious violence since 1958. McNamara's conclusion was that "there is a direct and constant relationship between the incidence of violence and the economic status of the countries afflicted."[23]

It is clear when violence and economic backwardness are linked in this fashion that economic assistance leading to advancement in the less developed countries is in the interest of the United States in its role as a leading power in the existing international system.

At least two specific expectations from economic assistance rise from the general belief among U.S. decision-makers that economic development is directly related to reduced violence. The first expectation is that, in preventing the frustrations generated by lack of progress, economic assistance which results in economic development can be a crucial factor in preventing Communist or right-wing take-overs of the less developed countries. By its contribution to the internal stability of less developed countries, economic assistance is expected to prevent the occurrence of conditions which could lead to revolution from within or subversion from outside. Gunnar Myrdal calls this the "insurance theory of aid."[24]

A second expectation is that economic assistance can help prevent the occurrence of a power vacuum in a less developed country which seems to result inevitably as an arena for conflict among the large powers of the world. It seems to be a fundamental trait in the behavior of powerful states to move into areas where order has collapsed or is in danger of doing so. Thus, when the Congo revealed its inability for self-rule after the abrupt withdrawal of Belgian power, Soviet, American, Chinese, and Belgian presence quickly flowed into the vacuum. Ultimately the United Nations assisted in the reestablishment of a modicum of order by filling the vacuum with its own presence, but only through a process which left the United Nations itself in severe financial and political disarray. The tendency of unstable less developed countries to provide the occasion and arena for conflict among the great powers has been called "passive provocation" by I. L. Claude.[25] Insofar as U.S. economic assistance can contribute to internal stability preventing passive provocation on the part of the less developed countries, aid performs a useful function in maintaining world order.

Economic assistance when thus conceived in terms of system maintenance becomes part of a significantly expanded definition of United States security. Security becomes less exclusively military and comes to involve the promotion of economic development through aid. Robert McNamara emphasized this point in his most remarkable Montreal speech:

In a modernizing society [and for the U.S. as a power interested in system maintenance], *security means development.*

Security *is* *not* military hardware—though it may include it. Security is *not* military force—though it may involve it. Security is *not* traditional military activity—though it may encompass it.

Security *is* development.

Without development, there can be no security.[26]

In summary, it becomes evident that economic and political development of the less developed countries is the primary goal of aid for cultural influence and system maintenance. United States economic assistance for development purposes in this case is given with the expectation that in the long run it can serve as a vehicle to transmit Western attitudes and structures to the less developed countries, to associate the United States with the interests of these countries, and to minimize frustration in the LDCs which might make attractive radical (and violent) solutions to economic and political problems. This type of aid is also largely preventive in that it seeks to guide the development process into channels which will result not in hostility between the United States and the less developed countries, nor in providing opportunities for Communist take-overs, nor in providing occasions for violent conflict among the LDCs or among the great powers over these countries. It is hoped that the ultimate result will be a stable world order consistent with basic Western and American interests.

Other Aid Programs

Finally, two aid programs other than present U.S. economic assistance have prompted the initiation and continuation of a substantial U.S. aid program in the less developed countries: the Marshall Plan and the Soviet aid program. American economic assistance to Europe under the Marshall Plan made possible the restoration of a modern, strong, self-sufficient industrial complex within a decade. This phenomenal success gave the United States confidence in the aid instrument and prompted economic aid to the less developed countries. When the problems of U.S. economic assistance are examined, we will return to the impact of Marshall aid on development assistance, but at this time it is sufficient to point out that America's success in Europe was a motivating factor in and stimulus to giving substantial aid to the less developed countries.

The Soviet aid program since 1954 has also provided an incentive for the continuation of American economic assistance. While there is little evidence to suggest that the United States has tried to match Soviet aid project for project, it is generally felt that it would be impossible to terminate U.S. aid extensions, for whatever reason, and thereby leave the Soviet Union as the major aid donor to the less developed countries.

Summary

It is clear from this discussion that there are a multiplicity of motivations and uses for American economic assistance—political influence of various types, anticommunism, security of the non-Communist world, economic benefit for the United States, humanitarianism, and cultural influence and system maintenance. All of these aspects can be found with varying degrees of emphasis for any time period during which one wishes to examine American economic assistance to the less developed countries, but their relative priorities change.

From 1949 when President Truman proposed Point Four through 1950 when the Korean War broke out, economic aid to less developed countries was characterized by emphasis on low-cost technical assistance, and humanitarianism was probably at its strongest as a motivating factor in the program. From 1951 to 1956 the emphasis of the program was economic assistance in the form of Defense Support to less developed countries which were allies of the United States. This was the period during which the United States forged its alliance systems around the Communist countries, and anticommunism and military security provided the dominant motivation for economic aid. From 1957 to 1961 serious reappraisal of the aid program by Congress and the Executive led to a gradual shift toward assistance for economic development in the form of Development Loans and increased shipments of food surpluses. Neutralist countries received more aid during these years than previously and the motivation for the aid program, while retaining its anti-Communist theme, began to substitute the more broadly conceived desire for cultural influence and system maintenance in place of the narrowly defined military security which had been characteristic of the previous five years. Since 1961, when AID was created, assistance for economic development has become the basic thrust of the program. Development loans and technical assistance in the areas of education, agriculture, and health have been emphasized. As a motivating factor in the program, cultural influence and system maintenance through economic development have become an increasingly important accompaniment to anticommunism. With the notable exception of Vietnam, economic assistance for the narrow purpose of military security has become progressively less significant as manifested by the attempt to phase out Supporting Assistance, the present equivalent of Defense Support.

This brief outline of various phases of the American economic assistance program to the less developed countries shows the change of relative priorities among the various motivating factors and uses of aid mentioned above. It should be reemphasized that while the priorities of the motivations change, all of these factors are present at any given time.[27]

It is unquestionably true that economic development of the less developed countries has been a central goal of American economic assistance. It is equally true that this goal has been pursued for a variety of reasons which we have discussed as motivations for economic aid. What should be evident is the fact that aid for economic development is not given selflessly or disinterestedly—U.S. economic aid is intensely political and exists because of the feeling that it is in the interest of the United States to conduct such a program.

This is not to suggest that the American program is peculiarly sinister; as we shall see, the Soviet economic aid program has at least as many political overtones as that of the United States. Indeed, without political and economic self-interest as basic motivating factors, it is highly improbable that the United States, the Soviet Union, or any other power would become major aid donors.

3

Motivations for
Soviet Economic Aid

‡ An attempt to analyze the motivations underlying the use of economic aid by the Soviet Union is even more difficult than in the case of the United States. The tendency toward reification is as prevalent as it is in an examination of the American program. But, in addition to the general problems of identifying motivations for any political program, American or Soviet, there is a paucity of detailed information on Soviet aid—particularly from Soviet sources, which are relatively few in number and extremely general and repetitious in content. Nevertheless, the principal motivations and expectations can be deduced from observing the manner in which Soviet aid has been implemented, combined with statements about the program by Soviet commentators, scholars, and decision-makers.

Some remarks concerning the general evolution of Soviet policy vis-à-vis the less developed countries since World War II will help to explain the emergence of economic assistance as an important instrument of Soviet foreign policy. Then the specific motivations for Soviet aid can be dealt with in detail.

Soviet Policy Toward the LDCs

The striking feature of Soviet policy toward the less developed countries after World War II was the shift from hostility to the

embrace of national bourgeois leaders of newly independent
states. In the immediate postwar period through the early fifties
the USSR viewed the emerging nations with suspicion and hostility because of the conviction that such states and their leaders
were still controlled by the West. Nehru, Sukarno, Nasser, and
other leaders were repeatedly vilified as "imperialist lackeys" and
"fascist usurpers." The USSR was imprisoned by the Stalinist
"two-camp" interpretation of the world which allowed no possibility for the existence of neutral states between the capitalist
West and Communist countries under the leadership of the Soviet Union. These convictions of the incompatibility of the USSR
and the emerging nations led to a policy of seeking to undermine
new governments and to institute Communist regimes in place of
national bourgeois leaders. The Second Party Congress of the
Communist Party of India and a youth congress, both held in
Calcutta in 1948, are often pointed to as the occasions for the
implementation of this policy, because within months after these
gatherings numerous Asian states were confronted simultaneously with overt Communist-led revolts. Such was the case in
Iranian Azerbaijan, the Philippines, Indonesia, Malaya, Burma,
and India (not to mention the struggle in French Indochina).

All of these attempts to capture power through internal rebellion ended in failure, except in French Indochina. In the latter
case the colonial power still ruled, allowing Ho Chi-minh to
become identified as the leader of national independence. In all
the other cases the countries were pushed closer to the West.

Another manifestation of militancy in Soviet policy of the period was, of course, the Korean War. The quick, surprising American and United Nations response was ultimately effective in
casting doubt on the efficacy of this type of behavior in addition
to internal insurrection.

During the period of Soviet militancy, roughly from 1948 to
1953, Soviet commercial policy viewed the former colonies as
convenient sources of various raw materials to be utilized when
the Soviet Union faced temporary shortages of those items. The
USSR usually paid for such purchases with proceeds from sales
made to the advanced nations of the West. There was virtually no

effort to enter into regularized trade with the less developed countries.

Between 1953 and 1956 several factors contributed to a significant alteration of Soviet policy toward the newly independent countries. Most important was the almost universal failure of internal rebellion and external aggression to yield gains for the Communists in the less developed countries. Stalin's death in early 1953 was also a factor in the policy shift. For, whereas Stalin undoubtedly recognized the failure of Soviet militancy and the need for a new approach, Malenkov's commitment to the New Course in Soviet domestic affairs provided the basis for a more fundamental change in foreign policy than Stalin probably would have attempted. Certainly, Malenkov's accession to power facilitated the change.

In addition, India's behavior during the Korean War demonstrated convincingly the possibility of there being a truly neutralist state in the cold war. India's refusal to support the West on the United Nations resolution branding Communist China an aggressor in Korea, and other independent actions, convinced the USSR that at least some former colonies did indeed possess a will independent of their former metropoles. This realization was crucial in allowing the Soviet Union to abandon the two-camp view of the world which had provided the basis for its hostility towards the less developed countries.

Finally, between 1952 and 1954 Soviet thinking on the nature and consequences of war in a nuclear era changed significantly. Until 1952 Soviet sources minimized the significance of nuclear weapons as a determining factor in military operations.[1] In addition the USSR did not expect that the United States would respond to Communist thrusts in the LDCs in a manner which would lead to general war. These two factors in combination contributed to the Soviet willingness to rely upon violence as a means of gaining influence abroad.

Perhaps because of the increase in Soviet understanding of the potential of nuclear weapons (which must have occurred by the time the USSR exploded a hydrogen device in August 1953), a basic shift occurred in Soviet thinking. At least one important faction in the Soviet leadership began to realize and publicize the awesome destructive power of nuclear weapons, as evidenced by Malenkov's famous statement of March 1954 (in spite of its subsequent retraction) that nuclear weapons do not discriminate among classes and that their use would mean the ruin of world civilization.[2] This increasing fear of nuclear weapons, plus the realization that the United States had indeed gone to war over Korea, undermined the basic assumptions underlying Soviet policy prior to 1952.

The combination of all these factors prompted the Soviet Union to abandon its almost exclusive reliance on violence as a means of influence in the less developed countries. Peaceful coexistence was the new policy adopted which would allow the USSR to exert influence in the third world while minimizing violence and its potential danger to the USSR. The essence of peaceful coexistence is the shift of East-West competition to nonmilitary spheres (such as cultural, political, and economic diplomacy) while still maintaining the legitimacy of wars of "national liberation" and of self-defense.[3]

The basic Soviet view of the less developed countries changed radically from that held in the period 1948–1953. The previously vilified national bourgeois leaders were now extolled as great patriotic leaders of gallant peoples, and the neutralist less developed countries were accepted as being politically independent of the West. The USSR came to believe that in the short term, at least, countries might exist which because of their own convictions and interests chose to be aligned with neither the West nor the Communist camp. This change in thinking necessitated the abandonment of the two-camp theory of the world. In its place was substituted what came to be called the "zone of peace" by the time of the Twentieth Party Congress in 1956. The "zone of peace" is the Soviet expression for what it views as a common position of the USSR and nonaligned less developed countries on matters such as peace, development, anticolonialism, imperialism, and disarmament.[4]

Concomitant with the basic shift in Soviet foreign policy outlined above was the increased reliance on economic means of influencing the less developed countries. A sweeping economic offensive in the third world emerged after 1953 in the form of numerous trade and economic aid agreements. The symbol of this change in policy and the initiation of the economic offensive was the speech of A. A. Arutiunian, the Soviet delegate to the United Nations Economic and Social Council on July 15, 1953, in which he announced that the Soviet Union would begin participation in the provision of technical assistance for the less developed countries by contributing the ruble equivalent of one million dollars to the United Nations Expanded Program of Technical Assistance (EPTA).[5] Within six months of this announcement the USSR had concluded trade agreements with Argentina and India and had announced a bilateral economic aid agreement with Afghanistan for the construction of grain silos, a bakery, and a flour mill.

Although in retrospect it is clear that the Soviet Union began a concerted economic offensive in 1953, it was not until several years later that the seriousness of its interest in the program was recognized in the West. Indeed, it was not until 1956 that the USSR publicized its commitment to trade and aid to the less developed countries through a statement made by Khrushchev in the report of the Central Committee to the Twentieth Party Congress:

These countries [LDCs] although they do not belong to the socialist world system, can draw on its achievements in building an independent national economy and in raising their people's living standards. Today they need not go begging to their former oppressors for modern equipment. They can get it in the socialist countries, free from any political or military obligations.[6]

A discussion of postwar Soviet policy in the less developed countries is necessary for any understanding of Soviet economic assistance as it has emerged and developed in the fifties and sixties. It is evident that before 1953 the basic orientation of the USSR towards the newly independent countries precluded even a desire to establish an aid program. Also, in light of the reasons for switching to the policy of peaceful coexistence, it is easy to see why trade and aid as instruments for influence outside the military sphere came to occupy a dominant position in Soviet relations with the less developed countries. With this background in mind it becomes easier to analyze some of the basic motivations for Soviet economic assistance.

Short-Term Political Influence

There are several forms of short-term political influence which constitute important factors in the extension of Soviet aid to the less developed countries. Among these is the use of aid, combined with trade, as a means of political entree to countries which previously have had no formal contacts with the USSR.

Prior to 1953 the USSR had virtually no contacts with the governments of the less developed countries, preferring instead to work with local Communist parties in these countries in an attempt to overthrow the national bourgeois leaders. After the abandonment of this policy, for reasons mentioned above, the Soviet Union sought through trade and aid agreements to forge regularized economic, diplomatic, and cultural channels between itself and the governments of the LDCs. On various occasions the USSR and other Communist countries have accompanied the establishment of diplomatic relations with trade and aid agreements. For example, in 1960 and 1961 Cuba signed separate credit agreements with the USSR, Communist China, East Germany, Bulgaria, Czechoslovakia, Hungary, Poland, and Rumania. In each case diplomatic relations were established within months of the aid agreements.[7] Regardless of whether or not Cuba is considered to have been solidly in the Communist orbit at that time, the example vividly illustrates the utility of aid agreements as a means of formal political entree.

Trade and aid have proved to be well adapted for establishing a Soviet presence in areas where its influence previously had been marginal or nonexistent. In the Near East and South Asia, particularly, the USSR has achieved notable success in such endeavors as reported by Robert L. Allen as early as 1957:

It has been more than a century since Russia has enjoyed its present influence in the Middle East. Four years of persistent effort, using credit for arms, capital goods, and technical assistance as one of the principal tools, has made it difficult to conceive of any solution to Middle Eastern problems without considering the USSR.[8]

What type of direct influence does the Soviet Union seek to exert with economic assistance once its presence is established? Certainly, one result desired from credit extensions to the less developed countries is the creation of goodwill and trust toward the USSR. This use of aid closely parallels that facet of the American program which stresses the promotion of friendship through aid. Like the United States, the Soviet Union hopes to be perceived by the LDCs as a champion of their aspirations for economic development and independence.

The USSR has used economic assistance as a means of demonstrating that, contrary to Western arguments, its intentions vis-à-vis the newly independent countries are honorable, its technology and equipment are sophisticated, and its agreements are advantageous to the LDC partner as well as to the Soviet Union. Thus, one motivation for Soviet aid has been to present the image of the USSR as a first-rate power rivaling the United States economically, technologically, politically, and militarily. At the same time it hopes to convince the LDCs that they can enter into regularized relations with the USSR without the fear that their independence or progress may be compromised in the process. Aid in this sense has a trust-building function enabling the Soviet Union to extend itself and to become accepted as a legitimate major power in world affairs.

Another aspect of direct political influence as a motivation for Soviet economic assistance is the desire to affect foreign policy positions of the less developed countries. The use of aid for this purpose is most clearly manifested in unreserved Soviet support of newly independent countries' espousals of neutralism, anti-colonialism and anti-Westernism. The Soviet aid program made neutralism pay as a foreign policy stance for less developed countries. Through economic aid to neutralist states the USSR provided an alternative source of capital and technical assistance which served to strengthen LDC bargaining power with the West.

The Soviet Union has used offers of economic assistance in an attempt to induce the adoption of a neutralist stance by less developed countries. In December 1959, when the USSR announced an agreement to provide Afghanistan with economic credits of $100 million, the neutrality and nonaggression pact between these countries was extended.[9] Similarly, the Soviet Union sent a high-level mission to Teheran in February 1959 to extend economic aid in return for Iran's signing a fifty-year nonaggression pact with the USSR and adopting a policy of neutralism.[10] The offer to Iran failed, but the attempt, along with the Afghanistan example and the overwhelming proportion of total Soviet economic assistance going to neutralist states, is convincing evidence that the desire to prompt LDCs to adopt a neutralist foreign policy constitutes a motivation for Soviet economic aid.

The desire for direct short-term influence in the domestic politics of less developed countries provides still another motivation for Soviet economic assistance. As is true of the United States, the Soviet Union attempts to influence the domestic political and economic development of its aid recipients by giving aid in forms which the donor feels will precipitate a desirable path of development for LDCs. For example, Soviet aid is concentrated in the state sector to strengthen the role of the government in national economic and political development and to preclude the development of private and local interests which might successfully challenge the priority of the state sector in the development process.

Another form of direct influence on the domestic politics of Soviet aid recipients is illustrated by the 1961 incident in Guinea, in which Sékou Touré accused the Soviet ambassador, Daniel Solod, of fomenting a teachers' strike and encouraging a coup.[11] The extent to which the accusation was valid is as yet unclear; however, it is evident that the Soviet Union had established many domestic contacts in Guinea as a result of its virtual aid monopoly in the country prior to 1961. Whether or not the USSR was actually involved in the strike or a coup attempt, Sékou Touré obviously was concerned about the extent of Soviet influence on domestic politics established through its aid presence.

Thus, like the United States economic aid program, Soviet aid is in large part motivated by the desire to exert direct political influence of various forms on the less developed countries. The desire to establish regularized economic and diplomatic channels with the LDCs, to generate feelings of mutual goodwill and trust between these countries and the USSR, and to exert influence on their foreign and domestic politics are all factors helping to explain why the USSR offers economic assistance.

Anti-Westernism and Soviet Security

Anti-Westernism plays a role in Soviet economic assistance very similar to the one anticommunism plays in the American program. Soviet behavior in connection with trade and aid agreements, as well as the anti-Western rhetoric which dominates all Soviet discussions of economic assistance, conclusively demonstrates that this is a basic motivation and use of Soviet aid. Soviet literature on economic assistance has as an underlying theme the defamation of American economic assistance. Surrounding almost every Soviet aid agreement is an attempt to portray U.S. aid as exploitative in its terms (high interest rates), antidevelopmental in its focus (nonindustrial projects), and dangerous to the recipient (political strings). The unrelenting abuse leveled against U.S. aid efforts suggests that one motivation for Soviet aid is the attempt to discredit the American and Western programs.[12]

A similar conclusion results from observations of the manner in which Soviet aid has been distributed. The USSR has characteristically extended credits closely following Western abandonment —particularly abandonment by the United States—of an aid package important to a less developed country. This has occurred with specific projects (such as the Bokaro steel mill in India and the Aswan dam in Egypt, which are both being financed by the USSR after the United States considered and rejected their support) and with entire country programs (such as Soviet aid to Guinea in 1958 after the Western nations at French insistence abandoned her).

There are also instances where the USSR stepped in to relieve serious problems faced by certain less developed countries when their primary products were unsalable in Western markets due either to boycott by principal buyers or to a surplus in the world market. Soviet purchases of Iceland's fish boycotted by Britain and of Cuban sugar boycotted by the United States provide examples of the former situation. Agreements involving exports of Burmese rice and Egyptian cotton provide examples of the USSR as a buyer of surplus goods.

The timing of Soviet purchases from less developed countries, the adoption of major aid projects following their rejection by the United States or the West, and the nature of Soviet literature on aid are all illustrative of the uses of Soviet economic assistance as an anti-Western instrument.

Soviet concern for its military security provides another impetus to the economic assistance program. Soviet support for neutralism in the third world and the distribution of most economic aid to neutralist states have been noted above. One reason for USSR interest in neutralism is that such a policy tends to preclude the formation of an alliance between an LDC and the West. Soviet discomfort about the U.S. alliance system surrounding the Communist world has been manifested in frequent attempts by the USSR to mobilize international opinion against the maintenance of overseas military bases by the Western powers. Through aid to neutralist states combined with other forms of support (military, diplomatic, economic, and cultural), the USSR seeks to prevent more less developed countries from joining the Western alliance system.

A more direct use of Soviet economic assistance for security reasons is the recent practice of distributing substantial aid to U.S. allies bordering the Communist world. The purpose of such aid offers is to penetrate and weaken the Western alliance system with the aim of enticing its LDC members to adopt a neutralist policy. This type of aid is designed to convince Western-oriented less developed countries that the USSR does not really constitute a threat to their independence. In 1965 the USSR extended about $655 million of new economic assistance: $540 million, over 80 percent of these new commitments, was concentrated in Iran, Turkey, and Pakistan.[13] Since previous credit agreements with the countries are very small in comparison to those negotiated in 1965, it seems reasonable to conclude that LDCs allied with the United States—in addition to neutralist countries—will be future targets of Soviet trade and aid. This new emphasis was corroborated by the 1967 agreement to extend *military* assistance of $110 million to Iran.[14]

Humanitarianism

Humanitarian overtones can be found in connection with Soviet aid to less developed countries. The USSR manifests what it generally calls the "internationalist duty of a socialist country" to help LDCs which have suffered at the hand of colonialism. Soviet humanitarianism is linked quite directly to anticolonialism,[15] but it still constitutes a form of humanitarianism. Evidence of such a motivation for Soviet economic assistance can be seen in statements like the following:

In giving aid the Soviet Union does not base itself primarily on consideration of commercial advantage. Guided by the principles of proletarian internationalism, the Soviet Union considers such aid important and necessary both from the standpoint of humanity and the solidarity of all mankind, and from the struggle for peace and peaceful coexistence between countries with differing social and political systems.[16]

There is a tendency to discount the humanitarian element as a factor motivating Soviet aid because it is usually accompanied by anti-imperialist, anti-Western rhetoric which obviously serves Soviet interests. However, as John Pincus has suggested in connection with large Western aid donors, the humanitarian sentiment is almost always "a judicious mixture of altruism and self-serving."[17] With limited funds any donor's first obligation is to those recipients and those causes with which its ties are closest.[18] Without attributing too much importance to the influence of humanitarian motivations on the Soviet economic aid program, it does appear that "the Russians feel they have an obligation [however small] as Communists and as human beings to facilitate the industrialization of these areas [LDCs].[19]

Economic Benefit for the USSR

The desire for economic benefit is another factor often mentioned as a motivation for Soviet trade and aid in the third world.

Due to the structure of Soviet economic investment and development it is argued that the relative cost of production in the USSR today is higher in the nonindustrial sectors (the extractive industries and agriculture) than it is in the industrial sector, particularly in heavy industry.[20] It seems, also, that the terms of trade between capital goods which the USSR exports and the primary goods which the USSR imports have not turned so as to affect the relative cost situation.[21] These two factors combined suggest that the Soviet Union can enlarge its total product by exporting increasing quantities of capital goods and importing greater quantities of raw materials and agricultural products.[22] The structure of Soviet trade with the LDCs arising out of the economic offensive is indeed consistent with this economic argument: the USSR generally exports industrial goods in return for agricultural products, raw materials, and semimanufactures.

An additional economic motivation for trade and aid is the fact that Soviet industrial products do not sell well in the highly industrial and competitive markets of the West while they are acceptable to and desired by many less developed countries. This problem is shared by the East European countries, and a Yugoslavian source explicitly gives this as a reason for their economic interest in the third world.[23]

The relationship of Soviet aid to the economic arguments outlined above lies in the fact that the only way the USSR and other Communist countries can conduct a program of industrial exports to less developed countries is by means of extending economic credits. The LDCs could not otherwise afford to purchase these products. Also, while they find Soviet products acceptable, the LDCs prefer Western goods of higher quality and with which they are generally more familiar. Soviet credits on easy terms serve as an inducement to purchase Soviet goods in place of Western products.

These are the basic arguments underlying the proposition that economic benefit is a motivating factor in the Soviet economic aid program and in Soviet trade. The USSR reinforces this explanation of its trade and aid by maintaining that Soviet economic relations with less developed countries are based on "mutual advantage." Through aid repayable in traditional exports of the recipient, the USSR obtains goods necessary for its own economy such as cotton, wool, natural rubber, hides, and cocoa.[24]

There is, however, much evidence to indicate that the economic criterion is not a determining factor in Soviet trade and aid policy. Several points should be mentioned with regard to the proposition that the relative cost situation dictates a Soviet trade policy focusing on the exchange of industrial products in return for nonindustrial imports from the less developed countries. First, the deficiencies in Soviet cost and price data probably make it impossible for even the USSR to calculate with any real accuracy the extent to which these relative cost differences actually exist and the extent to which trade should be restructured to increase the total Soviet product on the basis of this criterion.[25] Even if such calculations were reliably determined, there would have to be some indication that the USSR intended to reorient domestic production to benefit from the cost advantage in industrial production, if the economic criterion were to be considered a determining factor in trade and aid to the LDCs.

In fact, the USSR apparently is still not willing to substitute the acquisition of nonindustrial goods through trade with the less developed countries for domestic production of the same goods. Soviet domestic production of synthetic rubber, cotton, wool, sugar, and other goods which figure prominently in its trade with the LDCs has continued to expand, and the purchase of these products in the third world provides a supplement to Soviet production rather than a substitute for it. Thus, it appears that whereas the structure of Soviet trade with the LDCs is consistent with the economic argument for Soviet trade and aid in the third world, this economic logic can explain but a small portion of Soviet behavior in its relations with the less developed countries.

The evidence suggests that economics is not the main reason the USSR is in the aid business. Though there are many Soviet assertions that trade and aid with the less developed countries are "mutually advantageous" and desired by the USSR on economic grounds, there are also numerous statements in Soviet literature that credits to the LDCs are uneconomical to the USSR. Khrushchev, for example, made the statement:

While the Soviet Union and other socialist countries consider it their duty to help underdeveloped countries . . . we cannot say that our economic relations are based on mutual advantage. Generally speaking from the commercial standpoint our economic and technical assistance to underdeveloped countries is even unprofitable for us.[26]

In light of these statements, we have to look beyond considerations of relative costs and economics to find the motivation for Soviet economic assistance. Khrushchev confirmed that politics rather than economics provides the basis for Soviet trade and aid with the less developed countries in a statement to five U.S. senators visiting the USSR in 1955, widely circulated since then, that "we [the USSR] value trade least for economic reasons and most for political purposes."[27]

The timing of Soviet trade and aid agreements so as to maximize embarrassment to the United States and the West, the difficulty in calculating economically sound trade policy from Soviet cost and price data, and statements by Soviet scholars and leaders would all suggest that economic benefit to the USSR is by no means the most significant motivation for trade and aid in the less developed countries. Nevertheless, it is probably true that the Soviet Union can find some economic use for the products it obtains from the LDCs, and certainly the USSR seeks to enhance its economic benefit from a basically political economic aid program.[28] The economic offensive in the third world is not without sense economically even though economics is not the fundamental basis for the program.

Cultural Influence and System Conversion

The Soviet Union also seeks to promote through economic assistance long-term, indirect aims for cultural influence and system conversion. The nature of cultural influence and system maintenance, or system conversion as the case may be, was explained in chapter 2. There seem to be two relatively distinct phases associated with this motivation for Soviet aid: (1) the neutralizing of U.S. and Western influence in the third world and

(2) the ultimate commitment of the less developed countries to the Communist camp.

In spite of the change in thinking in the USSR which resulted in the conviction that newly independent, neutralist countries were not "lackeys of imperialism," there remained in Soviet thought a serious concern that Western control was being reestablished through economic means. Soviet leaders insist that (1) the nuclear and general military power of the USSR in support of LDC interests was instrumental in the destruction of colonialism after World War II and (2) the Soviet military threat is the reason the Western powers abandoned political control over the former colonies and have not been able openly to reassert their political influence.[29] It is claimed that this is the reason the West has resorted to trade and aid to reestablish control over the LDCs.

Through the economic offensive the USSR hopes to neutralize Western economic and cultural influence in the same way it feels it neutralized Western military influence and political control in the third world:

The aid rendered by the states of socialism to the liberated countries for the preparation of national cadres of specialists has inestimable importance.

The bonds with the socialist states create the opportunity for the liberated countries to neutralize, within certain limits, the colonialist aspirations of the foreign monopolies and compel the imperialists to make concessions, often substantial ones. . . .

It is increasingly difficult for the imperialists to use the lever of economic pressure [aid and private foreign investment] against the liberated countries. As the experience of Egypt, Guinea, and Cuba shows, the imperialists today are in no position to smother economically those countries that refuse to submit to them.[30]

The process by which the neutralization of Western influence would take place is a gradual infusion of Soviet presence in the less developed countries through economic assistance and trade. The USSR hopes that, once regularized contacts with the LDCs are established, they can be used to provide cultural, economic, social, and institutional alternatives to Western influences which have been dominant heretofore. More specifically, the USSR can use aid and the contacts aid programs provide to promote the state sector vis-à-vis private enterprise, to promote socialism as an economic and political system superior to capitalism, and to spread Marxist-Leninist thought as a conceptual means of dealing with all social problems. In many cases the promotion of such alternatives is simply a matter of reinforcing or slightly shifting the emphasis of programs and beliefs of leaders in the less developing countries who themselves often espouse variants of socialism and Marxist thought. Gradually the Soviet expectation is that Western influence will be eroded and replaced by a favorable disposition on the part of the LDCs toward the USSR as a state and to communism as a system of rule.

A manifestation of aid for such purposes is the concentration of Soviet credits for use in state sector projects, and the encouragement given to less developed countries to nationalize foreign private investment. Such efforts not only cut into existing private foreign investment, but undermine confidence in the future of the private sector and of private foreign investment in the third world.[31] By this type of policy the USSR seeks to destroy economic ties between the West and the less developed countries while simultaneously promoting socialism and pro-Soviet attitudes in these countries.

It is interesting to note the similarity between the long-term interest of the U.S. aid program and this first phase of Soviet aid motivated by the desire for cultural influence and system conversion. In each case the motivation seems strongest in its negative or preventive sense. The gradual enhancement of influence, indirect as well as direct, is desired by the USSR and the United States, but if either aid donor were confronted with the choice of enhancing its influence or of having the influence of the other eliminated, it would probably opt for the latter alternative. Along these lines, Herbert Dinerstein suggests that Soviet policy in the less developed countries "is largely pre-emptive, in that its success is measured in terms of opportunities denied to the capitalist world rather than gains for Communism."[32]

The second phase of the long-term motivation for Soviet economic assistance involves a desire to elicit the commitment of the less developed countries to the Communist camp and to complete the establishment of a new world order in which the role of capitalism and the West is severely circumscribed. During this phase the influence in less developed countries which the USSR hopes to attain through aid will be utilized to convince them that it is in their interest to join the Communist system rather than to join the West or even to remain neutralist.

The role that Soviet aid plays in this process can be appreciated when it is realized that the USSR appears now to be convinced that the less developed countries will not have to be converted to communism by force, but, rather, will choose communism of their own accord when they realize its advantages over capitalism. This is the essence of peaceful coexistence. Khrushchev vividly illustrated this point at the Twenty-first Party Congress in 1959 when he declared that the ultimate victory of communism over capitalism and America will be achieved "not through armed interference by the socialist countries in the internal affairs of the capitalist countries," but rather through the conclusive demonstration that "the socialist mode of production possesses decisive advantages over the capitalist mode of production."[33]

Trade and aid are the instruments by which the Soviet Union expects to familiarize the LDCs with the decisive advantages of the socialist mode of producton. Through these mechanisms Soviet goods, technology, ideology, and social, economic, and political structures can be gradually introduced to and hopefully accepted by the third world. For example, India established a state trading agency to facilitate growing economic relations with the USSR and other Communist countries; and in 1962 Brazil created a high-level government committee (Coordinating Group of Commerce with the Socialist Countries of Eastern Europe— COLESTE) to facilitate trade.[34] In both cases the creation of a state trading agency was in response to the increase in trade with the USSR and East European countries as a result of trade and aid agreements. This type of behavior does not necessarily suggest the adoption of the Soviet model by less developed countries. However, it does suggest that through trade and aid agreements the USSR has given certain less developed countries the incentive to establish, voluntarily, political and economic structures consistent with socialism as opposed to capitalism.

This ultimate expectation of a Communist victory in the third world through peaceful coexistence and the economic offensive is the underlying factor for Soviet aid as it relates to system conversion. By gradually winning the allegiance of the less developed countries with the help of economic assistance, the Soviet Union hopes to marshall the economic, military, and political strength peacefully to reconstruct the existing world order which until recently it has viewed as being essentially Western in character and dominated by the United States. The USSR hopes to convert the present system to one that is predominantly pro-Communist and that looks to the Soviet Union for leadership.

The peacefulness with which this system conversion is to proceed is, of course, relative. The USSR no longer views violent conflict with the West as inevitable, yet it contends that it will support "just" wars of "national liberation" and self-defense. What does seem clear is that since the basic policy shift in 1953, and particularly since the initiation of a limited rapprochement between the United States and the USSR after 1962, the Soviet Union manifests an interest in minimizing military conflict during the process of system conversion. The role played by the USSR in the Tashkent Agreement between India and Pakistan following their clash in 1965 would indicate that in addition to the desire of the USSR to minimize an opportunity for Chinese influence, for the present, at least, it is not attempting to change the world order more to its liking by a program of indiscriminately generating chaos.

Other Aid Programs

Finally, brief mention should be made of the American and Chinese aid programs as motivating factors for Soviet economic assistance. The United States aid program definitely played some role in the Soviet decision to initiate its own program, and it constitutes a factor prompting the USSR to continue its efforts. It has been noted that the Soviet Union has viewed U.S. and Western aid as a means to exert influence and control over the less developed countries in lieu of formal political ties. In addition, the USSR recognized that Point Four technical assistance and U.S. contributions to the United Nations aid programs were generating enthusiasm on the part of the LDCs for economic development assistance. The United States until 1953 continually called attention to the fact that the USSR had no bilateral aid program and did not contribute "one Red ruble" to the UN Expanded Program of Technical Assistance. The American aid program's influence and popularity in the third world (probably overestimated at the time by both the United States and the USSR) certainly contributed to the initiation of Soviet bilateral and multilateral economic assistance. Also, once established as a major aid donor, the USSR has undoubtedly been reluctant to discontinue aid because of the political repercussions it would bring from former and potential recipients and because the Soviets do not want the United States and the West to have once again a monopoly in the aid business.

Particularly since 1960 the Chinese aid program has been a factor motivating Soviet economic assistance. In Africa, Asia, and Latin America the Chinese have been attempting to replace the USSR in its leadership of local Communist movements and in exerting influence on government leaders. Statements accompanying Chinese aid offers are as often directed against Soviet aid and Soviet policies as against those of the West. The USSR has acted in ways which give clear evidence that its aid is in part an instrument for combatting Chinese influence around the world. The USSR is at least as afraid to give the Chinese the opportunity to become the major Communist aid donor as it is to give the United States an aid monopoly. In this sense, Chinese, as well as U.S., aid is a motivating factor for continued Soviet economic assistance in the less developed countries.

Summary

The discussion above suggests that the motivations underlying Soviet economic aid to less developed countries are more numerous and complex than most Western, or Soviet, scholars indicate. Soviet economic assistance is essentially a politically motivated program; however, this observation does not distinguish Soviet aid from its American counterpart, nor does it provide us with any real understanding of Soviet aid efforts. An attempt must be made to identify more specifically what the USSR expects to achieve through the distribution of economic assistance.

It is becoming increasingly unsatisfactory to avoid the distinction between the interests of the USSR as a state and its interests as a leading exponent of communism. Soviet economic assistance appears to be primarily an instrument for the advancement of Soviet state interests—particularly when viewed from the perspective of its short-term motivations and uses. The USSR has used economic assistance to forge regularized contacts with governments of the less developed countries, to establish itself as a great power whose presence and influence are felt the world over, to gain respect and friendship in the third world, and to maintain its security. Since the twenties the USSR has subordinated the interests of Communist movements to its interests as a state: the aid program is no exception. The Soviet Union has continued to give substantial economic assistance to countries like India, Egypt, and Iraq which openly suppressed domestic Communists during the tenure of the aid agreements.

The relationship between Soviet economic assistance and the promotion of communism will be the focus of the following chapter. At this point let us merely note that in addition to the uses of aid in promoting Soviet state interests, the USSR has operated on the assumption that communism abroad will benefit from Soviet aid relations with the countries of the third world. Aid recipients would presumably forge strong economic links with Communist countries and adopt Soviet methods of economic and political development. Gradually these processes precipitated by Soviet economic assistance would result in many LDCs joining the Communist camp. Such expectations, however, reflect an indirect, secondary role for aid as means of promoting communism. The linkage of economic assistance to Soviet state interests is much more dominant and direct.

Because of the multiplicity of motivations as well as the dichotomy between Soviet state interests and the interests of international Communist movements, one should be wary of statements which drastically oversimplify the purposes and nature of Soviet economic assistance in the manner of this statement: "The purpose of Soviet economic activity is to spread communism throughout the world. Moscow seeks to promote instability instead of stability in less developed parts of the world. It strives to destroy regimes rather than strengthen them."[35]

Conclusions

The Soviet and American economic aid programs differ in their primary aims, to be sure. The USSR hopes through aid and other means to create a world which is predominately pro-Communist, pro-USSR, and anti-Western in its mode of thought, behavior, and organization; America seeks exactly the reverse. This fundamental difference in the ultimate aims of the two programs, the apparent incompatibility of the systems of rule championed by the United States and the Soviet Union, and the differences observed in the operation of Soviet and American economic assistance programs have led most analysts (both Soviet and Western) to conclude that they are entirely alien in character. Given such a focus on the aims of the programs, the conclusion that they are essentially different is quite justifiable. However, if one chooses instead to compare the programs as instruments of foreign policy many similarities (previously overlooked) become evident.

Students of aid have tended to point to the complexities and contradictions arising from the multiplicity of purposes in American economic assistance while at the same time portraying the Soviet program as a narrow and carefully conceived political instrument, distinguished from its U.S. counterpart by its singleness of purpose and essential simplicity. For example, John D. Montgomery in an astute analysis of U.S. economic aid suggests that "in contrast to the apparent disorder of American purposes, Soviet foreign aid appears simplicity itself, serving immediate political objectives in the hope of achieving eventual domination."[36]

This asymmetry is more imaginary than real, and it leads Western scholars to attribute much more order and design to Soviet aid than probably exists. This is a natural development because the American program is so visible in all its positive and negative aspects whereas in comparison the Soviet program is shrouded in secrecy. The result is all too often an oversimplification of Soviet aims and an overestimation of Soviet capabilities when compared to the very familiar complexities, limitations, and frustrations experienced in American aid efforts.

Upon closer examination of the motivations and uses of Soviet economic assistance, one is struck by a multiplicity of purposes rivaling in complexity and number those of American aid. In addition, it is possible to discuss Soviet aid motivations in the terms commonly used to appraise the American program. Thus it is most improbable that complexity, ambiguity of specific purpose, and an overall lack of precise design are problems unique to American economic assistance.

The Soviet aid program is more eclectic and pragmatic than is generally presumed. Rather than giving a specific credit with a clear design behind it, the USSR may simply be attempting to establish a foothold in the third world through association with development aspirations of less developed countries. The goodwill or influence which is achieved in the process can be used to Soviet advantage in connection with whatever concrete developments unfold in the future.[37]

When viewed in terms of long-range motivations both American and Soviet economic assistance are essentially efforts in the pursuit of milieu goals.[38] Such a policy involves an attempt by a state to change the international environment so as to increase the likelihood that its own interests can be attained efficaciously. The United States and the USSR hope that economic aid will condition the international environment by making it conducive to their respective concepts of desirable social, political, and economic progress.

This aspect of aid motivations is particularly useful in helping to explain why the United States and the USSR continue to distribute aid in spite of the fact that aid seldom is accompanied by a congruence of the policies of the recipients and the donor. Aid as an instrument in the attainment of milieu goals requires neither a complete compatibility of interests between donor and recipient, nor a relationship of dependence. As long as the donor is convinced that economic assistance will ultimately result in the improvement of the international environment, the requirement of support from aid recipients on a wide array of contemporary political issues need not be paramount.

Thus, while the two economic assistance programs are different in their objectives, the uses of aid as an instrument of foreign policy reveal some essential similarities. An analysis of the motivations for aid reveals some of these similarities. More will emerge in our subsequent examination of the implementation, problems, and results of Soviet and American aid.

4

Economic Assistance and the Development Process

‡ The United States and the Soviet Union distribute economic assistance to the less developed countries with the assumption that a certain path of development will be promoted in the process. The development models promoted by these aid donors take very different forms.

American Aid and the Development Process

The initiation by the United States of Point Four technical assistance in 1950 was accompanied by high expectations and served as a prototype for more sophisticated development schemes later in the decade. In the early fifties it was suggested that relatively small sums of money in the form of technical assistance for pilot projects could yield substantial developmental results. The LDCs were portrayed as anxiously awaiting the discovery of new economic, organizational, and political methods which, when demonstrated by the United States or other aid donors, would be adopted wholesale and diffused throughout society. By means of technical assistance the political, social, and economic framework would be created which would then allow the financing of large capital goods projects primarily from public or private loans to be repaid by the recipient.

This great optimism in early U.S. aid to less developed countries is clearly reflected in a statement by Henry Bennett, administrator of the Technical Cooperation Administration at the time:

> Whenever possible, the projects have been geared to have an impact through a dramatic demonstration or pilot operation. . . . Through extension instruction and the use of information media on training, it is hoped that the new and better ways of doing things will catch on, so that in the course of a few years there will be less need for outside technical experts. . . .
>
> As point 4 is successful, the popular understanding and support of the people for their governments will be increased, which will make for stability and be an effective deterrent to Communist propaganda. The governments, in turn, will be more likely to embark on enlightened policies of improvements of standards and conditions, and there will be started a much-needed feeling of responsibility for the well-being and welfare of the people. . . .
>
> . . . Once the pilot projects, and the surveys, have been completed, it is hoped that conditions will be ripe for undertaking the large-scale agricultural, water, industrial and other expansion schemes which are needed. It is believed that the benefits of the pilot projects, and projects which the governments themselves have been stimulated to undertake in the next year or two, will result in improved earnings of the governments so that, to a maximum extent, the large-scale projects may be financed from loans, either private or public.[1]

This rather lengthy quotation demonstrates the high expectations characteristic of the early American approach to aid. Note the instances where Bennett suggests that just one, two, or a few years of technical assistance will succeed in reducing the need of the less developed countries for further aid. It is not fair to criticize such views on the basis of hindsight; the remarks are merely given to point out the early confidence that development problems were of a relatively short-term and manageable nature.

In 1957 the developmental model for American aid was more fully articulated in the work of Max Millikan and Walt Rostow[2] and in a collection of studies prepared for the Special Senate Committee to Study the Foreign Aid Program.[3] These and other studies provided the basis and the framework for the creation of AID in 1961.

The essential claim for U.S. development assistance is that it can provide the marginal capital and skill necessary, but not sufficient in itself, for attaining self-sustained economic growth in recipient less developed countries. It is assumed that the aid recipient is completely committed to the goal of economic development and will shoulder the greater part of the effort in the form of significant economic, political, and social reform. American aid is to be focused on the bottlenecks in facilitating and balancing the development process. Thus, capital and technical assistance from the United States would be designed to substitute temporarily for indigenous shortages in investment capital, foreign exchange, certain types of production, and technical and administrative skills until the LDC can acquire these in amounts adequate to permit self-sustained economic growth. It is assumed that economic aid if properly designed and administered will have a catalytic effect. "Though it would [not] assure the certainty of successful economic growth . . . in most of the countries concerned, especially in the most important ones like India, it would turn a 'close thing' into an excellent bet."[4]

American economic assistance is also expected to contribute to the development of politically mature and stable democratic societies in the third world. Through the aid instrument itself the United States hopes to promote options consistent with Western ideas as to the nature of a successful democratic process. For example, private enterprise is promoted on the grounds (among others) that it helps create nongovernmental institutions and elites which can act as a counterweight to governmental power. Similarly, community and institutional development are promoted in the hope that people at the grass-roots level of society will become directly involved in the modernization process and feel a sense of commitment and pride in development through democratic means. In these and other ways American aid attempts to contribute directly to the establishment of attitudes and institutions supportive of stable democratic processes.

An indirect, but heavily relied upon, consequence of American aid is the contribution of aid-stimulated economic growth to the development of stable democracies in the third world. It is assumed that political stability and democracy are fundamentally a result of the level of economic development of a state. Aid which leads to economic development is expected to reduce the gap between aspirations and economic performance characteristically found in less developed countries. This gap is felt to be a source of great political instability, and to the extent that it can be reduced the chances for moderation and successful operation of democratic processes are enhanced. If economic growth can be achieved through democratic means with the help of American aid, the appeal of radical programs of the political left or right should be minimized.[5]

If lack of violence is viewed as a manifestation of political stability, it is clear that Robert McNamara, for example, views economic development (and U.S. aid to that end) as crucial for the ultimate attainment of political stability and democracy in the third world.[6] His views are indicative of the importance attached to economic development by most U.S. decision-makers as a requisite for political stability.

The basic claim regarding the political development consequences of American aid is most salient in its negative sense. It is not so much that economic development will inevitably lead to the establishment of stable democratic societies, as it is that without U.S. aid and economic growth, the establishment of democracies among the LDCs is unlikely to occur. For example, David Bell, administrator of AID, asserted as an underlying premise of U.S. economic assistance that, "while there is no guarantee that improved political institutions will follow in an automatic way, it seems clear that without economic progress the chances for strengthening democratic processes in the less developed countries would be greatly diminished."[7]

These developmental assumptions underlying American economic assistance have great appeal to Congress and the attentive public. They offer the prospect that economic assistance to the less developed countries need not be an interminable phenomenon. A supreme confidence is asserted that all LDCs can ultimately attain self-sufficient economic growth and economic and political independence. In addition, these assumptions allow the conviction that aid distributed on purely economic criteria can produce desirable political development results. Aid distributed in this manner is viewed with favor by most American decision-makers because it seems to be visible, concrete, measurable, easily transferable, simple, and nonpolitical—whereas aid expressly for political development purposes is viewed as intangible, abstract, unmeasurable, difficult to transfer, complex, and constituting political interference in the domestic affairs of the recipient.[8] Finally, these assumptions offer a positive approach for U.S.-LDC relations which as a rhetorical and operational framework for aid efforts is distinctly preferable to the policy of anticommunism which dominated the program between 1951 and 1957.

Evaluation of U.S. Aid Assumptions

It is interesting to note how the simple claim that the marginal contributions U.S. aid can make to the economic growth of the recipient builds through a series of interconnections among aid, economic growth, and political development to a much more significant claim that aid can lead to the establishment of politically stable, democratic societies. This approach to the developmental effects of economic aid reflects a highly complex view of the nature of society in which the economic and political spheres are clearly distinguishable and interconnected in manner such that primary, secondary, and even tertiary effects of a new stimulus (aid) to the society of an LDC become predictable.[9] This type of reasoning has led to the expectation (in spite of certain qualifications) of a semiautomatic development process in which a relatively small U.S. aid input generates a series of interactions within the economy and polity of the recipient ultimately resulting in self-sustained economic growth and, hopefully, a relatively stable democracy.

AID makes a practice of linking the types and quantity of aid to the level of development of the recipient.[10] The implicit assumption underlying this practice is that virtually every less developed country can successfully achieve self-sufficiency in the economic development process with the help of temporary U.S. economic aid before and during the early stages of takeoff. The length of time required to complete the difficult, but almost automatic, development cycle depends upon the country's initial stage of development and the vigor of its own efforts.[11] The possibility is nowhere addressed at length that self-sustained growth may be attainable in only certain LDCs.

The tendency to overstate the successful accomplishment of the economic development process is manifested in the emphasis AID places on former U.S. aid recipients which are now self-sufficient and require no further assistance. David Bell as administrator of AID presented a list of fourteen countries in this category.[12] The implication was that these countries were representative of what the U.S. expects or hopes to accomplish through economic assistance to the less developed countries. The interesting thing about the list is that twelve of the fourteen countries are in Western Europe and were aid recipients under the Marshall Plan; Japan and Lebanon are the two others. Japan is not generally considered to be in the less developed country category. Lebanon was the recipient of only marginal U.S. aid, and its self-sufficiency is attributable less to U.S. aid than it is to its position in international banking. Therefore, the fact that these countries no longer require U.S. economic assistance has little bearing on the prospects of the less developed countries.

Since 1963 Israel, Taiwan, and Greece have been classified by AID in this category of successfully completed aid programs. These states are more like the LDCs in general, but uncommon endowment of human resources or untypically large amounts of per capita assistance separate these countries from most U.S. aid recipients. In addition, some U.S. assistance is still flowing to these countries through Export-Import Bank long-term loans or Food-For-Peace, even though AID funds have been terminated.

Certainly it is true that American aid has contributed to the development of many countries in the third world, but in terms of expecting self-sustained economic growth the examples given of successfully concluded aid programs seem to be the exceptions rather than the rule. Continued reference to the prospects for terminating U.S. economic assistance on these grounds tends to generate false hopes about the certainty of the development process and the quantity of American aid which is likely to be required in the future.

The prospects for ensuring or facilitating the creation of political stability and democracy through U.S. economic assistance inspire no more confidence than the prospects for aid-generated, self-sustained economic growth. Numerous scholars have noted a rough correlation between the level of economic development and the existence of democratic (competitive) political systems.[13] Similarly, political stability as reflected in fewer incidents of political violence and deaths therefrom seems to be correlated to the level of economic development.[14] These data tend to corroborate the assumptions underlying American economic assistance to the less developed countries, but some important qualifications alter the picture considerably.

It is necessary to distinguish between the level of economic development and the process of economic development. Whereas there may be a positive correlation between the former and political stability and competitive (democratic) political systems, there may be a different relationship between the process of development and these two variables. Charles Wolf makes this distinction and points out that there may well be an inverse relationship between the process of economic development and democratic political development and stability. In its initial stages "higher rates of economic development may lead to the breakdown of existing social structure and to the end of prospects for evolutionary development toward more open and competitive institutions. Revolution may be the result, either accompanied by authoritarian control or followed by authoritarian reactions."[15] Russett supports Wolf in suggesting that deaths from domestic group violence tend to increase in low-income states during the process of economic development.[16]

On a more general plane, Samuel Huntington convincingly argues that economic and political development do not progress at the same pace—the former proceeds faster than the latter.[17] Much like Wolf, he goes on to argue that as a result of economic development "rapid increases in mobilization and participation, the principal political aspects of modernization, undermine political institutions. Rapid modernization, in brief, produces not political development but political decay."[18]

Thus far the analysis has focused exclusively upon economic

development's contribution to political stability and democracy. There is also the question of aid's direct impact on the political development process. A student of political development doctrines in U.S. economic assistance suggests that in 1963 neither highest level foreign policy elites nor middle level operational elites in AID and the Department of State were paying much attention to the political development process and the effect of aid upon it.[19] Political development concepts were salient only to a small group within the research and planning units of the Department of State and AID.[20] Moreover, among most aid officials economic development criteria alone constituted the basis for determining how aid can be distributed to maximize both economic and political development:

Criteria for aid, except when they are short-term political, tend most often to be economic criteria, such as cost-benefit ratios and prospective contribution to GNP. Among the officials interviewed, and in the hearings, typologies of recipient countries tend to be based primarily upon the country's economic-development situation. Even where more elaborate criteria are stated, political development standards are almost wholly lacking.[21]

Since this statement was written, a new chapter has been added to the aid statute which calls for efforts on the part of AID to emphasize the development of democratic institutions in recipient states.[22] This vague guideline for political development activities has resulted primarily in a six-weeks conference at Massachusetts Institute of Technology on the application of the new chapter, in a series of seminars for mission directors and other principal AID and State Department officers on issues of political development, and in a series of in-depth country analyses relating to the effects of common AID projects on the development of democratic institutions in several states.[23]

But the lack of explicit political development criteria in the distribution of American economic assistance to the LDCs suggests that the contribution of U.S. aid to political development must come primarily from the indirect and unpredictable results of aid-supported economic growth. In light of the ambiguous relationship between economic development and political stability and democracy, the political development assumptions underlying American economic assistance seem to be as questionable as those relating to the prospects for self-sufficient economic growth in the third world.

Most Western literature on economic and political development in recent years has evidenced a retreat from the optimism present in the development model for American economic assistance. Hirschman's view of economic development as an imbalanced, eclectic process which proceeds in fits and starts[24] seems more relevant today than Rostow's view of steady, unilinear, semiautomatic development[25] which has permeated American aid rhetoric and operations. The work of Samuel Huntington, Robert Packenham, Charles Wolf, Bruce Russett, and others casts serious doubt upon the political consequences commonly expected to result from the distribution of American aid.

Continued reliance upon the optimistic development model underlying American aid has generated some negative results. It leads to frustration, disenchantment, and erosion of domestic political support for the aid program when the development process in the third world in fact reveals itself as a painful, uncertain, and seemingly interminable enterprise. It also tends to generate the belief that poor organization, administration, and personnel are the cause of the problems in the development process, because the certainty of development has been overstated in aid rhetoric. AID personnel are increasingly aware of the limitations surrounding the aid instrument,[26] but presentations of the program to Congress and the attentive public have not sufficiently stressed them.

Soviet Aid and the Development Process

The point of departure for Soviet treatment of the economic and political development process in less developed countries is the basic Marxist-Leninist model of the two-step revolutionary process in which colonies at a feudal stage of development pass through capitalism to become socialist states. The first step involves the seizure of power and the development of capitalism under the leadership of the national bourgeoisie. The second step is the socialist revolution which occurs at that indeterminate time when the capitalist system and the national bourgoisie no longer constitute a "progressive force" in the development process. Classical Marxism-Leninism demands that this stage of the revolution can occur only under the leadership of the proletariat and the Communist Party as its vanguard.

Since the initiation of its economic assistance program the USSR has gone through an interesting series of alterations and refinements of this basic model for economic, political, and social development in the less developed countries. It is this evolution in development doctrine which we wish to examine here.

From the beginning of the aid program until 1960 Soviet discussions of development in the LDCs relied heavily upon the basic Marxist-Leninist model outlined above. Leaders such as Nehru, Sukarno, and Nasser were viewed as national bourgeoisie constituting a progressive force in the development process. As such, these and other non-Communist leaders of less developed countries (particularly those adopting a neutralist position in matters of foreign policy) were considered deserving of Soviet support through economic and military assistance, trade, diplomatic, and other means. The main tasks of the national bourgeois leaders included the consolidation of political independence from the colonial powers and the management of the capitalist stage of development, both of which would serve to prepare the LDCs for the socialist revolution.

During this period Soviet spokesmen did not depart from the basic concept that significant economic, political, and social development could take place only with persistent pressure and support from a strong proletariat under local Communist direction. Consistent with the basic Marxist-Leninist model, there was, of course, no possibility of reaching the socialist stage of development except under Communist leadership.

Within this framework the USSR could distribute economic assistance to less developed countries without sacrificing ideological purity. Soviet economic aid insofar as it contributed to the industrial growth of recipients would serve to improve the conditions necessary for the formation and strengthening of the working class and its vanguard, the local Communist party. Through channeling aid to the state sector of the LDCs the Soviet Union could preempt development of the private sector and Western economic influence concentrated therein. Thus, the LDCs would be increasing their economic independence along a path consistent with future aims of the socialist stage of the development process.

The distribution of aid to national bourgeois governments allowed the USSR to pose as a champion of LDC development aspirations and as a protector of the third world from Western economic pressures. The USSR could claim at least partial credit for whatever economic progress its aid recipients achieved. At the same time, should economic stagnation and frustration result instead of growth, the USSR could point to the inability of the national bourgeoisie leaders to solve the difficult development problems facing the less developed countries and encourage the proletariat and local Communist parties to assert themselves and take control of the development process.[27]

In December 1960 at the Moscow Conference of Communist and Workers Parties the new formula of national democracy was introduced by the USSR as a model for the transition from national bourgeois leadership to Communist leadership of the LDCs. A national democratic state was defined as one whose political basis consisted of a coalition of Communist and non-Communist progressive forces, "struggling for complete national independence, for broad democracy and for the prosecution of the anti-imperialist, antifeudal, democratic revolution to its conclusion."[28] This coalition was to be led by non-Communists since it was recognized that in many countries of Asia and Africa the proletariat and local Communist parties were not yet strong enough to lead the masses.[29] The types of policies implemented by a national democratic state would include

the liquidation of all remnants of colonialism and all forms of pre-capitalist attitudes, the passing of agrarian reforms, the expropriation of major land holdings, the seizure of property from foreign monopolies, a change in the structure of industrial and agricultural production and orientation toward the states of the socialist camp in the development of economic ties with the outside world.[30]

The national democracy formula was initially applied to Indonesia, Cuba, Ghana, Guinea, and Mali as states on the noncapitalist path of development. It represented a substantially more optimistic view of the prospects for achieving socialism than the basic two-stage model for development used prior to 1960. In the national democracy formula it was proposed that a coalition under non-Communist leadership could move a less developed country onto the noncapitalist path of development, thus skipping the capitalist stage.[31] This was possible due to the absence of clearly defined class divisions within states of the national democratic category combined with the existence of the world socialist system which protects LDCs from imperialist intrusions.[32] Still, however, socialism was held distinct from the noncapitalist path of development, and only under Communist leadership could the former be attained.[33] Moreover, the various national socialisms espoused by many Afro-Asian leaders were attacked for being permeated with a "petty bourgeois spirit" and containing "Utopian" elements. Every effort was made to distinguish these types of socialism from the scientific socialism of Marxism-Leninism.

The national democracy concept was, in effect, a program for Communist revolution (though not necessarily violent) in the developing countries. However, Soviet spokesmen used it through 1963 primarily to emphasize the immediate tactical desirability of supporting non-Communist leaders of LDCs through aid, trade, and other means.[34] It was hoped that local Communists would play an active role in the politics of national democratic states, but Soviet credits were in no way conditional upon the increase of Communist influence in these countries. "The concept of national democracy [was] intended as a signpost for Communist strategy within the ex-colonial nations, not as a classification for the disbursement or refusal of Soviet credits."[35] Aid was distributed as a means of inducing less developed countries under non-Communist leadership to follow the noncapitalist path of development.

Hardly two years after the promulgation of the national democracy formula Soviet scholars and decision-makers became involved in a debate over the prospects for rapid economic, political, and social development in the less developed countries.[36] At issue was the fact that some LDC regimes (the United Arab Republic under Nasser and Algeria under Ben Bella) which had banned independent Communist activity put through unexpectedly radical domestic reforms and were increasingly at one with the Communist camp on issues dividing the East and the West.[37]

Some scholars such as G. Mirsky were suggesting by 1964 that it was possible for certain non-Communist leaders (revolutionary democrats) to carry out functions traditionally performed only by Communists and the proletariat in the Marxist-Leninist model. Mirsky held that revolutionary democrats could "begin the transition to socialist revolution," and in those cases where proletarian leadership was not yet mature the world socialist system could perform the function of the proletarian vanguard in the revolutionary process.[38]

This group was opposed by a section of the Party apparatus in the USSR in charge of external questions and contact with non-bloc Communist parties. M. A. Suslov, B. N. Ponamarev, and A. M. Rumiantsev preferred to emphasize interests of local Communist leaders in less developed countries who were often being suppressed by the very revolutionary democrats Mirsky and others were supporting.[39] Khrushchev until late 1963 remained in a centrist position between these two extremes, but during 1964 until his ouster from power he embraced the Mirsky position.

By 1964 revolutionary democracy thus came to replace the national democracy concept as a guideline for Soviet relations with the most progressive LDCs. In the spring of 1964 Mirsky gave what "constituted the first Soviet endorsement of a non-Communist country [Algeria] as having 'embarked upon socialism.'"[40] Shortly thereafter, when Ben Bella visited Moscow, Khrushchev awarded him the decoration of Hero of the Soviet Union and the official citation of the award referred to Ben Bella as Comrade.[41] These virtually unprecedented steps were followed later in 1964 by the awarding of the same honor to Nasser, and during his trip to Egypt Khrushchev made several speeches in which he declared that the United Arab Republic was "embarking on the path of socialist construction."[42]

The concept of revolutionary democracy as espoused by Mirsky and reflected in Khrushchev's policies during 1964 represents the high point of Soviet optimism concerning the development process in the less developed countries. The distinction between the noncapitalist and socialist paths of development was considerably softened in comparison to the national democracy formulation. But most startling was the proposition that non-Communist, revolutionary democrats could move a less developed country to the socialist path in the absence of a mature proletariat or local Communist movement.

Like national democracy, the USSR could and did use revolutionary democracy as a justification for continued aid to progressive non-Communist less developed countries whose one-party regimes made no allowance for local Communist political activity. It provided a convenient framework within which to distribute aid to Nasser's Egypt, Ben Bella's Algeria, Ne Win's Burma, Sékou Touré's Guinea, and Nkrumah's Ghana. While never explicitly articulated in this fashion, revolutionary democracy constituted the ultimate tribute to Soviet economic assistance activities as a catalyst for economic, political, and social development in the less developed countries. The concept implicitly suggested that, using aid as a primary instrument, the USSR could provide direction for the movement of an LDC from a semifeudal stage of development to the path of socialism without the need for local Communist direction of the process.

The post-Khrushchev era witnessed a marked retreat from the optimistic 1964 view of the development prospects for less developed countries and revolutionary democracies in particular. No clear-cut line has emerged, and no new concept has been formulated for Soviet relations with the LDCs since Khrushchev's removal; however, discussions of the development process since 1964 have been more liberally sprinkled with qualifications serving to dampen expectations for immediate and easy successes in the third world.

Evidence of this more cautious tone in Soviet development literature can be seen in the stress on the duality of the petty bourgeoisie (from which revolutionary democratic leaders emerge) and its tendency to waver in its conduct of the revolutionary process.[43] There have been warnings that the speed and facility of the first stage of the revolution involving the decolonization of most LDCs has led to an excess of optimism in the prospects for completing the transformation to socialism in the third world.[44] There has been increased emphasis on the absolute necessity of a strong working class and leadership by mature local Communist parties within the LDCs as a precondition for the construction of socialism in the third world.[45] It has also been explicitly suggested that, "owing to a number of factors, the period of the new states' transition to Socialism bypassing capitalism will be quite long."[46]

All these assertions have appeared before in Soviet literature, but their recent frequency in contrast to discussions of development prospects at the height of the revolutionary democracy phase in 1964 makes them noteworthy. They represent a specific manifestation of a more general trend in post-Khrushchevian Soviet foreign policy commentary which "retained the insight that ours is a revolutionary epoch while simultaneously pushing the time when the international relations of a new type would be created so far into the future as to be of little if any operative significance for Soviet foreign policy in the late 1960s."[47]

In spite of this more cautious appraisal of immediate revolutionary prospects in the third world since 1964, Soviet economic aid commitments and disbursements have continued at high levels. Thus, as has been the case since the initiation of the program, the revolutionary outlook seems to have little direct effect on economic aid operations.

Evaluation of Soviet Aid Assumptions

A most remarkable evolution has taken place since World War II in Soviet assessments of the role to be played by local Communist parties in the overall development process of less developed countries. Prior to 1953 the USSR backed local Communists against national bourgeois governments throughout Asia in a direct, violent assault for the capture of power. Non-Communist governments were viewed as reactionary, pro-Western, and incapable of directing economic, political, or social progress. With the initiation of the aid program after 1953, and particularly after 1956, Soviet spokesmen recognized national bourgeois leaders as being capable of asserting their independence from the West and of guiding their states through the capitalist stage of development. In 1960 with the formulation of the national democracy concept the USSR held out the possibility for non-Communist leaders, with active local Communist support, to direct less developed countries to the noncapitalist path of development. Finally, by 1964 Khrushchev and some Soviet scholars suggested that even in the absence of a local proletariat or a functioning Communist party it was possible for radical non-Communist leaders (revolutionary democrats) to lead a semifeudal LDC to the socialist path of development.

Thus, within a twenty-year period the USSR shifted from complete commitment to the necessity for local Communist leadership of all stages of the revolution (including the development of capitalism) to virtual abandonment of meaningful support for local Communists and the conviction that non-Communist leaders can guide the development process even to the point of preparing for the transformation to socialism and alignment with the Communist camp.

This evolution in Soviet doctrine reflects a continued effort to reconcile Moscow's ideological perception of the development process to the reality of the third world. Under Khrushchev's leadership this involved periodic reassessment of the revolutionary capacity of non-Communist leaders such as Sukarno, Nasser, Ben Bella, and Sékou Touré. When such men took steps which were seemingly beyond their prescribed role in Soviet development doctrine, the doctrine was simply revised to incorporate their acts into a Soviet model for a revolutionary process ultimately to result of the building of a socialist state.

As a consequence of this tendency Soviet doctrine by 1964 was overly optimistic almost to the point of losing its connections with the basic Marxist-Leninist model of the two-stage revolutionary process and the role of the working class and the local Communist party in it. With Khrushchev's removal there has been a tightening-up of ideology designed to correct this excess of optimism and, simultaneously, a striving for greater realism in assessing the overall development prospects of the LDCs.[48]

Greater realism and significant qualification regarding the specific results of Soviet economic assistance to the less developed countries can also be seen. Some of the basic tenets of aid were seriously questioned by Soviet scholars even during the period of Khrushchevian optimism. G. I. Mirsky and R. A. Ulyanovsky, for example, have pointed out the inapplicability of the Soviet experience for many less developed countries, and they warn against an indiscriminate copying of this experience by the LDCs. Since conditions are often unfavorable for the immediate construction of heavy industry, it is suggested that infrastructure projects and light and extractive industry might better be emphasized during the initial stages of development. Indeed, "premature attempts to set up heavy industry may discredit the idea of industrialization itself."[49]

Soviet scholars have also suggested that USSR aid to the state sector of some less developed countries may in fact serve to subsidize the expansion of the private sector.[50] The Indian example is most frequently cited in this regard. Soviet aid to India's state steel industry is said to result in the production and sale of steel at low, state-fixed prices which are, in effect, subsidies to the fabricating plants in the private sector which process the steel and sell their products at free-market prices.[51]

Still another set of questions revolves around the value of the private sector and private foreign investment to the LDCs and the dangers of premature nationalization. Some Soviet scholars have emphasized that the LDCs need all the capital and technical assistance they can get, and as long as Western investments through public and private channels are carefully controlled by the recipient these sources can contribute valuable foreign exchange and technical training to the LDCs. Since the Soviet Union is not in a position to substitute its own aid for Western aid and private foreign investment in more than a handful of countries, the LDCs are warned against premature nationalization efforts which might cut off these flows from the West.[52] Premature nationalization is also discouraged on the grounds that should inept management by local governments result in gross inefficiencies and economic decline in LDCs, these states might be soured on the socialist model altogether.

Recent changes in Soviet perceptions of the prospects for political, social, and economic development in the third world, as well as of the specific contributions Soviet aid can make to this development process are indications of Soviet efforts to adjust doctrinal preconceptions to the reality of the LDCs in the late 1960s. Earlier Soviet expectations of aid and the overall development process overestimated the degree to which local Communist parties would be allowed to develop by non-Communist leaders of the LDCs, and the degree to which the LDCs are willing to recognize the contribution of the USSR (or any aid donor) to whatever success is achieved in the development process. Nasser, Ben Bella, and other LDC leaders, for example, in spite of substantial aid from the USSR, effectively throttled local Communist activity. Similarly, with regard to recognition afforded to USSR aid, a Soviet reporter wrote in *Izvestia* with some dismay that on sightseeing tours of the Aswan dam the Egyptian guides did not even allude to the fact that it was being built with Soviet specialists and financial aid.[53] The Egyptian government was taking the credit for the project.

The crux of the problem is that while Soviet aid may help non-Communist leaders cope with the problems of development, withstand pressures from the West, and indirectly facilitate the creation of a strong proletarian base for local Communist parties, this aid also serves to strengthen non-Communist leaders against domestic difficulties, including challenges from local Communists. So in aid the USSR faces the same type of difficulty that frequently has arisen in past attempts to cooperate in other contexts with national bourgeois leaders of early stages of the revolutionary process—for example, Chiang Kai-shek and Mustafa Kemal. Soviet assistance in the form of organizational techniques, advice, and financial resources is as frequently utilized against local Communist competitors to non-Communist leaders as it is against the common enemy which ostensibly accounts for the assistance program in the first place.

Soviet economic assistance as it relates to the development process in the LDCs reflects the adoption by the USSR of a strategy for the revolutionary process which tends to preclude the necessity of assuming risks inherent in an aggressive policy vis-à-vis the less developed countries.[54] This approach at once incorporates Soviet recognition of the weakness of Communist parties in the third world and Soviet confidence that time, neutralism, and the superiority of the socialist economic system will be decisive in the ultimate conversion of the LDCs to the Communist camp.[55] Soviet economic aid is symbolic of a view of the revolutionary process which is inclusivist, gradualist, and minimally violent in character.

Conclusions

The development models espoused by the United States and the Soviet Union provide the basis for expectations concerning the contribution their economic assistance can make to the development process of less developed countries. The attractiveness of these models to the United States and the USSR lies in the fact that they offer the hope for significant political and economic development along predictable paths with relatively modest aid outlays and little direct control from the donors.

In recent years, however, aid experience and increased awareness of the difficulties inherent in the development process of the LDCs has eroded the optimism which, during earlier periods, characterized Soviet and American perceptions of economic aid and its contribution to development. It is now apparent that neither model describes the nature of the development process in most LDCs. More important, both models have proven to be of limited utility in prescribing U.S. and USSR aid policies capable of generating the developmental results desired by the donors in the third world. As a consequence, increasing caution is voiced in connection with the prospects for self-sustained economic growth and the establishment of stable democracies in discussions of aid within the United States. Similarly, Soviet spokesmen are portraying the revolutionary process in the third world as an increasingly more difficult, long-term process,[56] and the results of aid are being reexamined.

There seems to be an implicit assumption in the Soviet and American development models that there must be some more or less universal development recipe in whose service economic assistance can be most effectively utilized. On the other hand, the record suggests that

when one starts searching for causes, a country's rapid progress will always turn out to be closely related to very special and favorable circumstances in its location or heritage. The most admirable achievement seems least susceptible of imitation. What is encouraging is the length and diversity of the list. There is clearly no single pattern of modernization.[57]

This increasing appreciation of the uniqueness in the political and economic development process of various less developed countries has contributed greatly to the recent erosion of Soviet and American development models and the doubts concerning aid's effectiveness.

Quite aside from the congruence, or lack of congruence, between the development models of the donors and the reality of third world experience, there is the question of the extent to which the models have been reflected in actual Soviet and American aid practices. The criteria consistent with American economic and political development assumptions are more decisive in the selection of the type and content of aid provided to an LDC than they are in the selection of the countries which are to receive it. For whatever reason aid is offered, and through whatever funding category aid is disbursed, the United States evaluates and attempts to maximize the contribution of its aid to the economic development of the recipient. However, the economic performance of an LDC does not necessarily determine whether or not it will receive American aid.

Jacob Kaplan points out, for example, that on grounds of economic development Pakistan was deserving of a substantial aid pledge by the United States in 1965, but, nevertheless, the United States was reluctant to offer a pledge at the Pakistan Consortium meeting scheduled for mid-1965.[58] This behavior on the part of America suggests that Pakistan's decision to enter into closer relations with Red China and to threaten the use of force in Kashmir was more crucial in the determination of how much economic assistance the United States was willing to give than was Pakistan's economic development progress upon which the program was ostensibly based.

By the same token, Soviet economic aid in practice manifests the operation of well-defined revolutionary criteria more in the determination of the type of assistance to be given than in the selection of countries to receive it. As we have seen, the USSR continued to deliver aid in substantial amounts to countries such as India, Egypt, and Algeria while they exercised severely restrictive policies on the activities of local Communists. Also, it is difficult to explain recent Soviet economic and military aid to Iran, Turkey, and Pakistan primarily in terms of Soviet perceptions of the development process in third world countries. Like the United States, the Soviet Union probably attempts to maximize the contribution its aid can make to the development (in this case the achievement of socialism) of recipient countries, but decisions concerning allocation of aid between countries do not seem to turn primarily upon assessments of revolutionary prospects.

At best an examination of the developmental assumptions underlying Soviet and American economic assistance to the less developed countries can lead to a partial understanding of programs. For a more complete picture we must turn to a discussion of actual aid operations. To this end the next several chapters will focus upon the scope and magnitude of the programs, their administration, their operational emphases, their financial terms, and some of the problems which have arisen in Soviet and American aid efforts.

5

The Magnitude and Scope
of the Aid Programs

‡ A precise and universally acceptable definition of what constitutes aid has yet to be formulated and no such attempt will be
made here, but depending upon the purpose for which it is used
a satisfactory definition can be determined. With regard to the
impact on the recipient's economic and political development it
would seem that the transfer of resources (capital, technical, and
human) by any and all means from one country to another would
constitute economic assistance. By this definition private as well
as official (public) transfers on virtually any terms would be
included. If the purpose of the analysis were the evaluation of the
contribution of foreign resources to the economies of the less
developed countries, this approach might be useful; however, we
are viewing economic assistance as an instrument of foreign policy of the donor country.

For our purposes, economic assistance will include the official
transfer to the less developed countries of capital, goods, and
services which they could not obtain through normal commercial
means. This eliminates the consideration of transfers through
regular export earnings and through capital obtained on commercial terms or by foreign private investment.[1] Aid, therefore,
would involve official medium- and long-term loans, grants, loans
repayable in the recipient's currency, the sale of products for
local currency, credits repaid directly with the exports of the
recipient, and publicly financed technical services.[2]

There are two basic reasons for the decision not to include commercial flows as a form of economic assistance. First, while trade, short-term commercial credits, and private foreign investment contribute to the development of the recipients, such transfers are not generally initiated by enterprises in the advanced market economies for the specific purposes of economic development or forging political ties. By focusing upon official transfers of capital, goods, and services, one can get a sense of the donor's public interest in and commitment to the less developed countries which cannot be found in normal commercial transactions.

Second, less developed countries view some type of sacrifice by the donor as implicit in the meaning of aid. Normal commercial transactions imply no such sacrifice on the part of the donor who is assumed to be undertaking the loan, trade, or investment because of an expectation of personal (or corporate) gain. The LDCs, which tend to equate gain by a foreign private enterprise with exploitation, simply do not view transfers through normal commercial channels as aid—except perhaps to the donor who is felt (rightly or wrongly) to be the greatest beneficiary in such transactions. Given this fact, it is difficult to conceive that the types of results the United States or the USSR expects to obtain through economic aid could be realized through regular commercial channels. Official transactions, on the other hand, are usually considered by the LDCs as involving some sacrifice for the donor, because in one form or another the terms of the transfer are easier on the recipient (lower interest, longer repayment period, and repayment in local currency, for example) than regular commercial terms.

American Economic Assistance

Because of the ambiguity in the funding categories, the changes in these funding categories over a period of time, and the multiplicity of programs which have been lumped together under the rubric of foreign aid, it is difficult to arrive at an exact figure for total American economic aid to the LDCs. Total U.S. foreign aid from 1946 through June 30, 1968, amounts to $133.5 billion; but this figure includes military assistance, aid for relief and rehabilitation following the war, Marshall aid for European reconstruction, and other programs which clearly do not belong in the category of economic assistance to the less developed countries.[3] In order to derive an approximate figure for aggregate U.S. economic assistance to the less developed countries let us examine this figure for total U.S. foreign aid in more detail.

Aggregate Data

Table 1 represents an effort to break down total aid figures to suit the purpose of our examination of American economic assistance to less developed countries. While total U.S. aid since World War II amounts to some $133.5 billion, military and economic aid in all forms to countries other than the LDCs comes to $56 billion. Included in this figure are the postwar relief and rehabilitation programs, aid to Europe, and aid to Israel, Japan, and the Republic of South Africa which are not considered as less developed countries in this analysis. This portion of American military and economic aid does not concern us.

Thus, total U.S. aid to the less developed countries from fiscal years 1945/46 to 1967/68 is $77.5 billion; but included in this figure is military assistance totaling $19.3 billion. Pure military aid is only indirectly related to economic assistance, so we will ignore the military component of aid to the less developed countries. This means that $58.3 billion is the approximate figure for cumulative economic assistance to the LDCs as of June 30, 1968. Of the $58.3 billion total, all but $5 billion consists of bilateral economic assistance.

The Programs and Funding Categories

Food-For-Peace,[4] long-term loans made by the Export-Import Bank, and aid disbursed by AID and its predecessor agencies constitute the three basic channels for U.S. economic assistance to the less developed countries. Let us examine these channels in some detail.

AID and its predecessor agencies have administered those funds provided specifically by foreign assistance legislation since 1949; Food-For-Peace and the Export-Import Bank are techni-

TABLE 1

Cumulative U.S. Economic and Military Aid Commitments
Fiscal years 1946–1968
(In Millions of U.S. Dollars)

Recipient	AID[a]	Food-For-Peace	Export–Import Bank[b]	Other Economic[c]	Total Economic	Military	Total Economic and Military
LDCs							
Near East and South Asia[d]	$10,178.5	$ 7,455.9	$ 1,093.8	$ 982.9	$19,711.1	$ 7,379.6[e]	$ 27,090.7
Latin America[a]	4,673.8	1,722.7	4,302.2	2,389.1	13,087.8	1,118.0	14,205.8
Far East[f]	10,586.9	2,396.2	553.3	2,689.7	16,226.1	9,789.3	26,015.4
Africa[g]	2,158.5	1,235.0	312.0	217.9	3,923.4	274.9	4,198.3
Nonregional[h]	2,966.2	501.5	0.0	1,835.2	5,302.9	705.4	6,008.3
Total LDCs	$30,563.9	$13,311.3	$ 6,261.3	$ 8,114.8	$58,251.3	$19,267.2	$ 77,518.5
Non-LDCs[i]	$16,182.1	3,095.7	$ 4,438.7	$12,758.2	$36,474.7	$19,510.8	$ 55,985.5
Grand Total	$46,746.0	$16,407.0	$10,700.0	$20,873.0	$94,726.0	$38,778.0	$133,504.0

SOURCE: Data derived from U.S., Agency for International Development, *U.S. Overseas Loans and Grants and Assistance from International Organizations, Special Report* prepared for the House Foreign Affairs Committee, May 1969.

a. AID and its predecessor agencies.
b. Includes only long-term loans by the Export-Import Bank.
c. Two to three dozen grant and loan operations including the Peace Corps, capital subscriptions to international organizations, post-World War II relief and rehabilitation, etc.
d. Excludes Israel. See Appendix A for states included.
e. Includes military aid to Israel for fiscal year 1968 only.
f. Excludes Japan. See Appendix A for states included.
g. Excludes the Republic of South Africa. See Appendix A for states included.
h. Contributions to nonregional, multilateral programs including those of the United Nations family and administrative expenses of aid to LDCs.
i. Includes aid to all states not listed as LDCs in Appendix A.

cally separate programs under separate legislative statutes which are not included in the annual foreign assistance acts. AID and its predecessor agencies have disbursed $30.6 billion to the less developed countries since 1949. But the nature of the assistance distributed through this channel is so heterogeneous that we must break this $30.6 billion figure into several component parts to understand what type of assistance is being given.

Funds for AID and its predecessor agencies have been appropriated through funding categories which are good indicators of the different types of economic assistance provided by AID. Defense Support, now called Supporting Assistance, has accounted for approximately $14.1 billion or 46 percent of the economic assistance to less developed countries through these agencies.[5] This type of aid is given in the form of either loans or grants and is "provided to further urgent United States national security and foreign policy objectives."[6] During the fifties this type of aid went primarily to countries receiving U.S. military assistance, as was pointed out earlier. While every effort is made to give Defense Support/Supporting Assistance in a form which will contribute to the economic growth of the recipient,[7] it is not primarily an instrument for economic development.

Development Loans comprise another funding category through which AID and its predecessor agencies have distributed about $9.5 billion in economic assistance to the less developed countries.[8] While this figure is only 31 percent of the total aid given by these agencies, it should be noted that Development Loans did not begin until 1958, and such aid became the priority funding category with the creation of AID in 1961. Development lending is the type of economic assistance upon which the United States would like to model its entire aid effort. Aid in this form is given for the specific purpose of economic development, and of all the funding categories appropriated to and administered by AID, Development Loans come closest to being disbursed on the basis of economic development criteria. Development lending is the mechanism through which the United States usually finances large capital development projects in the less developed countries.

Development Grants for technical cooperation comprise another $3.0 billion, or 10 percent, of the total economic assistance disbursed by AID and its predecessor agencies to the less developed countries.[9] This type of aid is used primarily for the purpose of developing human resources in the areas of health, education, and agriculture. Along with Development Loans for capital assistance, Development Grants for technical assistance have taken on more importance in the U.S. program during the sixties, particularly under the Johnson administration which stressed health, education, and agriculture as the primary targets of American economic assistance.

Though this discussion has oversimplified the complexities within the various funding categories making up the program administered by AID and its predecessor agencies, it is sufficient to indicate the overall nature of the types of economic assistance flowing through this channel. Supporting Assistance, Development Loans, and Development Grants comprise 87 percent of the $30.6 billion in economic aid given by these agencies to the less developed countries. The remaining 13 percent is primarily accounted for by administrative expenses and the Contingency Fund which is used by the President to meet urgent and unforeseen requirements for economic assistance such as emergency relief for natural or certain political disorders.

In addition to the $30.6 billion in commitments by AID and its predecessor agencies, the United States has distributed $13.3 billion worth of economic assistance to the less developed countries under the Agricultural Trade Development and Assistance Act of 1954 (P.L. 480). Under this act and subsequent amendments to it, the United States has used agricultural surplus commodities for several purposes. Title I provides for the sale of these commodities for local currency which, in turn, is: (1) returned to the less developed country in the form of a grant or loan for use in economic development projects or for military purposes; (2) loaned to private American and, in certain cases, foreign enterprises; (3) used by the U.S. government to pay for part of its administrative and other expenses within the less developed country. Title II authorizes the use of surplus agricultural commodities for famine relief or other emergency assistance. Under Title III these commodities can be donated to voluntary relief agencies, such as CARE, for distribution to needy people abroad. Finally, Title IV allows for credit sales (repayable in dollars) of agricultural surplus commodities.

Of the $13.3 billion given to the less developed countries through P.L. 480, almost $10 billion has been delivered under Title I with the bulk of the local currency obtained having gone back to the LDCs in the form of grants and loans.[10] The remainder of P.L. 480 aid to less developed countries is largely accounted for by Title III contributions of surplus agricultural commodities to voluntary relief agencies.

It seems apparent that P.L. 480 represents a case in U.S. economic assistance where virtue was made of necessity. When the law was enacted, the United States was confronted with embarrassing quantities of agricultural surplus commodities which were held by the Commodity Credit Corporation at great expense to the government. Through the Agricultural Trade Development and Assistance Act of 1954, a means was found to reduce these stocks of agricultural surplus and lower the expense of storage, while simultaneously using the surplus to help meet the genuine need for agricultural commodities in the less developed countries. Thus, the sale of these goods on easy terms to the less developed countries provided America with an attractive aid instrument which had added appeal at home. Unlike other aid which seemed to impose a burden on the taxpayer, P.L. 480 was presented as a means of reducing U.S. government expenditures on agricultural surplus storage.

Assistance through P.L. 480 was explicitly linked to surpluses which could not be marketed through regular commercial channels. A cursory glance at the legislation reveals that P.L. 480 was primarily designed to promote trade and other outlets for agricultural surplus and only secondarily designed to provide economic assistance to the less developed countries.[11] On the other hand, this does not mean that P.L. 480 was of little or no use to the recipients; indeed, the $13.3 billion worth of agricultural commodities delivered to the less developed countries through this channel was crucial in facilitating economic growth in numerous LDCs and in preventing mass famine as a result of the inability of agriculture to keep pace with the population explosion in the third world.

It should also be pointed out that in the Food-For-Freedom Act of 1966 the United States has seriously attempted to give priority to the economic assistance and development aspects of agricultural commodity aid. Food shipments to the less developed countries are to be directly linked to U.S. production rather than to existing agricultural surpluses, which are largely depleted. The seriousness of the problem of food production as it is linked to population growth in the third world is considered explicitly, and U.S. food shipments and aid in agricultural development are to play a greater role in the American economic assistance program.

The third basic channel of U.S. economic assistance is Export-Import Bank long-term (five years or more) loans to the less developed countries. The Export-Import Bank was first created in 1934 to stimulate U.S. exports by providing loans to foreign governments and businesses for purchases in the United States, but since the mid-fifties it has increasingly focused on making loans to less developed countries enabling them to finance imports from the United States for economic development purposes.[12] The Export-Import Bank has made long-term loans to the less developed countries in the amount of $6.3 billion. The main purpose of the institution is still to facilitate and encourage foreign purchases of U.S. exports, but its long-term loans to the LDCs constitute a significant means of providing them with the economic assistance important for their development.

Other economic aid, totaling $8.1 billion, is not to be examined closely in the present analysis because it consists primarily of stopgap programs in the 1940s designed to ease the problems of relief, rehabilitation, and reconstruction which emerged after the Second World War. This type of assistance has now been virtually eliminated. The overwhelming proportion of the category in recent years has involved U.S. capital subscriptions to the International Bank for Reconstruction and Development and other international financial institutions.

Therefore, through AID and its predecessor agencies, Food-For-Peace programs, and the Export-Import Bank, the United States had extended $50.1 billion in economic assistance to the less developed countries as of June 30, 1968. When other bilateral economic aid programs are added to this figure the overall amount of U.S. economic aid to LDCs comes to $58.3 billion. These data represent commitments rather than actual expenditures; however, in the United States aid program expenditures have generally kept pace with commitments, a factor most unlike Soviet aid. In the case of AID and its predecessor agencies, for example, total aid expenditures as of June 30, 1968, amounted to 86 percent of total aid commitments to the less developed countries.[13] Expenditures for all U.S. economic assistance to LDCs, including P.L. 480 and Export-Import Bank long-term loans, amount to approximately 90 percent of total commitments.[14]

From the presentation of the overall aid program it should be evident that much of American economic assistance to the less developed countries has not been offered for the primary purpose of the recipients' economic development. While this may be lamentable from the point of view of those in who wish to see substantially more aid offered on the basis of economic development criteria, it does not necessarily constitute grounds for wholesale criticism of American economic assistance. The fact remains that the billions of dollars which flowed to less developed countries through the various U.S. economic aid channels contributed to whatever economic growth these nations have experienced since 1946. The benefit to the recipients might have been greater had more aid been designed specifically for development purposes; however, American interest in promoting the disposal of surplus agricultural commodities, the sale of U.S. exports, and the security of the West served to generate more funds which could be used for economic development than would ever have been provided by the United States for the primary purpose of the third world's economic growth.

The Direction of American Aid

Several interesting facts emerge from an examination of the areas to which American economic assistance has been distributed. From Table 1 it is clear that the Near East and South Asia and the Far East are the primary targets of U.S. economic aid; countries in these regions have received some $35.9 billion in American economic assistance. This represents over 60 percent of U.S. aid to the LDCs; however, it should be pointed out that these areas contain two-thirds of the population of the less developed world, so we should expect the concentration of aid here. Also, of course, these regions along with Europe surround the Communist countries, and it is interesting to note that 12 less developed countries[15] which are contiguous to the Communist bloc countries have received one-half[16] of total U.S. economic aid to the third world.

A closer look at the geographical distribution of American economic assistance is afforded by Table 2. An examination of the data over time using the years 1953–57 as a base reveals certain changes in the thrust of U.S. aid to the LDCs. Most notable, perhaps, is the emphasis on aid to Latin America since the initiation of the Alliance for Progress; the increase evident in the figures after 1961 is striking evidence of the impact of the Alliance for Progress on the aid program. Africa has also come to play a more important role in U.S. economic assistance than it did prior to 1959. This is most directly a result of the fact that only since 1959 have the majority of African states gained their independence.

American economic assistance to the Far East as a percentage of total aid to the LDCs revealed a decline from 1958 to 1965; however, the trend was reversed by the United States military commitment in South Vietnam, and since 1966 the Far East has reemerged as a major claimant upon American economic aid resources. Finally, the Near East and South Asia has replaced the

TABLE 2

Trends in American Economic Aid Commitments to LDCs by Geographical Area
(In Millions of U.S. Dollars)

Fiscal year	Near East and South Asia		Latin America		Far East		Africa		Total[b]
	Amount	% of Total[a]	Amount	% of Total	Amount	% of Total	Amount	% of Total	
1953–1957	$ 2,710	30	$ 1,775	19	$ 4,393	48	$ 226	2	$ 9,104
1958	878	41	354	17	794	37	100	5	2,126
1959	1,040	39	576	21	887	33	185	7	2,688
1960	1,427	53	341	13	707	26	208	8	2,683
1961	1,378	40	851	25	719	21	460	13	3,408
1962	1,826	47	1,016	26	590	15	487	12	3,919
1963	1,594	43	979	26	699	19	469	13	3,741
1964	1,539	42	1,190	33	567	16	356	10	3,652
1965	1,555	42	1,161	32	636	17	324	9	3,676
1966	1,429	34	1,227	29	1,240	29	366	9	4,262
1967	1,222	30	1,404	35	1,031	26	381	9	4,038
1968	1,202	32	1,362	36	905	24	337	9	3,806
Cumulative 1946–1968[b]	$19,711	37	$13,088	25	$16,226	31	$3,923	7	$52,948

SOURCES: Data for 1953 to 1961 are from U.S., Agency for International Development, *U.S. Overseas Loans and Grants and Assistance from International Organizations*, Special Report prepared for the House Foreign Affairs Committee, 1968. Data for 1962 to 1968 are from the 1969 edition of the same title.

a. Percentages may not add to 100 due to rounding.
b. Included in the regional and total figures are the following programs: AID and its predecessor agencies, Food-For-Peace, Export-Import Bank long-term loans, and other U.S. economic programs (see note c of Table 1).

Far East as the largest regional recipient of U.S. economic assistance since 1958. As the emphasis of the aid program changed to economic development, more funds were made available for this purpose and the largest development programs—notably those in India, Pakistan and Turkey—have emerged in this area.

In addition to the observations regarding the geographic distribution of American aid, it is interesting to note that 62 percent of total economic aid to 92 less developed countries through fiscal year 1967 was received by the 28 LDCs which are allies of the United States.[17] These 28 allies received U.S. aid in the amount of $62 per capita in contrast to the remainder of the LDCs which received $19 per capita.[18] These statistics definitely indicate that, in terms of maximizing economic aid from the United States, it generally pays for a less developed country to become an ally rather than to remain a neutralist.

Finally, it is interesting to note the contribution various aid channels make to the regional totals. Referring back to Table 1, it is clear that the bulk of Export-Import Bank long-term loans to less developed countries has gone to Latin America. Thus, even though this region has been afforded a higher aid priority since 1961, much of the assistance has been distributed on a relatively hard-term basis. The Near East and South Asia has benefitted most from the Food-For-Peace program. More P.L. 480 aid has gone to this area than has gone to all other regions combined.

Soviet Economic Assistance

There is an overwhelming asymmetry in the amount and type of data on the American and Soviet economic aid programs. In the case of the United States the plethora of programs and funding categories within programs makes it difficult to arrive at precise aid figures. The Soviet program, on the other hand, is still more difficult to analyze because of the paucity and lack of specificity in relevant data.

Nowhere has the USSR published comprehensive data on economic assistance such as that annually provided for U.S. aid by AID. Soviet literature on economic assistance usually gives an aggregate figure for cumulative Soviet economic assistance since 1954 and then reverts to a discussion of the number and types of projects undertaken in various less developed countries with the help of Soviet aid. For example, the figure given by almost all Soviet sources for total Soviet bilateral economic aid to less developed countries through 1965 was $4 billion.[19] This is approximately $1 billion less than the best Western estimates of total Soviet economic aid at the time.[20]

There are probably two reasons for this difference. First, Soviet sources usually cite United Nations literature as documentation for the aid figures presented, and UN sources give the $4 billion figure for total Soviet aid through 1965.[21] Second, the general paucity of specific information in Soviet literature would indicate that the USSR is not prone to divulge to the Russian public the full magnitude and scope of its economic assistance, thus, the pressure may well be toward understating rather than inflating Soviet aid figures.

Aggregate Data

Comprehensive data on Communist economic and military aid are presented in Table 3. Military aid and East European and Communist Chinese economic assistance are included to give an indication of the total Communist aid effort, but our focus will remain the economic assistance program of the USSR.

From Table 3, we see that the Communist countries have made economic aid commitments to 42 less developed countries in the amount of $9.7 billion since the economic offensive began in 1954. The USSR accounts for 65 percent of these commitments, having offered $6.3 billion in grants and long-term credits through 1968. However, unlike American economic assistance, Soviet expenditures are far below aid commitments. Through 1968 the USSR has delivered at most about $3 billion (somewhat more than 47 percent of its total economic assistance commitments) to the less developed countries of the non-Communist world.[22] Thus, it seems that, over all, the USSR is slower in implementing its aid commitments than the United States. Moreover, aid to three countries—Afghanistan, India, and the United Arab Republic—has accounted for 75 percent of USSR aid expenditures.[23]

TABLE 3

Cumulative Soviet and Other Communist Aid to the LDCs, 1954–1968
And Cumulative U.S. Aid to the LDCs, Fiscal years 1946–1968
(In Millions of U.S. Dollars)

Recipient	Communist Military Aid Commitments	Communist Economic Aid Commitments				USSR[b]	United States	
		Total	Com. China	East Europe[a]	USSR	Cat. 16 Exports	Economic	Military
Africa	$ 360	$1,502	$296	$ 348	$ 858	$ 137	$ 2,685	$ 229
Algeria	250	304	50	22	232	13	192	0
Cameroon	0	8	0	0	8	0	29	*
Central African Republic	0	4	4	0	0	0	5	0
Congo (Brazzaville)	*	34	25	0	9	3	2	0
Ethiopia	0	119	0	17	102	12	229	136
Ghana	10	231	40	102	89	21	240	*
Guinea	10	123	25	25	73	34	74	1
Kenya	0	62	18	0	44	0	63	0
Mali	*	101	23	23	55	22	19	3
Mauritania	0	7	4	0	3	0	3	0
Morocco	40	79	0	35	44	0	652	55
Nigeria	0	14	0	14	na[d]	0	229	2
Senegal	0	7	0	0	7	0	32	3
Sierra Leone	0	28	0	0	28	0	39	3
Somalia	30	94	22	6	66	18	73	0
Sudan	0	49	0	27	22	8	107	2
Tanzania	10	79	53	6	20	0	62	0

(Continued on following page)

TABLE 3—*Continued*

Recipient	Communist Military Aid Commitments	Communist Economic Aid Commitments				USSR[b] Cat. 16 Exports	United States	
		Total	Com. China	East Europe[a]	USSR		Economic	Military
Tunisia	0	105	0	71	34	7	564	27
Uganda	10	31	15	0	16	[e]	30	0
Zambia	0	23	17	0	6	0	41	0
Far East	1,350	944	239	294	411	71	1,161	158
Burma	0	124	84	26	14	4	100	0
Cambodia	10	80	50	5	25	1	254	87
Indonesia	1,340	740	105	263	372	66	807	71
Latin America	0	443	0	256	187	0	6,915	792
Argentina	0	54	0	9	45	0	700	117
Brazil	0	312	0	227	85	0	3,410	350
Chile	0	60	0	5	55	0	1,456	132
Colombia	0	2	0	0	2	0	979	103
Ecuador	0	5	0	5	0	0	249	50
Uruguay	0	10	0	5	0	0	121	40
Near East and South Asia	3,800	6,816	414	1,562	4,840	1,722	18,609	7,018[f]
Afghanistan	250	737	28	12	697	239	382	4
Ceylon	0	123	41	52	30	18	136	[e]
Greece	0	84	0	0	84	0	1,883	1,952
India	610	1,948	0	355	1,593	764	7,806	na
Iran	110	839	0	331	508	27	998	1,209
Iraq	650	184	0	0	184	108	56	47
Nepal	0	82	62	0	20	0	126	na

Recipient	Communist Military Aid Commitments	Communist Economic Aid Commitments				USSR[b] Cat. 16 Exports	United States	
		Total	Com. China	East Europe[a]	USSR		Economic	Military
Pakistan	40	343	109	56	178	24	3,631	na
South Yemen	0	12	12	0	0	0	0	0
Syria	460	418	16	169	233	49	63	[c]
Turkey	0	218	0	8	210	7	2,462	2,964
United Arab Republic	1,550	1,679	106	562	1,011	468	1,023	0
Yemen	100	149	40	17	92	18	43	0
Total	$5,480	$9,705	$949	$2,460	$6,296	$1,930	$29,370	$ 8,197
Other LDCs	$ 30[e]	0	0	0	0	0	$28,881	$11,070
Grand Total	$5,510	$9,705	$949	$2,460	$6,336[h]	$1,930	$58,251	$19,267

SOURCES: Data for Communist military aid derived from U.S. Department of State, Bureau of Intelligence and Research, *Communist Governments and Developing Nations: Aid and Trade in 1967*, RSE-120, August 1968. Data for Communist economic aid derived from ibid., *Communist Governments and Developing Nations: Aid and Trade in 1968*, RSE-65, September 1969. (Years cited are calendar years.) Data for American aid derived from U.S. Agency for International Development, *U.S. Overseas Loans and Grants and Assistance from International Organizations*, Special Report prepared for the House Foreign Affairs Committee, 1969. (Figures are aid *commitments*.)

a. Bulgaria, Czechoslovakia, East Germany, Hungary, Poland, and Rumania.
b. Table A in Appendix B. Through 1967. Totals differ from Appendix B due to rounding.
c. Less than $5 million.
d. Not available. Estimated at $140 million in the *New York Times*, November 22, 1968, p. 1.
e. Less than $500,000.
f. Data for U.S. military aid to India, Nepal, and Pakistan are classified. A rough estimate of military aid to these states through FY 1967 can be found in regional figures for the Near East and South Asia. The figure comes to $842 million through FY 1967 (see AID, *U.S. Overseas Loans and Grants*, 1968, p. 27). This accounts for the large Asia figure for U.S. military aid in spite of the lack of country data.
g. Cyprus.
h. Includes $40 million in multilateral aid. See Table 11.

A minimum estimate of the drawings on Soviet credits and grants by less developed countries can be derived from Soviet trade statistics. Category 16 of Soviet export data (Equipment and Material for Complete Plants) is believed to be almost entirely financed through economic assistance.[24] Cumulative Category 16 deliveries of the USSR to all the less developed countries receiving Communist aid since 1955 are presented in Table 3; these deliveries through 1967 total $1.9 billion. The difference between this figure and estimates of total Soviet aid deliveries is accounted for by the fact that some goods financed by Soviet aid move under other export categories. The Category 16 data also reflect the preponderance of Soviet aid deliveries to Afghanistan, India, and the United Arab Republic. A complete year-by-year summary of Category 16 deliveries to LDCs is presented in Appendix B.

The Direction of Soviet Aid

The geographical distribution of Soviet economic assistance indicates that Asia and the Middle East have been the major recipients of Soviet aid, accounting for some 82 percent of total commitments. Thus, Soviet as well as U.S. economic aid is flowing primarily to those countries surrounding the Communist camp. From Table 4 it is obvious that during the early period of Soviet economic assistance, Asia (India, Afghanistan, and Indonesia in particular) was the major recipient by an overwhelming margin, accounting for 73 percent of total aid commitments through 1957. Though relative to other areas Asia's importance in the overall program of the USSR has declined since that time, it still remains as the largest regional recipient of Soviet economic assistance.

The figures for the Middle East reflect the manner in which the Soviet Union has established a presence in the area through the use of economic (and military) assistance. Since 1956 Soviet aid has increased to the point where in 1965 the Middle East constituted almost as large a proportion of cumulative aid commitments as did Asia. However, large commitments to India in 1966 destroyed the temporary parity between the Middle East and Asia as Soviet economic aid recipients.

TABLE 4

Trends in Soviet Economic Aid Commitments to LDCs by Geographical Area
(In Millions of U.S. Dollars)

Year	Africa		Asia		Latin America		Middle East		Total
	Amount	% of Total[a]	Amount	% of Total	Amount	% of Total	Amount	% of Total	
1955–1957	$ 0	0	$ 496	73	$ 0	0	$ 183	27	$ 679
1958	0	0	37	10	45[b]	13	278	77	360
1959	137	16	577	67	0	0	141	16	855
1960	69	12	255	43	0	0	270	45	594
1961	193	35	354	65	0	0	0	0	547
1962	24	45	27	50	0	0	2	5	53
1963	100	42	53	22	0	0	83	35	236
1964	206	21	262	26	0	0	530	53	998
1965	0	0	64	10	15	2	574	88	653
1966	75[c]	8	660[e]	69	85[b]	9	139[c]	14	959
1967	9[b]	3	5[b]	2	55[b]	20	200[d]	74	269
1968[d]	140[e]	31	127	28	2	0	178	40	447
Cumulative									
1954–1968[f]	$998[g]	16	$2,929	46	$187	3	$2,322	36	$6,436[g]

SOURCE: Leo Tansky, "Soviet Foreign Aid to Less Developed Countries," in U.S., Congress, Joint Economic Committee, *New Directions in the Soviet Economy*, 89th Cong., 2d sess., 1966, pt. 4, p. 951—except where noted.

NOTE: *Asia* includes Afghanistan, Burma, Cambodia, Ceylon, India, Indonesia, Nepal, and Pakistan. *Middle East* includes Greece, Iran, Iraq, South Yemen, Syria, Turkey, United Arab Republic, Yemen. *Africa* and *Latin America* include the states listed under those regions in Table 3.

a. Totals may not add to 100 due to rounding.
b. U.S., Department of State, Bureau of Intelligence and Research, *Communist Governments and Developing Nations: Aid and Trade in 1967*, RSE-120, August 1968.
c. Ibid., *Communist Governments and Developing Nations: Economic Aid and Trade*, RSB-80, July 1967.
d. Ibid., *Communist Governments and Developing Nations: Aid and Trade in 1968*, RSE-65, September 1969.
e. Estimate in *New York Times*, November 22, 1968, p. 1.
f. U.S., Department of State, RSE-65, 1969. Figures may not coincide with totals by column because of revised estimates of earlier aid commitments.
g. Includes *New York Times'* estimate for Nigeria during 1968.

Until 1967 Latin America played a very small role in the total Soviet aid effort. The two major credit extensions prior to that year were to Argentina in 1958 and to Brazil in 1966. In 1967, a Soviet credit of $55 million to Chile was exceeded only by the credit extended to Turkey. It is interesting to note that Soviet and East European aid to Latin America is taking the form of commercial credits at higher interest rates and shorter periods of amortization than is characteristic of basic Soviet aid packages. This practice seems to reflect a preference by Latin American countries for Soviet aid in a form which brings a smaller number of Communist technicians to the field.[25] In spite of an increasing Soviet interest in forging trade and aid ties with Latin American countries, with the exception of Cuba, the United States until very recently has virtually preempted Soviet aid efforts in this traditional American sphere of influence. Developments in Peru and Bolivia during 1968 and 1969 may result in the forging of significant trade and aid ties between these states and the USSR and Eastern Europe.

Soviet aid to Africa followed much the same pattern as that of the United States: there was no aid to this area until 1959 because most countries had not yet achieved independence. As the decolonization process proceeded, the USSR moved into Africa with economic assistance. As a percentage of total aid the USSR has made a larger commitment to Africa than has the United States during the 1960s. In 1968 the USSR gained a firmer foothold in Africa through a major economic aid commitment to Nigeria.

The Soviet program is smaller and more selective than American economic assistance in that it has operated in only 38 less developed countries (compared to the 99 LDCs which have received U.S. aid). Also, the Soviet program is more concentrated as revealed by the fact that five countries have received 66 percent of total Soviet aid commitments—India, the United Arab Republic, Afghanistan, Iran, and Indonesia. This concentration is even more salient in an examination of actual aid deliveries, of which three-fourths have gone to only three countries.

Until the aid offers to Iran, Turkey, and Greece in 1965, Soviet economic assistance had gone almost exclusively to less developed countries which were not militarily aligned with the United States. The USSR has focused its aid agreements in the neutralist countries. Whereas the USSR favored a pro-Soviet policy on the part of the recipients, there has been no systematic attempt to bring the neutralist aid recipients into military alliance with the Soviet Union through economic assistance.

Much has been said in Western literature about the selectivity and concentration of Soviet economic aid, with the implication that its focus represents a singleness of purpose and a clear design in the use of the aid instrument by the USSR. The selectivity and focus of Soviet aid in a relatively small group of neutralist countries is partly a function of the less developed countries' receptivity to Soviet economic overtures. The USSR probably would have given more aid to more countries had the opportunities been present.[26] The Soviet Union has offered economic aid to Iran, Turkey, and Latin American states in the past, for example. But these countries felt it unwise to accept large offers until the mid-sixties when the USSR was perceived as being a less serious threat. Thus, the focus of Soviet aid in neutralist countries is partially explained by the refusal of LDCs closely associated with the West to accept offers of assistance from the USSR.

In order to compare the magnitudes of Soviet and American economic assistance to less developed countries, data on U.S. economic aid commitments to all countries which have received Soviet aid have been presented in Table 3. Since 1946 the United States has given $29.4 billion in economic assistance of various types to the less developed countries which are Communist aid recipients. The U.S. figures constitute commitments, but since expenditures have totaled approximately 90 percent of commitments we can treat the American data as roughly representing both commitments and expenditures. This $29.4 billion in U.S. aid to recipients of Soviet aid compares very favorably with Soviet economic aid commitments of $6.3 billion and deliveries of perhaps $3 billion. In one sense this basis of comparison favors the United States because the USSR only began giving aid in 1954; but it favors the Soviet Union in that total U.S. economic aid to these countries *plus* those in which there is no USSR program amounts to $58.3 billion. This means that in aggregate terms U.S. economic aid to less developed countries has been over nine times that offered by the USSR and about eighteen times that delivered.

Soviet Aid to Communist Countries

So far we have discussed only Soviet aid to less developed countries, but in order to fully comprehend the magnitude of Soviet aid something must be said of aid to other Communist countries. Total Soviet economic aid to Communist countries from 1945 to 1966 amounts to between $8.5 and $8.7 billion as shown in Table 5. In addition to actual loans this figure includes grants in the special forms of Soviet cancellations of debts, reparations, and Soviet shares in joint stock companies.

The significance of Soviet economic aid to other Communist countries is qualified by the fact that the USSR extracted an estimated $15 to $20 billion from Eastern Europe in the decade following World War II.[27] These extractions took the form of reparations payments, dismantlings of industry, occupation costs, and exploitative prices in trade, as well as the seizure of control over much East European industry in the form of joint stock companies. Indeed, it was not until 1954 that initial Soviet economic concessions to Eastern Europe were implemented, and the 1956 crises in Hungary and Poland provided the occasion for the USSR to reverse the flow of capital which previously had been coming to the Soviet Union from the East European countries. On balance it would appear that the USSR has received more "aid" from Eastern Europe since World War II than it has given to other Communist countries, including Eastern Europe, during the same period.

While recognizing that this figure ($8.5 to $8.7 billion) for Soviet economic aid to other Communist countries is probably inflated and more than offset by flows in the opposite direction, it is still useful as a rough calculation of Soviet assistance efforts in the Communist world. In addition to this economic assistance the USSR has given military aid to other Communist countries in the

TABLE 5

Soviet Economic Aid to Other
Communist Countries
1945–1966
(In Millions of U.S. Dollars)

Recipient	Amount
Albania	$ 246
Bulgaria	902–1,174[a]
Cuba	609[b]
Czechoslovakia	62
East Germany	1,353
Hungary	381
Mainland China	790
North Korea	690
North Vietnam	1,169[a]
Outer Mongolia	1,158[a]
Poland	914
Rumania	189
Total	$8,453–8,725

SOURCE: Data are taken from George S. Carnett and Morris H. Crawford, "The Scope and Distribution of Soviet Economic Aid," in U.S., Congress, Joint Economic Committee, *Hearings, Dimensions of Soviet Economic Power*, 87th Cong., 2d sess., December 11, 1962, p. 474.

a. Marshall I. Goldman, *Soviet Foreign Aid*, (New York: Frederick A. Praeger, 1967), pp. 24–25. Data for 1963 to 1966.

b. Robert S. Walters, "Soviet Economic Aid to Cuba," *International Affairs* (London) 42, no. 1 (January 1966): 81. Cuban figures include agreements through 1964. Goldman indicates a Soviet credit to Cuba of $89 million in 1966 which would bring the Cuban total to $698 million; and the cumulative aid total would also be raised to $8,542–$8,814 million. Goldman, *Soviet Foreign Aid*, p. 25.

approximate amount of $12 billion through 1963.[28] These data when combined with the $6.3 billion in economic aid and $5.5 billion in military aid to less developed countries yields an admittedly rough total figure for Soviet bilateral foreign aid of over $32 billion.

The $32 billion in total Soviet foreign aid is a figure most closely analogous to the $133 billion in economic and military aid given by the United States to all countries since World War II. Soviet economic aid to Communist and non-Communist countries comprises $15 billion of the $32 billion total. Approximately 58 percent of this economic assistance went to Communist countries.

The data concerning Soviet economic and military assistance to other Communist countries have been presented only as an indication of the order of magnitude of the total Soviet aid effort. It must be emphasized that these figures are much less precise than those given for American aid because of the lack of adequate primary sources on the Soviet program and because data on all types of military and economic aid are not available through 1968. The Soviet figures have been systematically biased on the high side throughout this presentation so as to arrive at a maximum total. (For example, we used total Communist military aid to LDCs as an estimate of Soviet military aid to these states.) It is clear that by any measure the sum total of Soviet economic assistance is a fraction of American economic aid.

Soviet Trade

Trade is closely related to aid in the Soviet economic offensive and requires at least a brief examination in any discussion of Soviet economic assistance to the less developed countries. A parallel discussion was not undertaken in connection with U.S. aid because the state trading practices of the USSR make trade an instrument wholly controlled by Soviet foreign policy, a practice which has no analogue in the U.S.

Table 6 summarizes Soviet trade since 1955, the first year for which reliable statistics became available. Total trade turnover of the USSR in 1967 was almost three times that in 1955. While trade with all types of countries grew, it is interesting to note that Soviet trade with other Communist countries grew the least, and such trade as a proportion of total Soviet trade actually has decreased from 80 to 67 percent over the period examined. This decline is explained by the severe deterioration in Sino-Soviet trade since 1960 combined with the increased emphasis on trade

TABLE 6

Soviet Trade Turnover, 1955–1967

(In Billions of U.S. Dollars)

Trading Partner	1955	1956	1957	1958	1959	1960	1961	1962	1963	1964	1965	1966	1967	1967 as % of 1955
Communist Countries	5.1	5.4	6.1	6.3	7.8	8.1	8.4	9.4	10.0	10.6	11.1	11.0	12.2	239
Non-Communist Countries	1.3	1.7	2.1	2.2	2.6	3.0	3.3	4.0	4.2	4.6	5.0	5.6	5.8	446
Industrially Developed	1.0	1.2	1.4	1.3	1.7	2.1	2.2	2.4	2.7	3.0	3.1	3.5	3.7	370
Underdeveloped (LDCs)	0.3	0.5	0.7	0.9	0.9	0.9	1.1	1.6	1.5	1.6	1.9	2.1	2.1	700
Total	6.4	7.2	8.2	8.6	10.4	11.1	11.7	13.4	14.2	15.3	16.1	16.6	18.0	281

SOURCES: Data for 1955–1963 derived from USSR, Ministerstvo Vneshnei Torgovli, Planovo-Ekonomicheskoe Upravleniye, *Vneshnyaya torgovlya Soyuza SSR za 1959–1963 gody* (Moscow: Vneshtorgizdat, 1965), pp. 10–11. Data for 1964 and 1965 from ibid., *Vneshnyaya torgovlya Soyuza SSR za 1965 god*, 1966, p. 10. Data for 1966 from ibid., *Vneshnyaya torgovlya Soyuza SSR za 1966 god*, 1967, p. 10. Data for 1967 from ibid., *Vneshnyaya torgovlya Soyuza SSR za 1967 god*, 1968, p. 10.

NOTES: Turnover equals exports plus imports. Ruble figures are converted to dollars at official exchange rate. Totals may not add due to rounding.

with non-Communist countries. The bulk of Soviet trade with other Communist countries is conducted with Eastern Europe from which the USSR imports predominantly machinery and equipment and manufactured consumer goods in return for Soviet exports of fuels, industrial raw materials, and machinery.[29] Czechoslovakia, East Germany, and Poland are the three largest trading partners of the USSR among the Communist countries.

Trade with the industrialized countries of the non-Communist world currently constitutes about 21 percent of total Soviet trade. Characteristically, the USSR has exported raw materials (with petroleum and petroleum products the most important single category), wood and wood products, metals, and ores to the industrialized West in return for machinery and equipment imports. However, for several years following the poor grain harvest in 1963, imports of grain from the West became an important component of the Soviet import structure. The main trading partners of the Soviet Union among the industrialized Western countries have been Finland, the United Kingdom, West Germany, Japan, Italy, and France.[30]

Soviet trade with the less developed countries has increased sixfold between 1955 and 1967. Even though this growth rate is made high by the very small amount of trade in 1955, it is clear that trade with the LDCs has been the most rapidly growing element in Soviet trade over the period in question. Trade with these countries constituted 12 percent of total USSR trade in 1967, compared to less than 5 percent in 1955. Though Soviet trade with the less developed countries is growing, it leveled off after 1965 and the USSR still accounted for only 2 percent of total LDC trade during the period 1964–1966. The smallness of this figure can be appreciated more fully when it is realized that the share of other Communist states in the total trade of these countries in 1964, for example, was 3 percent, that of the industrialized West was 75 percent, and 20 percent was accounted for by trade among the LDCs themselves.[31] So the $2.1 billion in annual Soviet trade with the third world is not particularly impressive in itself.

What makes Soviet trade important beyond its size is its use, in careful coordination with Soviet economic assistance, as a flexible instrument of foreign policy. This orchestration of trade and aid is possible because USSR trade is state trade, unlike the situation in the United States where trade is manipulated by the government only through comparatively indirect controls.

The relationship between Soviet trade and aid is particularly close because most Soviet aid agreements provide for the recipient to repay USSR credits in traditional exports or in the output of enterprises constructed in the LDC and financed by Soviet aid. This relationship is manifested in the fact that whereas the USSR traded with 42 less developed countries in 1964, two-thirds of Soviet exports to, and over three-fifths of Soviet imports from, the LDCs were accounted for by only seven countries (India, the United Arab Republic, Afghanistan, Indonesia, Iraq, Brazil, and Malaysia).[32] These countries—except for Brazil and Malaysia, which figure prominently only in Soviet imports of raw materials —are major Soviet aid recipients.

If the assumption is made that the Soviet Union accounted for 75 percent of total Communist aid deliveries from 1960 to 1964 (as is the case for overall aid deliveries since 1954),[33] it has been estimated that for the period 1960–1964, an average of 44 percent of Soviet exports to LDCs were flowing under long-term economic credits.[34]

With regard to the proportion of Soviet imports due to the aid program, the USSR has revealed that in 1964 it imported from the less developed countries $132 million in goods as repayment of credits granted to them.[35] This means that in 1964, at least, about 20 percent of Soviet imports from the third world were attributable to repayments of Soviet credits by the LDCs.

These data on the proportion of Soviet trade with the less developed countries accounted for by economic assistance are presented as evidence of the close relationship between trade and aid in Soviet economic relations with the LDCs. The relationship is much more significant in the case of the USSR than for the East European countries where aid disbursements have constituted only 10 to 12 percent of exports to the less developed countries in recent years.[36]

The composition of trade between the USSR and the less developed countries is almost the opposite of that conducted by the Soviet Union with Eastern Europe and the industrialized West. Almost two-thirds of Soviet imports from the LDCs consist of primary products (natural rubber, raw cotton, and hides and skins), while foodstuffs account for another quarter. Manufactured goods comprise only about 13 percent of Soviet imports from the less developed countries.[37] The structure of Soviet imports from the LDCs is most significant in light of the fact that the USSR claims that it is a large purchaser of third world manufactures, unlike the United States, which the USSR presents as interested only in keeping the third world as a supplier of raw materials. In fact, U.S. imports of manufactures from less developed countries amounted to almost $1 billion in 1963 compared to USSR imports of $85 million in 1964.[38] Moreover, U.S. imports of LDC-manufactured goods comprised about the same percentage of its total imports from the LDCs as the 13 percent figure from the USSR. U.S. imports from the third world in 1964 amounted to $6.4 billion, compared to $663 million in the case of the USSR.[39]

Soviet exports to less developed countries have largely been manufactured goods (rolled iron and steel, textile fabrics, etc.) and machinery and equipment. Particularly since 1961, Soviet exports of complete plants (Category 16) have become very significant in the structure of USSR trade with the third world. This is, of course, a reflection of the increase in Soviet deliveries under its aid program. In 1965 the USSR made aid deliveries in the approximate amount of $375 million; $294 million of these deliveries was in the form of complete plants exported to the less developed countries, which comprised over one-fourth of total Soviet exports to the LDCs. In spite of increasing Soviet exports of complete plants and other forms of machinery and equipment to the third world, however, the USSR remains a net importer of capital goods due to its trade with the West and with East Europe.

For comparative purposes Soviet trade with the less developed countries leads us to the same conclusions we drew when Soviet aid was placed alongside U.S. aid. In terms of order of magnitude and of scope, Soviet trade is very small in comparison to U.S. trade. In 1964, for example, U.S. exports to the LDCs were over $8 billion, or more than 10 times the amount of Soviet exports to these countries. Also, in spite of Soviet claims that the United States tries to keep the LDCs in a dependent economic relationship by minimizing exports of machinery to the third world, the United States exported almost 10 times as much machinery to these countries as did the USSR in 1963.[40] However, machinery and equipment do comprise a larger share of Soviet exports to the LDCs than is the case in U.S. trade.

Conclusions

This statistical comparison of Soviet and American economic assistance has revealed two basic imbalances. First, there is an imbalance in the nature of the basic data on the two programs: the U.S. figures are complex to a point requiring us to examine different channels and funding categories within the overall aid figures, whereas the Soviet data are so general that it is difficult to understand their significance in terms of the types of aid they include. Second, there is an impressive imbalance in the scope and magnitude of the two programs. By virtually any measure chosen the United States economic aid program, as well as its trade with the less developed countries, is overwhelming in comparison to the Soviet program. This is true even though the Soviet data were systematically presented in a fashion most generous to the USSR.

The relative magnitudes of American and Soviet aid are most vividly exemplified in the fact that cumulative Soviet economic aid deliveries of $3 billion to the less developed countries from 1954 to 1968 amount to less than U.S. aid deliveries in fiscal year 1968 alone. In addition, U.S. aid commitments have been far less volatile than those of the USSR. During the sixties the level of Soviet aid commitments has ranged from $53 million in 1962 to $998 million in 1964.

It should be noted that in 1964 the GNP of the USSR was only about 46 percent that of the U.S.[41] Therefore, we should expect American trade and aid to be at least twice the size of the Soviet economic efforts in the third world. From the data presented in this chapter, however, it appears that U.S. trade and aid in the LDCs are probably more on the order of ten times larger than the USSR programs. So, in spite of the differences in the size of the Soviet and American economies, the basic conclusions regarding the scope and magnitude of the two programs seem justifiable.

Among the LDCs both Soviet and American economic assistance have been heavily concentrated in the Near East, South Asia, and the Far East (including Southeast Asia). In these regions U.S. aid has most predominantly flowed to countries in the Western alliance system, whereas Soviet aid has been concentrated in neutralist countries. However, India has been the largest single recipient of American economic aid even though it is neutralist, and U.S. allies among the less developed countries surrounding the Communist camp have recently received substantial Soviet aid offers.

Soviet trade has been demonstrated to be intimately related to the Soviet economic assistance program. While this should not be surprising in light of the nature of Soviet aid agreements (which usually provide for repayment in traditional exports of the recipient), the fact that the East European countries make similar aid agreements yet vigorously engage in essentially purely commercial trade indicates that Soviet trade is particularly important as an instrument of Soviet foreign policy. Of course a major reason for this difference between the USSR and East European countries is that the latter are less abundantly endowed with raw materials of great variety and have much greater economic need for commercial trade than does the Soviet Union. Although this may be more true for the 1950s than the 1960s, the USSR seems to trade in order to aid the LDCs (for whatever reasons), as distinct from the East European countries which seem to give aid as a means of generating trade with the less developed countries.

There has been much concern in the West regarding the use of trade and aid in order to bring less developed countries into a position of economic dependence upon the USSR and the Communist camp. Since the Soviet Union accounts for only two percent and the Communist countries combined accounted for only six percent of the overall trade of LDCs in 1966, the danger is obviously not very great. On the other hand, due to the concentration of Communist economic relations, the case is not so clear on a country-by-country basis. Let us assume that a less developed country is in danger of becoming overly dependent upon the Communist countries if over 20 percent of its imports or exports are directed toward them. If this is true, then eight less developed countries (Afghanistan, Ceylon, Guinea, Iraq, Mali, Syria, the United Arab Republic, and Yemen) were in danger of becoming overly dependent upon the Communist camp in 1967.[42]

The real danger to the West constituted by the Communist economic offensive would not seem to be too great even if the correctness of the assumption is granted. East European commercial relations, as distinct from aid, manifest strong indications of competition with each other and with the USSR, so the fact that the Communist camp accounts for a relatively large portion of an LDC's trade turnover does not necessarily indicate that a single influence is being exerted on the less developed countries by all its Communist trading partners. There is also little reason to believe China is cooperating with either the USSR or Eastern Europe. Thus, since the data above were for Soviet, Chinese, and East European trade as a portion of the LDCs trade turnover, the share of USSR trade alone would be less—and presumably the dependence of these eight less developed countries on the USSR itself would be less than the data indicate at first glance.

But, more fundamentally, it seems questionable that any arbitrarily selected share in the total trade turnover of a less developed country is a valid indicator of the influence of the USSR or any other country over the affairs of the LDCs. In the vast majority of cases even a poor nation would sever crucial economic relations rather than sacrifice its political independence beyond a point deemed by itself to be acceptable. The Soviet Union accounted for 60 percent of Communist China's imports and 52 percent of her exports in 1954.[43] China could not expect the United States or the West to replace the USSR as a major trade partner accepting such things as pig bristles in exchange for heavy machinery. Nevertheless, when China decided it was politically expedient to sever commercial dependence upon the USSR it was able to do so in spite of the economic difficulty involved. In 1956 the Chinese began exporting more to the Soviet Union than they imported, and by 1965 they had completely repaid their aid and commercial debts to the USSR.[44]

Similar behavior has been demonstrated by less developed countries largely dependent on Soviet economic relations. These countries, unlike China, are able to count on U.S. and Western help in attempting to decrease economic reliance on the USSR. In spite of very heavy economic commitments to the Soviet Union in 1961, Guinea found it possible to initiate a quick shift in its trade and aid contacts toward the United States when it decided the Soviet Union had too much influence in the country.

Thus it appears that the danger of Soviet dominance over less developed countries through the use of trade and aid is not too great in the short run. The danger, insofar as it exists, is that over a long period of time continued heavy trade with the USSR will result in the less developed countries' becoming accustomed to Soviet trade procedures, products, and markets to the point where they either must or prefer to depend on the Soviets for spare parts and new goods out of habit or from the lack of contacts in the West. However, even this danger does not seem too salient in that the same relationship with the West has not prevented LDCs from securing trade relations with the USSR when they desired to do so.

These remarks lead us to the conclusion that the size of Soviet trade and aid with the less developed countries is not of a magnitude which should cause great concern in the West. The data suggest that the United States has an overwhelming economic advantage over the Soviet Union in the third world. Even in the very few specific cases where Soviet economic influence is predominant, the demonstration that the United States is willing to provide economic help, combined with the sensitivity of the LDCs to maintaining their newly won political independence, makes it questionable how much leverage the Soviets can exert by virtue of a local trade and aid dominance.

6

Administration
of the Aid Programs

‡ To outline in detail all the various aspects of Soviet and American aid efforts throughout the third world since the end of World War II would be an impossible task. Thus, we will attempt only to present the styles of the programs, by which we mean, simply, the characteristic modes of action employed by the donors in their distribution of economic assistance to the LDCs. Specifically, our attention will focus upon the administration, operational emphases, and terms of the programs.

The operations of P.L. 480 and the Export-Import Bank constitute a significant portion of American economic assistance efforts, as indicated in the discussion of the scope and magnitude of U.S. aid. However, these aid channels operate alongside of, and separate from, the core of the American economic aid program, which has been administered by AID and its predecessor agencies. Therefore, while P.L. 480 and Export-Import Bank activities will be mentioned from time to time, the discussion of U.S. aid will focus primarily upon the activities of AID and its predecessor agencies.

Administration of American Economic Assistance

Organizational Evolution

An impressive aspect of American economic assistance since the advent of Point Four, the first program designed primarily for aid to the less developed countries, has been the continued organizational reform of the agencies administering the programs. Since 1950 the American aid program has experienced the establishment and demise of the Technical Cooperation Administration (1950–1953), the Mutual Security Agency (1951–1953), the Foreign Operations Administration (1953–1955), the International Cooperation Administration (1955–1961), and the Development Loan Fund (1957–1961). This list is confined to those agencies whose operations are currently being performed by the Agency for International Development, created in 1961.[1]

The Mutual Security Agency (MSA) and the Foreign Operations Administration (FOA), which replaced it in 1953, were independent agencies located in the Executive Office of the President.[2] They were responsible for conducting economic assistance operations and coordinating economic and military assistance, the latter being administered by the Department of Defense.[3] The location of the principal aid agency in the Executive Office of the President during this period was designed to separate operational authority from policy-making, which was expected to come from the Department of State. This logic was particularly evident in the case of FOA.[4]

The creation of the International Cooperation Administration (ICA) in 1955 was primarily a response to congressional insistence that economic assistance could continue only if it were administered through permanent agencies of the government, rather than through a special independent agency such as FOA.[5] Thus, ICA was established as a semiautonomous agency within the Department of State to replace FOA, retaining, however, essentially the same functions that had been performed by FOA. Even though the Agency for International Development replaced ICA in 1961, it was placed in the Department of State and thus the arrangement has remained much the same as that created with the establishment of ICA in 1955.

This turnover in organizational form for American economic assistance has been paralleled by even more frequent change in the directors of the program. Since the creation of the Mutual Security Agency in 1951 the directors of the aid program have been Averell Harriman (1951–1953), Harold Stassen (1953–1955), John Hollister (1955–1957), James Smith (1957–1959), James Riddleberger (1959–1961), Henry Labouisse (1961), Fowler Hamilton (1961–1962), David Bell (1962–1966), William Gaud (1966–1969), and John Hannah (1969–present).

One factor contributing to the overabundance of organizational reform has been the dilemma of arriving at the proper relationship between the operation of, and policy formation for, the aid program. Specifically, the difficulty involves the relationship of the aid agency to the Department of State which provides policy guidance for the aid program. In 1953 the conviction that operational control of aid efforts should be divorced from policy guidance was a major consideration leading to the abolition of the Technical Cooperation Administration located in the State Department and the creation of FOA in the Executive Office of the President. The opposite impulse was evident just two years later in the creation of ICA as a semiautonomous unit within the Department of State. This dilemma has not been a determining factor in all reorganization efforts, but it has contributed at times to the motivation for administrative reform.

Congressional dissatisfaction on various grounds has been a second factor prompting reorganizations in the aid program. About the same time as the creation of FOA, Congress declared in the Mutual Security Act of 1953 that economic aid, as administered by FOA, was to be terminated within two years. As we noted above, Congress also insisted that if the President decided to continue aid beyond this time, it would have to be done through permanent agencies of the government rather than through an independent agency like FOA.[6] This led to the abolition of FOA and its replacement by ICA in 1955. Similarly, increasing congressional dissatisfaction with the aid program in the late fifties greatly influenced the decision to terminate ICA and replace it with AID in 1961, as the symbol of a new approach in the distribution of U.S. economic assistance.

This desire to mold a new aid image, for the benefit of Congress as well as for the benefit of countries abroad, constitutes a third factor contributing to repeated organizational reform. There seems to be a persistent desire to accompany a new policy emphasis in the aid program with a brand new agency having a clean slate and not being identified with whatever frustrations and problems are associated with the aid agency in existence. The creation of an agricultural surplus commodity export program (1954) and the Development Loan Fund (1957) as entities separate from the existing aid machinery is indicative of this tendency. But the best example is undoubtedly the creation of AID. The new agency was presented by the administration as a new departure in U.S. economic assistance which would emphasize economic development as the basic motivation and criterion for the distribution of aid. Presumably, the new agency, in addition to being organized differently from ICA, was to serve as a visible symbol of a new determination and focus in U.S. economic assistance which would not have been as evident had ICA continued to administer the program.

Still another factor inducing reorganization of American aid has been the desire to centralize the plethora of ad hoc aid programs which have grown up over the years. This was the motivation, in part, for the decision to merge the Technical Cooperation Administration and the Mutual Security Agency into the FOA in 1953. Also, a facet of the rationale for the creation of AID was to consolidate some of the various aid mechanisms into a single agency. The attempt was only partially successful, but the activities of ICA as well as those of the Development Loan Fund (DLF) were taken over by AID in 1961. The success of consolidation efforts has been limited because of interdepartmental jealousies and the countervailing tendency to create new aid instruments, like P.L. 480 and the DLF, outside of the existing administrative apparatus.

There have been serious negative effects within the aid agencies as a result of the frequent reorganization of the program. Each reorganization has been accompanied by significant delays in programming and implementing economic assistance because of the inevitable ambiguity in the definition of new responsibilities for personnel within the agency and for the agency in its relations with other parts of the government. Aid personnel have suffered a serious lowering of morale due to this constant reshuffling of responsibilities and the lack of confidence shown in the aid program by the need or desire to restructure it so often. Also, the general public cannot but question the quality and effectiveness of the aid program and its personnel, when, with each reorganization, the old activities are discredited and the new structure is oversold and unable to realize the expectations generated with its creation.[7]

The rapid turnover of the directors of American economic assistance has also produced negative results. An obvious difficulty is to obtain strong leadership from directors of the program who have such brief tenure in the position and who often are recruited into the job from outside the agency. Fitzgerald notes that in ICA a new country director did not usually reach his peak usefulness and competence until a lapse of two to three years of experience on the job;[8] few directors of the overall aid program have remained for that period of time, and those that have left shortly thereafter. Presumably, the timetable regarding country directors would constitute a minimum schedule for the development of the director of the entire aid program.

Another problem posed by the brief tenure of the aid directors is the fact that the members of congressional committees examining the aid program every year seem even more formidable by virtue of their continued observation of aid efforts in contrast with the relative inexperience of most new directors of the program.

Finally, a general result of the many aid reorganizations has been to focus undue attention and blame for difficulties in the program on administrative forms and personnel, rather than on the more basic substantive problems such as the inherent difficulties in developing human resources and institutions in the less developed countries. This tendency to believe mistakenly "that persistent and intractable problems of substance could be resolved by a radical change in the form of the organization"[9] is remarkably similar to the approach Khrushchev took to problem-solving in the USSR. It may be recalled that he was prone to tinker incessantly with the organization of the Party and the economy in attempts to rectify "persistent and intractable problems of substance."

The discussion of the evolution in the administration of American economic assistance has led us to the creation of AID, the present agency responsible for U.S. aid. Let us now examine in more detail the organization of AID in Washington and in the field.

The Organization of AID

AID is a semiautonomous agency located within the Department of State. The administrator, currently John Hannah, reports directly to the secretary of state and the President, and has responsibility for the formulation and direction of economic assistance policies as well as the coordination of economic and military assistance.

AID is organized primarily on a geographical basis to enable country-by-country programming of U.S. economic assistance. The chain of command runs from the administrator through the heads of the regional bureaus and then through the ambassadors, to the country directors of U.S. aid missions abroad (see Figure 1).[10]

The administrator plans, directs, and coordinates the operation of the agency with the help of program offices and staffs dealing with broad functional problems and interregional programs. Among the most important of these program offices are the Office of Program and Policy Coordination, the Office of Private Resources, and the Office of the War on Hunger. The Office of Program and Policy Coordination develops economic assistance program policies, coordinates and presents agency budget requests, recommends allocation of resources, provides guidance to the regional bureaus in development planning, and coordinates military and economic assistance.[11] It also coordinates U.S. aid programs with development assistance activities of multilateral organizations and other Western nations. The Office of Private Resources formulates policy, program guidance, and procedures for fostering overseas development through nongovernmental resources. This office is the focal point for AID contacts with the

FIGURE 1

The Organization of the Agency for International Development, 1967

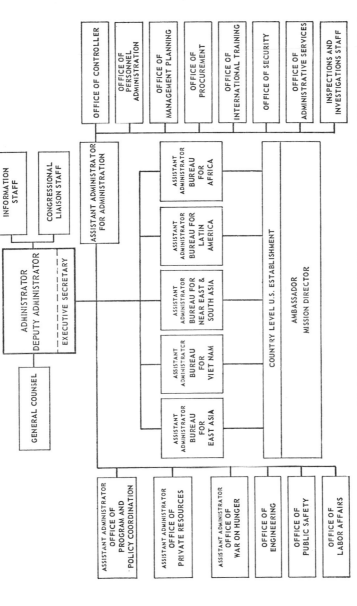

SOURCE: U.S., General Services Administration, National Archives and Records Service, Office of the Federal Register, *United States Government Organization Manual, 1967–68*, June 1, 1967, p. 637.

business community and it coordinates the various programs designed to promote private foreign investment in the less developed countries.[12] Some of these efforts will be discussed in the following chapter. The Office of the War on Hunger assists in the development of AID policies and procedures relating to agriculture, health, and population in the LDCs. It coordinates AID activities in these fields with the Department of Agriculture which administers P.L. 480 aid.[13]

The regional bureaus are the principal offices of AID which link Washington to the field missions in the less developed countries. They direct operations and formulate program policies for countries in their area in accordance with the guidelines set by the AID administrator. There are five regional bureaus: Latin America, the Near East and South Asia, Africa, East Asia, and Vietnam. The last two bureaus were created in 1967 out of what used to be a single bureau for the Far East. The step was made in order to deal more effectively with the Vietnam aid program which by fiscal year 1966 accounted for approximately twenty percent of AID funds and personnel.

In most countries receiving American economic assistance there is an AID mission attached to the U.S. embassy. The mission is usually composed of a mission director with a staff for program planning, accounting, and administrative support of various aid projects going on in the country.[14] The size of the mission varies with the size of the country program, and in cases where the program is very small (such as in some African nations) a small office or a single AID official may be attached to the embassy, as AID representative, to oversee the use of AID funds. The mission director or AID representative is in charge of aid activities in the field. The role of the mission and the relations among the various levels in the administration of U.S. economic assistance can best be understood by observing the programming process in which aid allocations are determined.

The Programming Process

At the beginning of each programming cycle the missions in the various countries have at their disposal standing policy guidelines set forth in the *AID Program Guidance Manual* as well as messages from the administrator and the regional bureau in Washington, pointing out subjects to which special attention should be given in preparing proposals for the coming fiscal year. This guidance, along with the country program agreed upon during the previous fiscal year, the desires expressed by the recipient, and the needs evaluated by the mission, constitute the basis upon which the various missions draw up program proposals for submission to Washington. The proposed country assistance program as drawn up by the mission is submitted to the ambassador, who reviews it in terms of its compatibility with overall U.S. policy in the recipient country and then sends it to AID-Washington with whatever comments he desires to make.

The proposed program coming from the mission in the LDC is reviewed in Washington by responsible officers in the regional bureau and a regional review culminates in an interagency meeting chaired by the regional assistant administrator and attended by representatives from the Departments of State and Defense, and usually the Bureau of the Budget. The decisions reached in this review process are reflected in a revised and approved Country Assistance Strategy Statement which states U.S. aid objectives in a particular LDC and sets out the strategy, magnitude, and content of the aid program through which the goals will be pursued. This approved statement is then sent back to the country mission through the ambassador. It provides guidance for operational decisions during the year and a starting point for the program-planning process the following year.

On the basis of the revised and approved Country Assistance Strategy Statements, AID seeks to reconcile its budget estimates with planning levels submitted to it from the Bureau of the Budget. Upon acceptance of the total AID budget by the Bureau of the Budget, AID presents its requests to congressional authorization and appropriation committees. This entire cycle from the missions' country assistance program proposals to presentation of the program to Congress takes approximately fifteen months.[15]

Turning from AID to the other two channels for American economic assistance, we will deal only with their administrative linkages to AID as the central U.S. aid distributor and coordinator.

Export-Import Bank long-term loans and AID Development Loans are used for similar projects and programs. Therefore, in order to avoid working at cross purposes the president and chairman of the board of the Export-Import Bank is a member of the Development Loan Committee (whose chairman is the AID administrator) which determines loan policies and utilization in the less developed countries. Through this contact, as well as through a liaison committee to coordinate AID and Bank activities on specific lending proposals, the activities of the two agencies are supposed to be harmonized.[16]

The relationship between AID and P.L. 480 aid has been in such a state of flux over the years that a detailed description of administrative responsibilities would be unnecessarily lengthy for our purposes. The basic arrangement has remained relatively stable, however. The Department of Agriculture determines the agricultural commodities and the quantity available for distribution under the Food-For-Peace Act and the nature and quantity of commodities which may be distributed to any specific less developed country under the act.[17] The primary interest of the Department of Agriculture in determining these factors is the avoidance of disrupting normal agricultural commodity trade patterns. The Department of State and AID determine the extent to which P.L. 480 assistance is consistent with overall U.S. foreign policy objectives and the economic development of the recipient.

Most of the local currency obtained by the United States through the sale of agricultural commodities under P.L. 480 is loaned or granted to the recipient. The programming of these funds is determined by an interagency committee of which the principal members are AID and the Department of Agriculture.[18]

Finally, the overall coordinator of Food-For-Peace assistance is the director of the Food-For-Peace program who has at various times operated out of the Office of the President and out of the Department of State and currently is located in the Office of the War on Hunger in AID.

Administration of Soviet Economic Assistance

Organizational Evolution

The evolution of the administration of Soviet economic assistance to the less developed countries has been less complicated
than that of the United States. Prior to 1955 when the USSR gave
little economic assistance to either Communist countries or non-
Communist less developed countries, a subordinate organization
of the Soviet Ministry of Foreign Trade, Tekhnoeksport, handled
Soviet aid efforts. This agency had central responsibility for planning and administering Soviet aid including functions such as the
furnishing of equipment for projects abroad, providing technical
assistance for the planning and operation of aid projects, and
supervising the training of foreign nationals from the recipient
countries in the Soviet Union.[19]

In 1955 the USSR established the Chief Administration for
Economic Relations with the People's Democracies (Glavnoe
Upravlenie po Delam Ekonomicheskikh Sviazei so Stranami Na-
rodnoi Demokratii [GUES]) as the primary agency for economic
assistance.[20] As its title suggests, the chief emphasis of Soviet aid
at the time was economic assistance to the Communist countries
of Eastern Europe; however, Tekhnoeksport was affiliated with
GUES and continued to handle aid to the less developed countries. In July 1957 GUES was reorganized and replaced by the
State Committee for Foreign Economic Relations (Gosudar-
stvennyi Komitet Sovyeta Ministrov SSSR po Vneshnim Ekonom-
icheskim Sviaziam [GKES]), which since that time has administered Soviet economic aid to Communist and non-Communist
countries. This creation of the State Committee in 1957 represented an upgrading of the assistance program in the USSR
administrative hierarchy and reflected the change in emphasis of
Soviet aid which by 1957 was focused on less developed countries, rather than on the People's Democracies. The head of the
State Committee in 1957 was M. G. Pervukhin, who was replaced
in February 1958 by the present Soviet aid administrator, S. A.
Skachkov.[21]

The long tenure of the head of the State Committee on Foreign Economic Relations and the durability of the State Committee itself contrast markedly with the American experience in the administration of economic assistance with its constant reorganization and turnover in top personnel. During the years in which Skachkov has directed the Soviet aid program, for example, the United States had had seven administrators for AID and its predecessor agencies.

The Organization of GKES

Very little concrete information is available from Western or Soviet sources on the structure and operation of Soviet economic assistance; however, enough is known to piece together a general picture of the aid program's administration.

The State Committee for Foreign Economic Relations reports directly to the USSR Council of Ministers, and Skachkov holds the rank of minister.[22] So, unlike AID in the United States, which is a semiautonomous agency within the Department of State, GKES is not a subordinate element of the Soviet Ministry of Foreign Affairs or of any other ministry.[23] While there is some question as to whether or not a body exists in the USSR which oversees and coordinates the activities of GKES with other Soviet programs in the LDCs (such as trade and cultural relations),[24] it is currently believed that no formal institutional device exists for this purpose. The Council of Ministers of the USSR upon which Skachkov sits would seem to be the place where this type of coordination takes place.

The internal organization of GKES is divided along geographical and functional lines. There are departments for the socialist countries, Africa, the Near and Middle East, and Southeast Asia.[25] Some of the functional divisions as they existed in 1958 were an administration for construction of enterprises abroad, a section for industry and transport, a section for agriculture, a section for finances and internal trade, an administration for matters of scientific-technical cooperation, a protocol section, a legal-treaty section, and a main engineering administration (believed to be in charge of Soviet military assistance).[26] These functional divisions seem to be substantially the same today (see Figure 2).

Attached to the State Committee for Foreign Economic Relations are four trade corporations which used to be part of the Ministry of Foreign Trade. Tekhnopromeksport (technical and industrial exports) handles irrigation and engineering work and was given initial responsibility for work on the Aswan Dam. Tekhnoeksport (technical exports) makes geological surveys, builds industrial plants, and undertakes work connected with transportation. Tiazhpromeksport (heavy industrial exports) is responsible for projects concerned with ferrous and nonferrous metals as well as coal and oil development. Finally, Promasheksport (industrial machinery exports) handles machine tools, radios, chemicals, and other machinery exports.[27]

Western knowledge about the organization and operations of GKES in the less developed countries receiving Soviet aid is as skimpy as that concerning the arrangements in Moscow. In the 1950s—it seems certain—the USSR had no real counterpart to the American aid missions which were in charge of overall U.S. economic aid efforts in the recipient country. Soviet aid, given on a project basis, apparently was organized through a process whereby each project was virtually self-contained administratively—somewhat like projects financed privately by Western firms.[28] However, as the size of the Soviet aid program increased, a more or less permanent staff attached to the Soviet embassy and not connected directly to any single Soviet aid project had to be maintained in the largest aid recipients (for example, India, the United Arab Republic, and Indonesia). These staffs assist in negotiations between GKES and the recipient[29] on new project agreements and on problems arising in connection with ongoing projects. In countries with small Soviet aid programs these duties are handled by one or a few persons in the Soviet embassy.

Only in those countries receiving large amounts of aid, and then only in a superficial way, does the organization of Soviet foreign aid resemble that of the U.S. program, with its missions and mission directors of AID attached to the American embassy. The USSR economic missions in these countries are presumably

FIGURE 2

The Organization of GKES, 1966

Government Committee of the Council of Ministers of the USSR for Foreign Economic Relations (GKES)

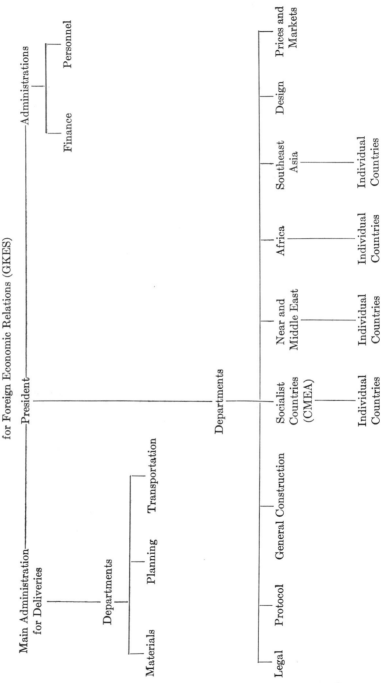

Source: Marshall I. Goldman, *Soviet Foreign Aid* (New York: Frederick A. Praeger, 1967), p. 77. Reprinted by permission.

staffed by personnel of the State Committee and are attached to the Soviet embassy. Although the exact nature of the linkage between Moscow and the field in the administration of economic assistance is unclear, the Soviet field staff connected with economic aid to less developed countries probably does not possess the authority and broad responsibilities held by a U.S. AID mission director who is in charge of the overall American aid effort in an LDC.[30]

Of course, this is to be expected since the USSR does not engage in overall country programming as does the United States, but relies almost exclusively on assistance of a nature which requires little coordination among various projects. Thus, the need for a local aid official or staff with wide discretion over the entire aid effort in the country is not as great in the Soviet program as it is in that of the United States. Because of this fact, and the smallness of the Soviet economic aid program, the size of the more or less permanent Soviet aid mission or staff in the LDCs is probably smaller than that of the United States. (This statement does not apply to the personnel attached to specific projects.)

The Programming Process

There is no precise analogue in Soviet aid to what in the U.S. program would be called the programming process, but the manner in which Soviet aid is given for specific projects is generally understood. The first step has traditionally been the conclusion of a general aid and technical assistance agreement which stipulates the overall monetary commitment the USSR will make to the recipient. During the Khrushchev era these larger credit-line commitments were reached by top Soviet leaders, such as Khrushchev and Bulganin in the case of the $100 million credit to India in 1955, and Mikoyan in the case of the $100 million credit to Cuba in 1960. Since Khrushchev's removal, the level of fanfare accompanying new agreements has diminished somewhat, but large credits are still negotiated by top-level personnel in GKES, very often by Skachkov himself.[31]

Upon the conclusion of the general credit agreement the less developed countries submit project proposals which they wish to be financed by the Soviet Union. The recipient "is not required to develop a general plan or framework for development in terms of which specific projects have to be justified,"[32] and there is no evidence to suggest that the USSR attempts to draw up such a plan for its own use in decisions as to which projects are more valuable for the overall economic progress of the less developed country. The USSR seldom recommends which projects should be submitted by the LDC, and the aid negotiators tend to confine themselves to the acceptance or rejection of the specific project proposals.[33] There are a few instances where Soviet advisors have assisted in the drawing up of development plans and influenced the selection of projects included;[34] however, this has not been typical of Soviet behavior vis-à-vis its aid recipients.

The following comment by I. Kapranov reflects Soviet aid behavior concerning project selection in aid to less developed countries:

In all cases, the recipient country itself decides what it should build in the first place. Soviet technical experts only help such countries, at their request, to determine the economic advisability of this or that enterprise, to fix its optimum capacity and also to solve other problems in making the plant profitable to operate.[35]

The USSR usually makes careful and thorough studies of costs and availability of human and raw material inputs from within the recipient country before signing specific project agreements under the general credit lines.[36] Though these studies have always been made, since the removal of Khrushchev the Soviet Union has been increasingly cautious in completing cost studies and surveys before announcing specific credits.[37] Thus, whereas the Soviet Union does not examine the overall development requirements of the recipient, its selection of projects is based on careful analysis designed to prevent Soviet support of enterprises which are economically unfeasible for the recipient to undertake.

Compared with United States aid, Soviet aid involves much less participation in the overall development planning and initiation of project proposals by the recipient countries. The United States actively encourages and assists less developed countries in evaluating their development requirements, while the USSR, unless requested to make proposals of its own, assumes a relatively passive attitude which places the responsibility for aid projects more squarely upon the recipient. However, to conclude that the United States accepts responsibility for its aid efforts, while the USSR does not, is too simple. It seems to be a general characteristic of aid that regardless of the donor country or its practices, the recipient accepts responsibility and credit for projects which are successful while the donor is held responsible and receives the blame for projects which fail.[38]

Because of the lack of concern for overall development requirements manifested in the administration of Soviet aid and the interest in political impact through timely assistance, the USSR is frequently portrayed as having more flexibility and speed in negotiating aid agreements than is the case in the American program, which seeks justification of all development projects in terms of their relation to the needs of the economy before an aid agreement is made. The speed with which the USSR moved to negotiate and implement the 1955 aid agreement with Afghanistan (five months) is illustrative of what the Soviet Union can do when it desires to act fast.[39] On the other hand, the Contingency Fund and Supporting Assistance are means by which American aid can be quickly channeled to less developed countries when the need arises. The United States moved rapidly in extending Supporting Assistance to Guinea in 1961 and 1962 when the chance to counterbalance Soviet aid presented itself. This form of American economic aid does not require the justification in terms of the overall development plans of the recipient which is necessary for Development Loans and Grants. So, whereas Soviet aid agreements may be negotiated with more flexibility and dispatch than is characteristic of U.S. development assistance, there are other American aid mechanisms which are prompt and flexible.

Conclusions

The most striking contrast in the administration of Soviet and American aid is, undoubtedly, the relative lack of organizational stability in the latter. The rapid turnover in the top administrative personnel and the continual restructuring of the aid agencies have generated results detracting from the performance of American assistance in less developed countries. The Soviet Union, on the other hand, has maintained the same aid agency since 1957, and has had the same director since 1958. This difference in the two programs is certainly not of decisive importance, but the incessant administrative tinkering with American aid gives the impression that the United States is still searching for a basis upon which to make a long-term commitment for distributing aid to the less developed countries.

On the other hand, the plethora of funding categories within AID and the existence of two additional aid channels (P.L. 480 and the Export-Import Bank) are manifestations of the complexity of American economic assistance efforts. This intricate mix of U.S. aid instruments necessarily requires a more elaborate and flexible administrative structure than the comparatively simple program conducted by the Soviet Union. It is also worth reemphasizing that in terms of actual annual aid deliveries to the less developed countries the United States program is at least ten times the size of its Soviet counterpart. Thus, the administrative requirements and problems in the distribution of American economic assistance are substantially greater than those facing the USSR.

The United States places much more reliance in its country missions abroad than appears to be the case in the Soviet program. U.S. missions are more or less permanently involved in evaluating development plans of aid recipients in order to suggest worthwhile aid projects or programs, and to prevent the United States from financing projects which are economically unfeasible. The Soviet Union tends to confine its activities in evaluating aid proposals to the assurance that they are economically practicable. All this indicates a general tendency for the United States to play a more active and forceful role than the Soviet Union in its aid relations with the less developed countries.

The difference in the stances taken by American and Soviet aid officials in their relations with recipient countries basically derives from the difference in priorities motivating the donors in the extension of aid. United States interest in economic development and the structuring of its aid program around this principle has led to the adoption of country programming, which requires the accumulation of massive amounts of information by AID for the purpose of addressing the needs of the recipient country in its development process. From this information AID arrives at decisions as to priorities among needs, and the agency attempts to prompt the LDC to go through a similar decision process with or without the assistance of American officials. In this manner, the economic development motivation for U.S. aid has necessitated an activist relationship vis-à-vis the recipient involving close contacts in the drawing up of overall development plans and the justification of specific aid projects in terms of the needs and priorities of the overall economy.

By contrast, the Soviet Union generally appears to show more interest in establishing a political and economic presence in the third world through economic assistance than in structuring its program around principles of economic development. Thus, the USSR usually tries to finance whatever project the recipient proposes, once it is determined through surveys that the project is economically feasible. This difference in the priority of economic development accounts for the relatively passive role adopted by the USSR in its relations with aid recipients.

The examination of the administration of Soviet and American economic assistance has focused strictly upon the aid programs themselves. In the final chapters some of the effects of the differences in the political systems of the donors will be discussed—such as the degree of centralization in the government, the exercise of government restraints on public expression, and the existence of Congress in the United States as opposed to the lack of a comparable body in the Soviet Union. Whereas these factors reflect significant differences in the styles of the political process in the United States and the USSR, our concern is with the nature of the relationships forged between these donors and the less developed countries as a result of economic assistance. As we shall see, the nature of these relationships is remarkably similar in spite of fundamental differences in the domestic political systems of the two donors.

7

Operational Emphases

‡ Knowledge of the scope, direction, magnitude, and administration of the Soviet and American aid programs tells us little about the nature of the economic assistance delivered to the LDCs. What types of activities are financed through aid? In what form is aid distributed? On what basis do the donors choose to give aid in one form versus another? These questions can be answered only by observing the manner in which U.S. and Soviet economic assistance have been implemented.

Operational Emphases of American Economic Assistance

AID

Substantial American economic assistance is distributed on both a project and a program basis. Project assistance is granted or loaned by the United States to cover the foreign exchange costs, and sometimes part of the local costs, of a specific project (such as a power plant, a steel mill, or an irrigation system). Assistance of this type is felt to have several advantages. First, project aid yields tangible results which have great public appeal in the donor country as well as in the recipient. Successful capital projects like a dam or a manufacturing facility provide visible evidence of the American contribution to the economic development of a less developed country.[1]

Second, project assistance provides a convenient mechanism for linking technical and capital assistance.[2] It is easier and more effective to provide technical assistance in connection with a specific project than it is to link technical assistance to general purpose program loans, for example. The project approach affords more focus to technical assistance activities.

The strongest factor motivating project assistance in American aid efforts is the desire to retain substantial accountability and control over U.S. aid expenditures.[3] It is much easier to follow and evaluate the use of aid funds when they are allocated for the construction of a specific project whose progress can be closely monitored by the donor.

Program assistance is not tied to a specific project. It is used primarily to cover the costs of importing from the United States raw materials, spare parts, machinery, and commodities which are necessary to keep the existing economic system of an LDC functioning.[4] Such general purpose aid helps less developed countries curb inflation, ease balance-of-payments problems, and combat other serious economic difficulties which are not readily amenable to treatment on a project basis.

William Gaud suggested that there are basically two categories of countries which receive program loans. First, there are countries (such as India, Pakistan, and Turkey) which are operating under plans for development which the United States has helped shape. AID is satisfied that the plans make sense and take account of the recipient country's overall requirements for foreign exchange.[5] In these cases where the recipient demonstrates its ability to handle funds for economic development, program loans are given to enable the host country to exercise greater flexibility in meeting overall resource needs, based on a rational assessment of overall requirements and resource availabilities. Program assistance has the advantage of providing resources to ease unforeseen difficulties in the development process which might not be accounted for in project assistance.

The second category of countries receiving program loans consists of cases (such as Brazil, Chile, and Colombia) where the loan is part of an overall agreement between the United States and the recipient designed to induce or facilitate basic economic reforms such as limiting debts, taking steps against inflation, tax reform, or whatever is important in the particular case.[6] Large general purpose program loans are felt to be more effective than project loans (which are usually smaller) in affording leverage to obtain better performance on the part of the recipient in using American aid to combat serious economic problems. In most cases involving this type of program aid, the loan is linked to adequate performance of specified tasks agreed upon by the United States and the recipient. For example, the United States may make the loan available in quarterly installments provided that the recipient takes certain steps to control inflation, follows sound fiscal policies, or takes other steps outlined at the signing of the loan agreement. The agreement may specify that at each quarter there will be a review of performance by the United States and the less developed country to evaluate the extent to which the recipient is living up to the agreement. If the terms are met, the next quarterly installment is provided by the United States; if the terms are not met, the funds are not transferred to the LDC. In this way program loans are a useful device for tying U.S. aid to performance of the recipient and for the accomplishment of basic reforms the United States feels are necessary for economic development.[7]

In 1965 the United States held up disbursements of such a program loan to Colombia when that country delayed decisions on budgetary and exchange rate problems.[8] But, in general, the United States has seldom refused to provide an installment of a project loan because of the failure of the recipient to meet the targets specified in the agreement. As long as the less developed country is taking some steps toward the accomplishment of the specific goals outlined—even if they are less decisive than the United States deems necessary—these program loans are still considered valuable in that the recipient government has explicitly recognized the need for certain basic reforms and has gone on record (in signing the aid agreement) as committing itself to their execution.

Another factor which provides inducement for the use of program assistance in American aid is its contribution to the private sector of the recipient's economy. When aid is given on a project basis, large public sector projects are often the best means of attracting economic aid for an LDC because state sector projects are the simplest activities for the LDC government to negotiate and control.[9] Smaller enterprises in the private sector which need spare parts and relatively small amounts of capital goods (compared to most project aid agreements) are often unable to benefit from project assistance focused on large state enterprises. By offering program assistance to finance general commodity imports, the foreign exchange is provided which allows local private sector enterprises to benefit from American economic assistance. William Gaud testified that during the 1960s about 90 percent of the commodities and materials imported under program assistance in a country such as India went into the private sector.[10]

It is clear that program and project loans have different strengths. Project loans may be advantageous because of their visibility, accountability, and contribution in focusing technical assistance. However, program loans have the advantage of focusing aid on fundamental economic reforms of various types, of being more flexible, and of contributing more to the private sector of the recipient country. American assistance as administered by AID has adopted a strategy of mixing the two types of loans since the disadvantages of each are most severe when one or the other is used exclusively, and the advantages of each can be achieved without excluding the use of the other.[11]

Over the past six years (fiscal years 1963 to 1968) a little more than half of the funds administered by AID have been committed in the form of program assistance.[12] Throughout this period program aid was steadily increasing relative to project assistance except for fiscal year 1967 when the trend was reversed temporarily by large commitments of Development Loans (in the Near East and South Asia) and Supporting Assistance (in Vietnam) on a project basis. Notwithstanding these developments it would appear that program assistance will come to play an increasingly larger role in U.S. aid efforts.[13]

In addition to the basic distinction between project and program assistance, the operational emphases of American aid can be more fully appreciated by examining the various funding categories within the program. Before proceeding, however, some comment is in order concerning the data in Table 7 which provide the basis for this discussion. The figures cover only project assistance since it is virtually impossible to trace the end-use of program aid by fields of activity. This gives us only a rough indication of the uses of aid, since about half of American assistance is given on a program basis. The data are presented for fiscal years 1963, 1967, and 1968 as they are the most recent years for which figures were available in the form presented here. Moreover, the data on the end-use of Soviet aid are available only for 1963, so it is desirable to cite the U.S. figures for that year.

Supporting assistance has been given for the general purpose of enabling certain LDCs to maintain military forces at the request of the United States which are in excess of the level they could afford to sustain on their own.[14] To this end the United States has given substantial aid to countries such as South Korea, Taiwan, Pakistan, and South Vietnam. In fiscal years 1967 and 1968 all economic assistance to South Vietnam administered by AID was in the form of Supporting Assistance.[15] With the exception of Vietnam since fiscal year 1966, Supporting Assistance has been given predominantly on a program basis. It has taken many forms including funds for general commodity imports, budgetary support, general balance-of-payments subsidies, and specific capital and technical assistance projects.[16]

Unlike Development Loans and Development Grants, Supporting Assistance to less developed countries does not require the imposition of development criteria in determining aid allocations. Virtually the same activities may be financed by Supporting Assistance as by these other funding categories, but the recipient of Supporting Assistance qualifies for U.S. aid on the basis of political considerations rather than its development performance.[17]

The data in Table 7 on Supporting Assistance are of marginal utility in assessing the end-use of these funds, since in fiscal year 1963 only 14 percent of Supporting Assistance commitments were

TABLE 7

U.S. Project Commitments, Fiscal Years 1963, 1967, and 1968

(Percentage by column)

Field of Activity	Supporting Assistance and Other[a]			Development Grants			Development Loans			Total		
	1963	1967	1968	1963	1967	1968	1963	1967	1968	1963	1967	1968
Food and Agriculture	6	14	4	16	16	14	11	14	14	12	14	10
Power	b	11	1	b	0	0	b	21	13	b	12	5
Other Industry and Mining	1	0	0	7	4	3	49	13	17	34	6	7
Transportation	36	3	7	5	3	2	19	20	8	16	10	6
Labor	1	0	0	1	2	3	0	0	0	0	1	1
Health and Sanitation	3	8	17	11	9	7	6	8	27	8	8	17
Education	8	6	5	19	14	14	2	6	8	7	8	9
Public Safety	15	8	14	4	3	2	0	0	0	2	3	6
Public Administration	0	2	2	6	6	5	1	1	2	2	3	3
Community Development and Social Welfare	6	5	10	1	1	1	0	2	0	1	3	4
Housing	0	0	1	1	1	0	9	1	1	6	1	1
Private Enterprise Promotion	b	0	0	b	3	2	b	11	10	b	5	4
General and Miscellaneous	5	17	26	18	26	30	4	4	1	8	14	18
Technical Support	17	25	13	11	14	14	0	0	0	4	12	9
Total (In Millions of Dollars)	$76.1	$421.4	$340.4	$334.3	$308.7	$288.1	$756.0	$501.2	$325.3	$1,166.8	$1,231.4	$953.8

SOURCE: U.S., Agency for International Development, *Operations Report, Data as of June 30, 1963*, 1963, p. 44; ibid., *Operations Report, Data as of June 30, 1967*, 1967, p. 29; and ibid., *Operations Report, Data as of June 30, 1968*, 1968, p. 29.

NOTE: Column totals may not add to 100 due to rounding.

a. Aside from Supporting Assistance, these data include the Contingency Fund and negligible amounts of other general types of funds.

b. Power and Private Enterprise Promotion were not listed separately in the 1963 data, but were included within the other fields of activity.

on a project basis. The 1967 and 1968 figures for the use of Supporting Assistance are swamped by the Vietnam program which stressed technical support and food and agriculture activities in fiscal year 1967 and health and sanitation, public safety, and technical support in fiscal year 1968.

The Contingency Fund is an emergency reserve set aside for the President to use in meeting urgent and unforeseen requirements for economic aid. Over the period 1963–1967 approximately 84 percent of Contingency Funds have been given on a program basis. Except for meeting problems created by natural disasters in LDCs, the Contingency Fund is used for the same purposes as Supporting Assistance.[18] Accordingly, it is included with Supporting Assistance in Table 7. The primary distinctions between these two funding categories are: (1) the Contingency Fund is smaller than Supporting Assistance and (2) the Contingency Fund is not programmed on a country basis since its uses are unforeseen, whereas the specific uses of Supporting Assistance are foreseen and programmed in advance by country.

Development Loans are intended to contribute directly to the economic development of the recipient, and strict development criteria are imposed in the distribution of these aid funds. Since the creation of AID in 1961 this funding category has accounted for the largest amount of U.S. economic assistance disbursements and commitments. Since 1963 Development Loans have been committed in the amount of $1 to $1.5 billion annually. Development Loans are distributed on a project and a program basis, with the latter exceeding the former since 1965.

From Table 7 we see that project aid in the form of Development Loans has been concentrated in the fields of power, industry and mining, transportation, and food and agriculture. These fields of activity accounted for 79 percent of Development Loan project commitments in fiscal year 1963, and 68 percent in fiscal year 1967. During 1968 the field of health and sanitation emerged as a major claimant of Development Loan resources.

Development Grants are used to finance the bulk of American technical assistance to less developed countries. These funds are designed to transfer skills and knowledge to the recipient which will result in increased efficiency and output for the economy. The emphasis is clearly upon the development of human resources in contrast to capital assistance (usually financed with Development Loans), which is designed primarily to increase the physical economic plant of the recipient.

During the period 1963–1967, 98 percent of Development Grants have been project-oriented. Over the years, Development Grants in particular, and U.S. technical assistance in general, have been focused on the fields of education, food and agriculture, technical support, and health and sanitation.

U.S. economic assistance financed through these various means involves sending Americans abroad to give instruction in the field and/or in the classroom and bringing LDC nationals to the United States for instruction. Let us examine briefly these personnel flows.

In June 1968 there were 7,758 U.S. technicians overseas connected with economic assistance activities.[19] Of this total, 5,248 were U.S. government technicians, and 2,510 were contract technicians.[20]

The government technicians are concentrated most heavily in the field of technical support which involves overall planning, coordination, and control of U.S. aid activities in less developed countries. Following technical support in terms of numbers of personnel are food and agriculture, health and sanitation, and public safety in that order. Together these categories account for 56 percent of U.S. government technicians connected with aid in the less developed countries.[21] Geographically, these government technicians have been concentrated in Vietnam since fiscal year 1966. In June 1968, for example, there were over twice as many government technicians in Vietnam as there were in any other *region* (Latin America, Near East and South Asia, East Asia, or Africa).

Contract technicians are personnel from universities, private firms, labor unions, and other organizations who are hired temporarily under contracts with AID, or employed under arrangements made between AID and the recipient, for specific projects or programs. Ranked according to number of personnel, contract technicians in June 1968 were concentrated in the fields of education, food and agriculture, technical support, and industry and mining in that order.[22] In terms of geographical distribution, these technicians were concentrated in Latin America and Africa.

In addition to U.S. technicians abroad, there is a reverse flow of LDC nationals to the United States financed through American aid. In 1967 there were 9,397 publicly financed students and 6,406 publicly financed trainees from the LDCs in the United States.[23] These LDC nationals were studying or training primarily in the fields of agriculture or education.[24]

Export-Import Bank and P.L. 480

Export-Import Bank long-term loans to less developed countries are usually made for industrial or public utilities projects needing considerable imports of capital equipment from the United States. These loans are for projects similar to those financed by AID Development Loans except that the latter can be used to cover part of the local costs of the projects, whereas Export-Import Bank loans can cover only U.S. dollar costs. Also, AID Development Loans can be used for a broader range of purposes.[25] Export-Import Bank long-term loans have been used, additionally, for extensions of general lines of credit in order to finance projects which may be agreed upon at a later date; for financing continued U.S. exports to countries with protracted foreign exchange deficits despite stabilization programs; and for easing general balance-of-payments problems.[26] As a general rule, AID Development Loans (which are made on easier terms) are not used when the Export-Import Bank will undertake the project or program.

The end-use of P.L. 480 assistance to less developed countries takes several forms. First, of course, there are the food commodities which are distributed to the LDCs on the basis of local currency sales, dollar sales, or gifts, depending upon the title under which the commodities have flowed. To date, however, most agricultural commodity assistance to the LDCs (approximately two-thirds) has been in the form of Title I sales for local currency, so our outline of the uses of P.L. 480 aid will be confined to these sales.

From the beginning of P.L. 480 through fiscal year 1968 the United States has made sales agreements for foreign currency with LDCs in the amount of $10 billion.[27] This local currency remains in the LDC under American control and is used in a variety of ways. Of the $10 billion in Title I sales to LDC's for local currency, $8 billion has been planned for country use, and the remainder has been used by the United States to cover local expenses of its embassy and other operations in the recipient country. In fiscal 1967, for example, 70 percent of the funds for country use were distributed as loans or grants for economic development, 21 percent were used for common defense, 6 percent were distributed as Cooley loans to private enterprises, and 3 percent were used for maternal welfare, child nutrition, and family planning.[28]

The Choice of the Aid Instrument

In the determination of what type of aid should be given and the funding category or channel through which U.S. economic assistance is to be distributed, an attempt has been made by AID to link the type of economic assistance given to the level of development of the less developed country receiving it. As a general rule, American economic assistance to countries in early stages of development is concentrated on technical assistance designed to develop human resources and institutions capable of supporting economic growth. U.S. aid to African countries is typical of this type of assistance, involving relatively small expenditures. As the countries gain the capacity to utilize larger capital projects of various types effectively, the United States shifts its aid emphasis to capital assistance which is much more expensive than technical assistance. Technical assistance is continued, but its emphasis usually shifts to specific bottleneck-breaking efforts, and the aid, then, is often linked to specific capital assistance projects.[29] Also, when the LDC demonstrates its capacity to utilize American economic assistance effectively within an overall plan of economic development which is deemed feasible by the United States, program assistance may be offered as a supplement to project aid.[30] India provides the most outstanding example of a more developed aid recipient country in which U.S. economic aid has often taken the form of capital projects and program assistance. This explicit linkage by AID of the type of aid to the level of development of the recipient is based largely upon the suggestions offered by Millikan and Rostow in the fifties.[31]

Once the decision is made by AID concerning the type of assistance with which the United States is willing to provide an LDC, the problem still remains as to which funding category or aid channel should be used to finance the effort. Among the funding categories of AID, Development Loans are clearly the preferential means of rendering U.S. economic assistance. There has been a serious effort since 1961 to phase out the Supporting Assistance category, and Development Grants are not used whenever the use of Development Loans is possible (that is, when the United States feels the recipient can afford to repay a loan for the project or program). The Contingency Fund is purposely kept at a minimal level since its function is to meet only unforeseen needs of less developed countries. Development Loans have emerged as the largest funding category of AID since 1961. All these factors together indicate a distinct preference to use Development Loans to the maximum extent.

However, Export-Import Bank long-term loans are deemed even more desirable than Development Loans by the United States, as manifested by the fact that AID does not normally offer Development Loans for projects or programs which the Export-Import Bank is willing to undertake.[32]

This preference is a manifestation of more recent thinking in the United States which seeks to make aid available on terms most closely resembling normal, private commercial transfers.[33] The financial terms of Export-Import Bank long-term loans are harder than those accompanying Development Loans, so they represent less of a subsidy on the part of the donor and they more closely approximate the commercial channels through which the

United States would like to see capital transfers flow to the less developed countries if and when they are able to service this type of debt. The precise terms of the various U.S. economic assistance funding mechanisms for bilateral aid will be dealt with in a separate section.

Private Enterprise

An important aspect of the use of American economic assistance concerns its allocation between the state and private sectors of the recipient countries. The United States has always attempted to maximize the contribution of its aid to the private sector of the recipient and to the promotion of American private foreign investment in the less developed countries.

An impressive array of instruments has been employed by AID to this end. AID publicizes investment data and specific investment opportunities in less developed countries to bring such information to the attention of American businesses seeking investment opportunities abroad. AID administers a program whereby it can share the cost of surveys by potential U.S. investors to determine the feasibility of specific investment opportunities. If, after the survey, the U.S. firm decides to invest in the project, it bears all the cost of the survey; if, on the other hand, the decision is made not to invest in the project surveyed, AID pays up to 50 percent of the survey costs and retains the survey results. Dollar and local currency loans are made by AID to U.S. private borrowers for investments in less developed countries. In approximately seventy less developed countries AID will issue investment guarantees to American firms to insure them against certain political risks (such as loss by expropriation, war, revolution, and inconvertibility of local currency receipts).[34]

The programs mentioned above are clearly designed to give direct help to U.S. firms that desire to make investments in less developed countries. In addition, the U.S. aid program seeks to improve the overall investment climate within the LDCs so as to attract private foreign investment without the need for inducements from AID. Attempts are also made to increase the reliance upon the private sector within the recipient's economy. Through its aid the United States has promoted the creation of lending institutions in less developed countries which can, themselves, finance local private investments. Program loans are used as mechanisms to give the private sector in less developed countries more benefits from foreign exchange provided by American economic assistance. Through its country programming process, AID helps to identify and provide resources to carry out reforms in governmental policies which have significant effects on the private sector; for example, tax reform, land redistribution, stabilization of exchange rates, and new investment laws may be emphasized by AID as being necessary for economic growth and for demonstrating self-help measures upon which the continuation of U.S. economic aid may depend.[35]

In spite of American interest in attempts to promote private enterprise in the less developed countries through the aid instrument, most U.S. economic assistance has gone directly to the public, rather than the private, sector. Leo Tansky in a study of U.S. aid to Turkey, India, and the United Arab Republic concluded that not more than 15 percent of U.S. aid to Turkey and 10 percent of U.S. aid to India went directly to the private sector; and virtually none went to the private sector in the United Arab Republic.[36] Unquestionably, the bulk of American economic assistance to the less developed countries has gone directly to the state sector and the United States recognizes the importance of the state sector in the development process; however, this assistance cannot necessarily be considered to have taken place at the expense of the private sector in the LDCs.

American aid for projects in the state sector of the recipient country contributes significantly to the development of the basic infrastructure of power, irrigation, transportation, and communications from which the private sector derives benefit in the form of external economies. Also, every effort is made by AID to induce recipients with explicit development plans, usually emphasizing the public sector, to incorporate and promote private sector activities in the overall development process.[37] For example, India is currently taking steps to reduce government controls on fertilizer prices, at least partially because of U.S. pressure, in order to attract private investment into such enterprises.[38]

A less obvious factor is involved in the manner in which U.S.

aid to the public sector can simultaneously help the private sector. Insofar as U.S. aid, even to the state sector, alleviates shortages in foreign exchange and resources of all types, the private sector benefits in an economy in which the public sector has clear priority—as is the case in most less developed countries. In the absence of aid this public sector priority might well result in even more severe restrictions on the development of private enterprise, because what foreign exchange and resources are available to the LDC are likely to be channeled exclusively into state activities. Additional taxation and deprivation of factor inputs of private enterprises might be used to help facilitate the realization of high priority state sector goals.[39]

The precise effect of U.S. economic assistance to the public sector on the private sector of the recipient's economy is very difficult to assess. However, insofar as the United States seeks to promote private enterprise and foreign private investment in the less developed countries, aid to the state sector need not result in weakening local private enterprise. Also, it is questionable that reducing or eliminating aid to LDCs which are public sector-oriented would result in increased reliance upon private enterprise.[40]

AID, in fact, operates on the assumption that in these ways aid to the state sector indirectly benefits private enterprise and foreign private investment in the LDCs. It is interesting to note that some Soviet scholars also harbor thoughts along these lines. We have seen, for example, in the discussion of Soviet development doctrines, how concern was expressed that Soviet aid to state sector projects in India might have the effect of subsidizing growth in the private sector. In effect, this constitutes an endorsement of AID's position on the general relationship between economic assistance and the state and private sectors of less developed countries.

Operational Emphases of Soviet Economic Assistance

The analyst of Soviet economic aid to the less developed countries is not confronted by the complexity of funding categories with differing purposes, end-uses, and financial terms found in the American program. He has the entirely opposite problem of trying to find some precision in incomplete and very general information. Thus, the discussion of the operation and terms of Soviet aid must necessarily be less specific than that in connection with the American program.

The End-Use of Soviet Aid

In terms of the program/project assistance distinction found in American economic assistance, the overwhelming bulk of Soviet aid is project-oriented. The best indicator of Soviet program assistance in any quantitative sense is the portion of Soviet aid allocated for commodity credits, which are used by the recipient to import commodities not connected with specific projects. This type of aid comprises only about five percent of total commitments since the beginning of the program.[41] Soviet program assistance is also reflected in the assignment of technical personnel not connected with specific economic aid projects. Since 1961 the USSR has engaged in an increasing amount of managerial, educational, medical, economic planning, agricultural, and other nonproject activities;[42] however, while program assistance is increasing it is still only a minor component of the overall aid efforts.

Most nonproject technicians have been employed in countries such as Africa which lack the skilled personnel necessary to provide local support for projects of the type the USSR generally finances through aid.[43] Thus, through technical assistance of this type the USSR can establish an aid presence, while simultaneously preparing the recipient for the time when larger capital projects would be feasible with Soviet financing. It is interesting to note that Soviet program assistance seems to flow predominantly to LDCs at the lowest stages of economic development, whereas U.S. program aid is concentrated in more advanced LDC economies.

Except for this small proportion of Soviet aid distributed on a program basis, economic assistance from the USSR to the less developed countries is linked to specific projects. The nature of the projects financed by Soviet aid can be seen in Table 8. These data include both Soviet and East European aid, but they should accurately reflect the end-use of Soviet economic assistance since the USSR program is so much larger than that of the East European countries, and since, in general, the emphases of the programs are similar.

TABLE 8

End-Use of Soviet and East European Economic Credits and Grants to Non-Communist Less Developed Countries as of December 1963

End-Use	% of Total Obligations
Manufacturing	53
Transport and Communications	14
Hydroelectric Power Development	12
Irrigation and Reclamation	10
Commodity Credits	4
Agriculture	3
Health, Education, and Municipal Services	3
Gold, Foreign Exchange, and Funded Trade Deficits	1
Total	100

Source: U.S., Department of State, Bureau of Intelligence and Research, *The Communist Economic Offensive Through 1963*, Research Memorandum RSB-43, June 18, 1964, p. 15.

From the table it is evident that the bulk of Soviet economic assistance has gone to the industrial sector and for social overhead investment (transportation, communications, power, irrigation, and land reclamation). While the data presented are for programs completed by 1963, the basic pattern of the distribution of Soviet aid by end-use, up to 1966 at least, has remained basically unaltered since 1959,[44] the earliest date when reliable estimates of this nature could be made on the relatively small and new Soviet aid effort.

The USSR is indeed interested in promoting the industrial sector of the less developed countries as manifested in innumerable statements on aid and in the large proportion of aid obligations going to manufacturing. However, it is not correct to assume that the USSR is totally preoccupied with an emphasis on aid to the industrial sector. The aggregate data presented on the end-use of Soviet economic assistance do not reveal the fact that India alone has received 45 percent of the total Soviet aid committed to heavy industry;[45] and, except for India, most Soviet aid to less developed countries is concentrated in transportation and multipurpose projects involving electric power, irrigation, and communications.[46]

In addition, Soviet spokesmen have explicitly recognized that economic growth in the less developed countries will not necessarily be achieved through exclusive or primary efforts in heavy industry. The chief Soviet representative at the 1957 Afro-Asian Conference in Cairo, A. A. Arzumanyan, made the following statement in this regard:

The development of various branches of the manufacturing industry cannot be effected otherwise than by expanding agriculture and the extracting industry. . . . It should be noted that agriculture and the extracting industry may become the basis for developing many other branches of the economy.[47]

Similarly, we have seen how G. Mirsky and R. Ulyanovsky have suggested that infrastructure projects, light, and extractive industry should be emphasized during initial stages of development since conditions are often unfavorable for the immediate construction of heavy industry.[48]

These statements and the record of aid obligations reveal a Soviet awareness of and interest in the importance of aid to sectors other than manufacturing and heavy industry in the less developed countries.

The Level of Development of the Recipient

In the United States aid program there is an emphatic doctrinal and operational link between the type of aid given and the stage of development of the recipient. This link is not nearly so explicitly articulated or emphasized in Soviet economic assistance, but it is clearly present. The USSR does not ordinarily extend assistance for projects it believes to be beyond the technical capacity of the recipient.[49] So, for cases such as India where the basis for advanced industrial enterprise is present, Soviet aid has taken the form of heavy industrial projects. At the other extreme, in a country such as Afghanistan, where the basis for industrialization does not exist, the USSR has concentrated on road construction, development of mineral resources, and multi-purpose projects. Those manufacturing units that are financed by Soviet aid in Afghanistan are usually small and do not require advanced skills for their continued operation. In Africa, also, Soviet aid has emphasized small projects and technical training.[50]

This rough correspondence between the type of Soviet aid and the level of development of the recipient is evident in Soviet literature on aid, as well as in the distribution of assistance. The following statement indicates Soviet interest in this problem:

The nature and purpose of Soviet economic and technical assistance are predetermined by the concrete conditions and level of development in each recipient country. . . . Such countries as India, the U.A.R., Iraq, and Algeria . . . are using Soviet assistance to create a diversified national economy, priority being given to industrial enterpirses. They are building metallurgical and engineering plants . . . to produce equipment.

Some of the developing countries, who have a small population and a comparatively narrow home market, consider it advisable at first to build factories for producing consumer goods and processing raw materials for export, and also to concentrate on agricultural production.[51]

The evidence suggests that the Soviet Union does not indiscriminately propose large industrial projects in less developed countries that are unable to support them. There is also little question that Soviet economic assistance contributes to the economy of the recipient. It is neither designed for, nor does it usually have the effect of, disrupting the economic growth of the less developed countries.

Soviet aid for "showpiece projects" of limited economic value, such as the hotel in Burma, the stadium in Indonesia, and the various hospitals and technological institutes which have often been extended as gifts to LDCs by the USSR, have received much attention in the West. It should be noted that these projects play a very minor role in the overall use of Soviet economic assistance. Frank Coffin as deputy administrator of AID indicated that such projects account for less than three percent of total Soviet and East European economic aid commitments.[52]

Soviet Technical Assistance and Aid Personnel

Soviet technical assistance is for the most part directly related to the projects implemented under the general credit lines. Technicians from the USSR make feasibility studies and initial project surveys, supervise the construction of Soviet aid projects, give on-the-job training to local technicians, and, in some cases, manage the completed installations until local personnel are able to take over.[53]

Between 1955 and the end of 1968 approximately 80,000 Soviet technicians have been employed in the non-Communist less developed countries.[54] During 1968 alone there were 9,820 Soviet technicians in the LDCs.[55] From Table 9 we see that during 1968

TABLE 9

Personnel Exchanges Between the USSR and the LDCs, 1968

Region	Soviet Technicians in LDCs	LDC Technical Trainees in USSR	LDC Students in USSR
Africa	3,300	220	6,080
Far East	200	5	635
Latin America	20	0	1,500
Near East and South Asia	6,300	730	3,565
Total	9,820	955	11,780

SOURCE: U.S., Department of State, Bureau of Intelligence and Research, *Communist Governments and Developing Nations: Aid and Trade in 1968*, RSE-65, September 1969, pp. 9–12.

the Near East and South Asia was the largest regional recipient of Soviet technicians.

It is interesting to note that the USSR had some 2,000 to 4,000 more economic aid personnel abroad than did AID in each of the years 1966, 1967, and 1968, even though the Soviet aid program was operating in less than half as many countries as the American program. The major reason for the relatively large number of Soviet technicians abroad is the fact that Soviet aid is more heavily project-oriented than the American program. This type of aid requires more personnel for surveying, planning, supervision, and construction than is the case with technical assistance in the form of pilot projects or assistance not related to the construction of large enterprises.[56]

It should be emphasized that the data for U.S. personnel abroad encompass only direct hire and contract technicians associated with AID. If the number of U.S. personnel abroad engaged in technical cooperation activities under the auspices of government agencies other than AID, of private foundations, and of private American corporations were included in the U.S. data for technicians abroad, the Soviet figure of 9,820 would appear to be comparatively small. The number of aid personnel abroad is of limited utility as an indicator of the donors' foreign influence.

Although no precise data are available, it appears that as of 1963, at least, the largest group of Soviet technicians abroad was engaged in planning and supervising the construction of industrial projects. The next largest grouping of technicians was employed in mineral surveys and prospecting. The remainder worked primarily on roads, harbors, and power projects.[57] The focus of Soviet technical assistance on industry and the development of mineral resources is quite different from that of American technical assistance efforts which in addition to technical support stress activities related to education, health, and agriculture.

Soviet experts abroad are by all accounts well qualified and competent in the tasks they come to perform. In general their performance seems to be equal to that of American technicians.[58] However, Soviet technicians are more narrowly trained and specialized than American experts, a factor which necessitates the use of more technicians per project than is the case with U.S. aid.[59] Another distinction between Soviet and U.S. personnel in the performance of technical duties is that the former are employed to perform a specific task in connection with a specific project and then return to the USSR after a relatively brief tenure. American aid personnel are employed with the hope that they will remain in the less developed country for about two years.[60]

As a rule there appears to be little contact between Soviet aid personnel abroad and nationals in the recipient countries aside from the relations on the job. The Soviet technicians "keep pretty much to themselves, living in self-contained enclaves, keeping their own schools, and shying away from social invitations."[61] In this respect they seem to resemble the large, self-contained American communities which are often found in less developed countries. The following description of the Soviet technicians at Aswan made by an Egyptian official shows this tendency: "The Russians are living in a self-contained world. . . . They have their stores in their own areas. They have their club. They have their post office, their schools. And they don't mix much with Egyptians after hours."[62]

Soviet aid personnel usually have not had language training for the less developed country to which they are sent. There are reports of some technicians who are fluent in languages such as Hindi, Persian, Pushtu, and Farsi, but proficiency in local languages is the exception rather than the rule. The USSR usually relies upon its own and foreign interpreters for communication between its technicians and their local counterparts.[63] An article in *Izvestia* corroborates the difficulty encountered by Soviet technicians abroad who do not speak the local language. Concerning Soviet experts at Aswan it was reported that "the unfamiliar language hinders them [Soviet specialists], but they can already explain some things in Arabic, and at any rate a working man shows with his hands and by action what is to be done."[64]

In addition to the problem of local languages, which effects the American program as well as that of the USSR, Soviet technicians probably have greater difficulty than U.S. specialists with the second language of less developed countries (such as English in India). Most Soviet technicians in Burma, for example, had to rely on interpreters, whereas Americans were able to converse in English because of its prevalence in the area.[65] Some Soviet personnel are competent in the Western languages best known in the foreign locality, but the evidence suggests that across the board

USSR experts experience more language difficulties than American personnel in AID, who have the second language advantage and are probably more often trained in the local language.[66]

The USSR also brings LDC nationals to the Soviet Union for training. In 1968 there were 955 technical trainees from the less developed countries receiving instruction in factories and training institutes within the USSR.[67] Most of the trainees came from the Near East and South Asia where the largest Soviet aid enterprises are located. An additional 11,780 students from LDCs were enrolled in Soviet academic institutions in 1968.[68] Unlike the technical trainees, the students were predominantly from Africa. Many of the students were enrolled in Friendship (Patrice Lumumba) University in Moscow which opened in late 1960. In 1966 this institution (created specifically for educating students from non-Communist LDCs) graduated 470 students, and its overall enrollment was 4,000.[69]

It should be emphasized that the U.S. data on LDC students in America cover only those who are publicly financed. In 1967, for example, there were some 48,000 students from the less developed countries studying in the United States,[70] but only 9,000 were financed through the aid program.

The State Sector

Virtually all Soviet aid efforts are directed toward the enhancement of the state sector in the less developed countries. The USSR operates on the assumption that the state sector is the only means by which an LDC can achieve economic growth independent from foreign (that is, Western) influence.[71]

One visible goal of Soviet emphasis on the development of the state sector in less developed countries is the elimination of traditional Western ties to these countries through private foreign investment. Soviet aid to India, for example, permitted the development of state sector production in petroleum and pharmaceuticals which had traditionally been preserved for private investment.[72] Also, through credits repayable in traditional exports the USSR familiarizes the recipient with Soviet products and procedures of state trade when implementing the aid agreements; and during the period of repayment the LDC redirects its exports from their traditional markets in the West to the Communist market. This process of changing marketing patterns among the less developed countries complements the Soviet attempt to decrease reliance upon private foreign investment in the economic growth of the LDCs by giving aid to promote the state sector. The creation of a state trading agency in India to facilitate economic relations with the USSR and other Communist countries is the type of effect the Soviet Union desires to generate through aid and trade with less developed countries.

The interest of the USSR in the promotion of the state sector of the LDCs is understood well enough to preclude the necessity for further elaboration here. On the other hand, it deserves reemphasis in this context since it represents a major thrust determining the style of Soviet economic assistance. Like American aid to the state sector, Soviet aid tends to be utilized for the development of the basic economic infrastructure which, depending upon the policies of the recipient, can contribute to the climate necessary to attract private investment in the less developed countries.

Production-Cooperation Agreements

During 1964 and 1965 a new thrust appeared in the theory of Soviet economic relations with the less developed countries which could, if implemented, substantially alter the nature of USSR aid efforts. The USSR and other socialist countries have proposed that LDCs abandon autarkical economic development and take advantage of the opportunity to engage in specialization and a partial international division of labor with the USSR and Eastern European countries. Through production-cooperation agreements the USSR would assist LDCs in expanding the production of certain commodities and manufactured goods if the LDC were well endowed for the production of these goods, and if Soviet imports of these goods would increase the efficiency of overall production in the domestic Soviet economy.

It is argued that this division of labor may make it more profitable for the USSR to import a number of important products from the LDCs than to produce them (or expand their production) in the USSR. "If a stable source for the receipt of an import item is ensured, production cooperation and the foreign trade conditioned by such cooperation may . . . be regarded as a branch of the national economy of the importing country [USSR]."[73]

The assertion is also made that the effectiveness of such options "may be assessed on the basis of criteria employed for the selection of variants of economic solutions inside the given socialist country [USSR]."[74] Thus, when determining where a capital investment should be made to meet the production requirements of the USSR in a specific item, the proposed production-cooperation variant in an LDC would be compared with domestic production variants using the existing method for determining the economic effectiveness of capital investments within the USSR.[75] Presumably, if the LDC variant is more effective than the domestic Soviet variant, the capital investment would be made in the LDC through implementation of a production-cooperation agreement.

Tentative estimates were drawn up by the Institute of Economics of the World Socialist System, USSR Academy of Sciences, and it was suggested that production-cooperation agreements between a number of LDCs and some socialist countries would be both possible and economically expedient with regard to oil, iron ore, cotton fiber, some nonferrous metals, and other commodities.[76] It is interesting to note that the early emphasis of such agreements would be in the extractive industries of less developed countries. The socialist countries have repeatedly attacked the West for investment in this sector of LDC economies.

A typical production-cooperation agreement would involve the extension of Soviet credits to a less developed country for the expansion of production and export capacity of a particular item, say cotton fiber. The LDC would retain sole ownership of the enterprise financed by the Soviet credit, and the credit would as a rule be repaid in the form of quotas from production of the constructed enterprise.[77] However, unlike Soviet aid in the past, these agreements would require the recipient to continue exports of production from the enterprise to the USSR after the credit had been entirely repaid.

This points to the characteristic of production-cooperation agreements which most clearly distinguishes them from traditional Soviet aid agreements. The former involve cooperation not only in the exchange of goods through trade and aid, but also in the production activities of the LDC and the USSR. Particularly in the field of manufactures, production-cooperation agreements would involve significant Soviet controls over the design of the product, the production process, the quality of the goods, and the assortment of production throughout the tenure of the agreement, even after the aid recipient had repaid the Soviet credit. Such controls would be necessary since the output of the LDC enterprise is to be an integral part of the Soviet economy under the production-cooperation agreement mechanism. Unlike past and present Soviet aid efforts, these new agreements would view foreign aid credits as an alternative to investment in the USSR, and the criteria of efficiency of investment would be applied to aid credits.[78]

The production-cooperation approach to foreign economic assistance offers several attractions to the Soviet Union. Aid distributed on this basis ceases to be an economic burden on the donor. Indeed, under production-cooperation agreements, aid to an LDC would theoretically contribute to the economic efficiency and total product of the USSR. Aside from this economic benefit for the Soviet Union, there is also the advantage that domestic Soviet opposition to the aid program would presumably be reduced since the cost of aid to the USSR would be minimal. Furthermore, if through aid the USSR is seeking to establish long-term contacts and exert influence over the development paths adopted by non-Communist LDCs, production-cooperation agreements would appear to be better suited for these purposes than the existing Soviet aid program.

Soviet spokesmen suggest that the LDC party to such agreements would benefit from stable prices on their exports during a period when world prices on a majority of goods exported from third world countries producing raw materials and food are displaying a downward trend. In addition, the LDC would benefit from a stable market for any goods produced under production-cooperation agreements. The problems of quality and trade restrictions which usually face LDC manufacturers in international commerce would be eliminated under the new Soviet aid scheme.[79] These agreements would also facilitate the expansion of the industrial sector in the LDCs.

In spite of the existence of these theoretical advantages to both parties to the production-cooperation agreements, there are some important factors which detract significantly from the prospects of implementing this scheme on a large scale. Apart from the question of the capability to compare with precision the relative effectiveness of LDC and domestic Soviet variants, there is the question of Soviet willingness to make critical investment decisions on this basis.

From the standpoint of the LDCs it is difficult to see why these young states, jealous of their economic and political independence, would wish to have major sectors of their economies integrated as branches of the Soviet economy through production-cooperation agreements. The political and economic implications of such a move are truly astounding, and it is doubtful that they would be overlooked by any less developed country. It is also doubtful that LDCs would like to see the prospects for Soviet financing of aid projects determined by the contribution the projects will make to the Soviet economy. Present Soviet aid practices would seem to be more attractive to the recipient than production-cooperation agreements.

At this time there are no known cases where the USSR has actually implemented a production-cooperation agreement with a non-Communist less developed country. While these agreements may appear in future Soviet aid efforts, it does not appear that they will significantly alter the basic Soviet approach to economic assistance.

Conclusions

The United States aid program is noteworthy for the number of mechanisms through which aid is distributed to the less developed countries for different end-uses, different levels of development, and different intentions. Thus, we can observe the use of

Supporting Assistance and the Contingency Fund in financing commodity imports or budgetary support for more or less avowedly political purposes with peripheral concern for extensive justification by the recipient as to the manner in which such aid relates to its long-term development plans. This type of aid, as exemplified in South Vietnam today and in Guinea in 1962, is generally quite flexible and rapid in its implementation. On the other hand, aid in the form of Development Loans is much more demanding of the recipient in terms of justifying requests on the basis of economic development criteria and provisions for overseeing its implementation; also, the programming process tends to be more rigid and takes longer. These various types of aid give the United States a great deal of flexibility in meeting assistance needs deemed important to American interests.

Soviet economic assistance seems to be less specialized and less formally structured in terms of differing mechanisms for the distribution of aid. Its small size relative to the American program enables Soviet aid to retain a certain flexibility and quickness of implementation when desired, without the real necessity for developing a plethora of funding categories.

Significant differences in emphasis are seen in Soviet efforts to champion the state sector of the recipient and virtually complete reliance on project assistance, as opposed to American efforts to promote the private sector through a combination of program and project aid. The USSR seldom engages in commodity import programs and budgetary support, both of which have played a large role in American economic assistance.

Neither Soviet nor American specialists abroad possess linguistic or technical skills inherently superior to those of the other country. Both countries' personnel tend to live in self-contained communities or enclaves. The USSR has more technicians abroad under aid auspices because their program is largely project-oriented, and due to specialized training it usually takes more Soviet technicians to complete a given job than it would for U.S. technicians.

Some observers of Soviet and American aid have suggested that there has developed an incipient pattern of specialization which manifests itself in decisions of LDCs to seek aid from the United States for the development of light industry and agriculture, while going to the USSR for large industrial projects in the state sector.[80] Whereas this type of specialization does reflect the ideological preferences and priorities of Soviet and American aid, in the final analysis the end-use of Soviet and American aid does not suggest that the two programs are essentially complementary to each other. The USSR gives priority to heavy industry, manufacturing, transportation, communications, and irrigation, while the United States has emphasized health, agriculture, and education in addition to efforts in industry, mining, and transportation. However, whereas the priorities in the programs may differ, the nature of the assistance overlaps considerably, with both the United States and the USSR giving substantial aid to the infrastructure of the recipients' economies—transportation, communication, irrigation, and electric power.

8

Terms of Aid

‡ The interest rates, repayment period, strings, and division of costs between the recipient and the donor are all important in determining the attractiveness of an aid program to the recipient. Let us examine the packaging of Soviet and American economic assistance to less developed countries.

Terms of American Economic Assistance

There are basically two types of expenses connected with an aid project—the foreign exchange costs and the local costs. Foreign exchange is necessary to cover the cost of whatever materials and equipment must be imported for the project as well as for payment of the travel and at least a portion of the salaries of the technical personnel from the donor country. The United States pays these expenses in connection with any aid project it undertakes.

Local expenses involve such items as the salaries of the personnel in the recipient country connected with the project, the costs of obtaining and transporting materials and equipment supplied from within the recipient country, and the costs of the property upon which the project is built. In its aid projects, the United States encourages the less developed country to cover these costs as much as possible. AID will generally consider requests to finance up to 50 percent of the local costs, but will not go beyond this amount except with extensive justification.[1] The feeling is that, for projects of relatively high priority, the recipient should be able and willing to finance at least this proportion of the aid effort. The local costs paid by the United States are financed from American holdings of local currencies generated by P.L. 480, Title I, sales or counterpart funds arising from grant assistance.

Regardless of what part of foreign exchange and local costs are paid by the United States in connection with an aid package, there is the question of the terms on which the financing will take place. In its broadest sense this involves a decision as to whether the assistance is to be in the form of a grant or a loan.

Loans versus Grants

Over the years the form of most U.S. economic assistance has gradually shifted from grants to loans. In the 1953–1957 period, for example, only 9 percent of the funds administered by AID and its predecessor agencies was in the form of loans. Since that time loans have accounted for an increasing proportion of economic assistance. During the period 1962–1968, 53 percent of the economic aid administered by AID was distributed as loans.[2]

During the early phases of American economic assistance to the less developed countries, several factors led to reliance upon grant assistance. Marshall Plan aid to Europe had been in the form of grants, and this precedent carried over to U.S. efforts in aiding the LDCs. Also, it was felt in the United States that the LDCs were unable to assume the burden of repaying the donor on commercial terms for assistance rendered; therefore it was deemed preferable to give aid as grants, rather than as loans which would not be repaid.[3] In addition it was assumed that the LDCs themselves would prefer grants to loans since the former precluded the need for using what limited foreign exchange they commanded to service a debt imposed by aid on a loan basis.

As economic assistance continued, however, and came to look increasingly like a permanent program instead of a temporary pump-priming operation, more pressure from within the United States favored the substitution of loans for grant assistance. The dominant impulse underlying this emphasis on loans was undoubtedly the desire of the United States to economize and be repaid for its aid whenever possible.[4] This desire is observable in many bilateral aid programs of donors in the East and the West.

Congressional pressure was a major factor in the shift to loans. Congressmen expressed the belief that if an LDC was given U.S. aid because its development potential was considered excellent, then it seemed reasonable to expect the recipient to accept aid on a loan basis—particularly if interest rates were lower and repayment periods longer than for normal commercial loans.[5] That part of American aid which was designed for and justified in terms of its contribution to economic development, as opposed to Defense Support of an admittedly political nature, was especially subject to demands for loan financing. Thus, with the creation of the Development Loan Fund in 1957 and of AID in 1961, a switch to loans in place of grant assistance was clearly visible.

Additional factors prompting U.S. reliance upon loan assistance were the success of the USSR in giving aid on a loan basis and a change in the feeling that aid recipients inherently preferred grants to loans. The Soviet Union apparently struck a responsive chord in the LDCs by offering aid credits on easy terms and emphasizing the businesslike nature of loans, as opposed to grants which were portrayed as charity placing the recipient in a dependent relationship with the donor.[6] The willingness of less developed countries to accept Soviet credits, as well as declarations of preference for loans over grant assistance by some LDC leaders[7] reinforced the impulse to shift U.S. economic assistance to a predominantly loan basis.

This combination of factors led to a gradual shift in American economic aid from grants to loans. But the process was tempered, as far as the hardness of terms is concerned, by the establishment of an array of financial mechanisms for distributing U.S. economic assistance which range from grants to loans repayable in dollars at rates close to commercial rates.

United States economic assistance loans are given in the form of dollars and local currency, interest rates vary from 2 to 6 percent, the period allowed for repayment varies from 1 to 40 years, and repayment takes the form of dollars and local currency. This range of terms makes a simple explanation of U.S. aid lending virtually impossible. In Table 10, however, an attempt has been made to list the main loan instruments of American economic aid and the usual terms associated with each.

TABLE 10

Terms of Various Types of American Loans

Loan Instrument	Currency of Distribution	Interest Rate (%)	Repayment Period (Years)	Currency of Repayment	Grace Period (Years)
Mutual Security Act (1954–61)[a]	Dollars or local	3.0–5.75	10–40	Dollars or local	1–7
Development Loan Fund (1958–61)[a]	Dollars or local	3.0–5.75	3–40	Dollars or local	1–7
Foreign Assistance Act (1961—)[b]	Dollars	2.5–5.75	15–40	Dollars	10
Export-Import Bank long-term loans[c]	Dollars	5.0–6.0	8–20	Dollars	2–3
P.L. 480: Cooley loans[d]	Local	Prevailing local rate	Up to 10	Local	1–4[e]
Foreign currency loans[f]	Local	4	Up to 10	Local	1–3

a. Leo Tansky, *U.S. and U.S.S.R. Aid to Developing Countries: A Comparative Study of India, Turkey and the U.A.R.* (New York: Frederick A. Praeger, 1967), p. 32.
b. U.S., Agency for International Development, *Principles of Foreign Economic Assistance*, 1965, p. 17.
c. Ibid., p. 44.
d. *Foreign Commerce Weekly*, vol. 63, February 8, 1960, p. 16.
e. U.S., Congress, House Committee on Foreign Affairs, *Hearings, Foreign Assistance Act of 1963*, 88th Cong., 1st sess., 1963, pp. 501–02.
f. Ibid., *Hearings, Foreign Assistance Act of 1965*, 89th Cong., 1st sess., 1965, p. 74.

Export-Import Bank long-term loans to less developed countries are given on terms approaching those characteristic of normal commercial channels and are the hardest form of assistance given by the United States. These loans are distributed and repayable in the form of U.S. dollars. In recent years the average interest rates of such loans to foreign governments and loans with government guarantees have been 5 to 6 percent.

Development Loans given under the authority of the Foreign Assistance Act of 1961 have flexible terms depending upon the ability of the recipient to service a debt, and upon the use of the loan. In most cases there is a 10-year grace period during which the recipient pays interest at a rate of 2 percent, then over a period of up to 30 years the loan is repaid with an interest rate of 3 percent. As a less developed country progresses toward self-sustained growth the interest rates are raised and the repayment period is shortened; for example, loans to Iran and Israel have had grace periods of 2 to 3 years, interest rates of 3.5 percent, and maturities of 15 to 20 years.[8]

Development Loans of the type just described are repayable in dollars. They have replaced Mutual Security Act Loans and the Development Loan Fund which were combined under the Foreign Assistance Act of 1961. The most notable difference between Development Loans and these previous loan programs is the fact that before 1961 such loans were sometimes repayable in the local currency of the recipient. In 1961 it was decided that loans repayable in dollars at lower interest rates were preferable to loans repayable in local currency. At that time Development Loans could be made at 0.75 percent interest. Over the years the rates have been increased, however, to 3 percent during the period of repayment and 2 percent during the grace period.

In addition to Export-Import Bank long-term loans and Development Loans which are given and repayable in the form of dollars, the United States makes loans to less developed countries in local currency generated from P.L. 480 sales and counterpart funds. These loans are repayable in local currency.

Because of the multitude of interest rates, maturities, and means of repayment, it is difficult to see the total picture of the terms of American economic assistance from looking at the various types of loans and grants. Some figures presented by the Development Assistance Committee of the Organization for Economic Cooperation and Development (OECD) on the average financial terms of official bilateral loan commitments are most helpful. During 1967 the weighted average maturity of U.S. loan commitments to less developed countries was 28.2 years, and the weighted average interest rate was 3.6 percent.[9] The comparable figures for the six-year period 1962–1967 are 30 years and 2.8

percent interest.[10] The 1967 figures indicate the extent of the general trend toward harder terms in U.S. aid lending since 1963 when the weighted average interest rate for U.S. loans was 2.0% and the weighted average maturity period was 32.5 years.

This general trend in hardening the terms of American aid was reinforced by the Food-For-Peace Act of 1966 which provides statutory authority for U.S. agricultural commodity assistance. Whereas food sales under Title I are made for local currencies, the 1966 act provides for the progressive transition from sales for foreign currencies to sales for dollars. By 1971 it is hoped that all sales will be on a dollar basis.[11]

This provision concerning agricultural commodity assistance, combined with the increase in interest rates on Development Loans and the basic shift in emphasis from grants to loans, are all symptomatic of a gradual hardening of terms for American economic assistance to the less developed countries. However, the terms of Western European aid donors, on the average, are still a little harder than those of the United States today;[12] and the average interest rate and maturity figures cited for American loans overstate the hardness of the financial terms for overall American aid, since 45 percent of all U.S. economic assistance in 1968 was given in the form of grants.[13]

Strings on U.S. Aid

Aside from the financial provisions accompanying economic assistance, the strings attached to the aid by the donor are an important aspect of the overall terms of an aid program. Since every aid donor must impose some conditions on its program merely to implement the transfer of resources involved and to arrange for repayment if the assistance is in the form of credits, the problem is not whether or not to tie strings to economic assistance, but rather the form which the strings will take.

In the case of American economic assistance many of the explicit formal restrictions on the eligibility for receipt of U.S. aid and on the manner in which U.S. aid can be utilized are found in the statutory authority for the aid program and congressional amendments to that legislation. While they constitute strings imposed on the recipient by the United States, they must also be considered as strings imposed on the American executive by Congress. The latter uses this device to influence directly certain aspects of the American aid program which it feels are particularly important. Congressional strings of this sort are exemplified in the prohibition against U.S. economic aid to countries which are furnishing assistance to Cuba[14] and the stipulation that subject to the availability of the ships, 50 percent of the commodities financed by U.S. aid must be shipped in American bottoms.[15]

More important than the branch of the U.S. government which imposes the strings, however, is the nature of the strings themselves. There are basically two types of strings to be considered —political and economic.

Political strings are those conditions imposed on economic assistance which have no bearing on the actual utilization of the aid by the recipient, but which commit the recipient to the support, at least on paper, of certain policies deemed important by the donor.

A salient example of the use of political strings in connection with American economic assistance is the stipulation in the Food-For-Peace Act of 1966 which prevents the United States from supplying food to countries that trade in any fashion with North Vietnam or that sell anything but medicine or nonstrategic food and agricultural commodities to Cuba. India was forced to accept these restrictions in order to get American grain which it desperately needed in early 1967. Resentment over this "sacrifice of national honor" to obtain American aid was shown during the Indian election campaign in January 1967. The Prime Minister, Mrs. Indira Ghandi, countered the opposition by pointing out the fact that India did not trade with North Vietnam and that only jute—which the United States classed as nonstrategic—was sold to Cuba. Thus, she emphasized that accepting the conditions really meant no change in the policy already being followed by India.[16]

This example vividly demonstrates a basic problem in the attempt to impose political strings on an aid recipient. The stipulations tend to be either redundant, in those cases where the recipient is already pursuing policies consistent with the donor's, or meaningless, when potential recipients would rather refuse assistance than accept it with political strings contradictory to their policy interests.[17] Therefore, the results seems to be the generation of hostile feelings toward the donor, even in instances where the stipulations do not require an alteration of policy.

Economic strings are conditions imposed on economic assistance designed to affect directly the manner in which aid is utilized by the recipient. In the American aid program economic strings are imposed to increase the efficiency of the recipient's use of the aid or to protect certain public and private interests of the United States.

The United States employs economic strings in the distribution of program and project assistance. By making program assistance contingent upon the demonstration of progress in implementing basic internal reforms necessary for economic growth, the United States seeks to increase the effectiveness of its overall aid efforts and the general efficiency of the recipient's economy. Economic strings are also imposed on project assistance where the recipient is required to explain the utility and necessity of the project in terms of its contribution to the overall development needs of the country, to demonstrate its economic feasibility, and to account periodically for the use of aid funds in the actual construction of the project.

These types of economic strings are clearly designed to increase the efficiency of American economic aid and are now felt by AID to be acceptable to most recipients.[18] They are considered an important component of the self-help efforts of the less developed countries upon which the United States in its aid program is placing increasing emphasis.

Economic strings are also used in American economic assistance as a means of protecting certain private and public interests of the United States. Stipulations such as the 50/50 shipping clause,[19] the requirement to notify small American businesses of purchases to be made with aid funds in order to let them participate in the bidding,[20] and prohibition of the use of P.L. 480 aid to encourage the production of commodities that would compete with commercial sales of U.S. products[21]—all are designed to help private interests in the United States.

Still another use of economic strings has been to minimize the burden of giving aid. Due to a deterioration in the U.S. balance-of-payments position in the late fifties, for example, aid was tied to purchases in the United States. The effort's success is reflected in the fact that during 1959 only about 40 percent of American aid funds were spent in the United States, whereas in fiscal year 1968 the figure was over 90 percent.[22] This policy was not without its costs, however. The recipient and the United States, as an aid donor, get less per aid dollar when tying is involved, because goods and services which are obtainable in third countries at less cost than in the United States can no longer be purchased with American economic assistance.

An aid controversy in Bolivia affords a notable example of the burden placed on the recipient by these American practices. The United States required Bolivia to spend on U.S. goods an amount equal to the local cost part of the aid loan. Moreover, the American goods purchased had to come from a list of U.S. products that were doing poorly in international commerce because of their high prices. Thus, the United States urged Bolivia to purchase ore carts costing three times as much as a similar Belgian product and to buy American oil-well casing costing 60 percent more than comparable Argentine pipe.[23]

The practice of tying aid has its most serious consequences when aid is given on a project basis. This "double tying" of U.S. aid to (1) purchases in the United States and (2) purchases for a specific project creates a situation minimizing the cost savings from competitive bidding by potential suppliers of equipment necessary for the project. It is very difficult to estimate precisely the excess costs of tied aid to the recipient, but in a recent study by the United Nations Conference on Trade and Development, it was estimated that, overall, tied aid raises costs approximately 10 to 20 percent.[24]

Tying has less severe consequences in program assistance than in project assistance. Under program aid the recipient of U.S. aid and similar aid from other donors can get competitive bids from numerous countries for a specific piece of equipment; if the prices in the United States are much higher than elsewhere, the less developed country can put the American program loan on the shelf, use another credit, and buy from another country. Thus, U.S. aid is not spent for purchases elsewhere, but it does not place the recipient in the position of having to buy U.S. goods for a particular project when the same goods are obtainable in third countries at lower prices. This flexibility and means of savings is denied to the less developed countries under project assistance.[25]

The various types of political and economic strings attached to American economic assistance, and to that of other donors, all have the effect of extracting some form of concession from the recipient in return for the aid given. The problem is that there is some limit to the amount of control a less developed country is willing to allow an aid donor to exercise, and if the strings imposed on aid go beyond that limit, the LDC would rather do without the aid than accept it. This behavior on the part of the potential recipients suggests a necessity on the part of the donor to impose only those stipulations which are absolutely necessary to accomplish the goals desired through giving aid. All additional strings result only in the using up of what limited *quid pro quo* can be extracted through aid. Thus, if the goal of the donor is to secure the political allegiance of the recipient, the latter's support of the donor on foreign policy issues constitutes the *quid pro quo,* and strings on the manner in which the aid is utilized may appear uncalled for to the recipient. On the other hand, if the goal of aid is to promote the economic development and independence of the recipient, the institution of basic reforms necessary for economic growth and the efficient use of aid funds constitutes the *quid pro quo,* and strings concerning the stance of the LDC on foreign policy issues might appear unacceptable to the recipient.

At the bottom of any attempt to attach stringent political and economic conditions to an aid package is the implicit assumption on the part of the donor that economic development is of utmost priority among the various interests of the recipient country. Indeed, economic development in general, and the desire for foreign aid in particular, are among the primary concerns of virtually all less developed countries; however, the extent to which these interests are actually paramount over others—such as nationalism, neutralism, sovereignty, and the aversion to even the appearance of a colonial relationship—is certainly debatable. Consequently, the attempt by an advanced nation to impose numerous visible strings on economic assistance may reflect a serious overestimation of the priority of development assistance in the policies of most LDCs.

The United States has attached to its aid program strings which are designed to increase the effectiveness of the recipient's use of the aid, to influence certain foreign policies of the recipient, to help certain private interests in the United States, and to minimize the burden of giving aid upon the U.S. balance of payments. Certainly, an important factor responsible for the number and scope of conditions imposed on U.S. aid is the desire of Congress to exert direct influence on the program by means of legislation outlining activities which must be promoted by the executive. This impressive scope of conditions imposed along with U.S. aid is by no means completely dysfunctional to the program, however. Particularly in the case of strings designed to increase the efficiency of the use of aid, some controls are essential for the proper utilization of the funds and resources made available through aid.

Terms of Soviet Economic Assistance

The USSR provides economic credits which cover only the foreign exchange costs of projects financed by Soviet aid, and the recipient is expected to finance all local costs. A Soviet writer has described the responsibilities of the recipient as follows:

The governments of these countries [LDCs] undertake to provide (through their local building agencies) the labor and all the work to construct the industrial and other projects with technical assistance of Soviet specialists. Financing in local currency all the expenses connected with the construction and other related jobs is an obligation of the country that receives the credits. These conditions in granting Soviet credits permit them to be directed into purchases of essential equipment and materials for a maximum number of projects.[26]

Whereas the United States prefers and encourages the less developed countries to finance the local costs of aid projects, it is realized that the recipients do not always possess the resources to do so; consequently, the United States often finances part of these local expenses. The Soviet Union's general unwillingness to underwrite local costs is in part responsible for the relatively slow rate at which Soviet credit agreements have been drawn upon, since recipients are frequently unable to meet the companion domestic costs of aid projects.[27] Only in rare instances, such as with Afghanistan on several occasions, has the Soviet Union helped its recipients defray local costs of aid projects.[28]

Loans versus Grants

Unlike the American program which underwent a transformation from primary reliance upon grants to extensive use of loan assistance, the USSR has always given aid on a predominantly credit basis. Only about 4 percent of total Soviet aid commitments from 1954 to 1965 have been in the form of grants.[29] The nature of the efforts undertaken in connection with grant assistance varies considerably. Grant aid has been used to finance "gifts" such as a radio station in Conakry, hospitals in Cambodia, Nepal, and Lebanon, equipment for a technical institute in Bombay, a technical school in Ethiopia,[30] and a hydroelectric power station in Nepal.[31]

Such assistance is only a minor part of the overall Soviet economic aid program. Grants are used primarily as a gesture of Soviet generosity and goodwill toward the recipient. Credit assistance as distinct from grants is always discussed in Soviet literature as the form of aid designed to assist the less developed countries in their economic development.

The reasons for the decision to distribute Soviet economic aid to the LDCs on a credit basis are not definitely known, but several factors suggest themselves as a partial explanation for it. First, since USSR assistance to Communist countries has been given in the form of credits, it is doubtful that the Soviet Union would desire, or find it politically feasible, to grant aid to the non-Communist less developed countries on substantially easier terms than those provided to less developed Communist states. Second, the method devised for repayment of Soviet credits (described below) is well suited to establish continued contacts between the Soviet Union and the countries of the third world. If Soviet aid were given on a grant basis, the contacts generated by the program would last only through the period of implementation of the projects (perhaps five years), whereas through credits the contacts remain intact through the period of implementation and repayment (generally about fifteen years). This is an important factor since a major motivation for Soviet aid has been to establish permanent relations with a part of the world from which it was previously isolated. A third factor involved in the Soviet preference for credit over grant assistance is the psychological benefit derived from the practice of presenting aid on the basis of mutual advantage, equality, and businesslike arrangements which is a characteristic feature of the Soviet program mentioned previously. Grant aid is not conducive to this line of argument. Finally, there is the important fact that credit aid is less costly to the donor than grants.[32]

The financial terms of Soviet economic credits to the less developed countries are quite uniform. The credits at 2.5 percent interest are usually made in the form of rubles[33] and are repayable in the traditional exports of the recipient, or occasionally, in the output of the project financed. Repayment is made in equal installments over a period of twelve years, beginning one year after the completion of the project for which the credit was extended. There are, however, some qualifications and exceptions which should be noted in connection with these characteristic terms accompanying Soviet aid. Occasionally, for instance, assistance is given on more lenient terms when the recipient is felt to be particularly important to the interests of the Soviet Union and is unable to service a credit on the terms generally used in Soviet aid. Thus, for example, Afghanistan was given a $100 million credit in 1955 which carried an interest rate of only 2 percent and which was repayable in 22 years, commencing after an 8-year grace period.[34] Also, in 1959 when Afghanistan insisted that it was financially unable to assume more foreign debts, the USSR provided a grant of $129 million—a concession very unusual for the Soviet aid program.[35] On the other hand, the USSR has begun to extend trade credits on harder terms for LDC imports of machinery and equipment which carry interest rates of from 3 to 4 percent and maturities of 8 to 10 years.[36]

In most credit agreements there is a provision for repayment either in the form of local currency to be used for the purchase of commodities in the LDC for export to the USSR, or in convertible currency.[37] The USSR has seldom exercised the option of demanding repayment in convertible currency, and in the case of India even formally agreed not to insist on sterling convertibility.[38] But this option is maintained in most Soviet aid agreements, and insistence upon repayment in convertible currency would substantially alter the financial terms characteristic of Soviet economic assistance at present and in the past.

In spite of these exceptions and qualifications, the characteristic financial terms of Soviet economic assistance are as stated above, and they will be used as the basis of comparison with American aid.

Soviet versus U.S. Financial Terms

The relative stringency of the financial terms accompanying Soviet and American aid to the less developed countries is difficult to determine in any precise sense because of the variety of instruments used by the United States, the changing market conditions facing the less developed countries in their attempt to export commodities for foreign exchange, and the occasions when both the USSR and the United States have rescheduled or altered repayment obligations in the face of economic difficulties confronting aid recipients.

An attractive feature of Soviet aid, which is repeatedly emphasized in Soviet literature, is the provision for repayment in the form of traditional exports and/or goods produced in factories built with Soviet aid. This arrangement purportedly eliminates the problem of the recipient's having to finance its aid debt with foreign exchange, which is desperately needed and in short supply for most LDCs. In fact, the degree to which the use of foreign exchange is involved in commodity repayments to the USSR depends upon the marketability of the specific commodity in the West. To the extent that the goods cannot be sold in the world market for foreign exchange, the terms for repayment of Soviet aid are more favorable than the terms of those U.S. credits requiring repayment in dollars. If there is no problem in marketing commodities, the effect is identical to repayment of Soviet aid in foreign exchange.

Nevertheless, there is always great uncertainty on the part of the LDCs as to the performance of commodity exports in the world market from year to year and the ability to raise adequate amounts of convertible currency through commodity sales to service foreign debts. The repayment provisions of Soviet aid virtually eliminate LDC anxiety concerning this problem as it relates to debts incurred through receipt of Soviet credits.

The uncertainty of the commodity markets in the West makes this provision of Soviet aid more attractive than the terms of American credit assistance which are increasingly emphasizing repayment in dollars. However, it must be noted that since the beginning of the program, approximately two-thirds of cumulative American economic assistance distributed through AID and its predecessor agencies to the less developed countries has been in the form of grants, requiring no repayment.[39] Also, P.L. 480 sales under Title I have been for local currency, not dollars: therefore, in terms of the currency of repayment, the Soviet arrangements do not seem, overall, to be significantly more lenient than those of the American program.

With regard to interest rates and the period of repayment of U.S. and Soviet aid it appears that the American program is less demanding than that of the USSR. The 2.5 percent interest rate of most Soviet credits to the LDCs is often compared in Soviet literature to U.S. loans through the Export-Import Bank carrying interest rates of from 5 to 6 percent. While this contrast is striking, we noted previously that the average interest rate of U.S. credits to less developed countries during the period 1962–1967 was 2.8 percent.[40] These figures indicate that U.S. loans to LDCs have not carried interest rates substantially higher than those accompanying Soviet aid. In addition, the large portion of U.S. aid which has been distributed on a grant basis would significantly reduce the interest rate of American aid if the interest payments were calculated over total aid given. This would not be the case with Soviet aid, since only four percent has been distributed on a grant basis.

The period of repayment for American assistance in the form of credits also compares favorably with that for the Soviet program. Soviet credits are generally repayable over a 12-year period. The average repayment period for U.S. credits to the less developed countries has been 30 years for disbursements between 1962 and 1967.[41] Thus, it would appear that Soviet aid terms are, on the whole, harder on the recipient than those of the U.S. program.

It might be argued that such a comparison on the basis of average financial terms in the sixties is misleading, since U.S. terms are hardening year by year. On the other hand, if Soviet credits to Latin American states in 1967 at 3 to 4 percent interest, repayable in 8 to 10 years,[42] are an indication of a shift in basic Soviet aid financing, the terms of U.S. aid in 1967 still compare favorably with the Soviet program.

The terms accompanying technical assistance in Soviet and American aid programs require special attention. Among Western scholars of aid it is generally believed that Soviet technical assistance is basically different from that provided by the United States, in that the former is paid for by the recipient with credit funds provided by the donor, whereas the latter is given on a grant basis requiring no repayment by the recipient.[43] This was, indeed, the case through the 1950s before the United States began to rely increasingly on credit assistance. It is still largely true at present since Development Grants are used primarily for technical assistance and do not require repayment by the recipient, whereas Soviet technical assistance is handled almost exclusively on a credit basis. On the other hand, not all U.S. technical assistance is given in the form of grants. American aid projects financed on a credit basis through the Development Loan funding category often involve substantial technical assistance. This technical assistance is covered by the credit, and the less developed country is obliged to repay the costs of these technical services.[44]

Strings on Soviet Aid

As in the case of American aid, certain strings accompanying Soviet economic assistance must be considered along with financial arrangements in an examination of the terms upon which aid is given to the less developed countries.

The USSR has generally avoided the imposition of political strings on its economic assistance to the LDCs. The Soviet Union indeed has focused its aid on those countries pursuing a neutralist or pro-Soviet foreign policy; and there have been occasions involving Afghanistan and Iran when an aid offer was linked to signing a neutrality and nonaggression pact with the USSR.[45] But, these occasions are rare, and as a rule the USSR has conspicuously sought to avoid the imposition of explicit political stipulations (such as those mentioned in connection with American food aid to India) which prescribe a specific stance on some foreign policy issue by the recipient. This is not to say that the Soviet Union has no political interest in the distribution of aid. Rather, the evidence suggests that the USSR feels its political interests in the less developed countries are best served by minimizing the strings accompanying aid.

It appears that from the beginning of its aid program, the Soviet Union realized the antagonism generated in the less developed countries by the more obtrusive stipulations attached to American aid and sought to avoid this problem while at the same time deriding U.S. practices. Thus, on many occasions one can find statements such as that made by the Soviet delegate to the Afro-Asian Solidarity Conference in Cairo:

Russia is now ready to grant Soviet aid to Afro-Asian nations to hasten the development of their economies. Tell us what you need and we will help you. We are ready to send you experts, to supply you with equipment and instructors without any strings attached.[46]

With regard to economic strings, the USSR does not make aid conditional upon basic reforms by the recipient, as the United

States does in some of its program assistance, nor does the Soviet Union require the extensive justification of a project in terms of its role in the overall development plan of the recipient, as the United States does in project assistance. If the recipient requests aid for a specific project and the USSR determines by surveys and studies that the project is feasible, aid is usually given.

Soviet economic assistance is not without strings, however. Credits offered to the less developed countries are, with rare exception, tied to purchases in the USSR. Before 1959, this practice compared most unfavorably with U.S. aid which was not tied to purchases in the United States. Even after the United States began tying aid to purchases, with over 90 percent of American aid being spent in the United States, the Soviet program has been more confining as virtually 100 percent of the credits given to the less developed countries have been used for purchases of goods and services in the USSR. This tying of aid is accomplished by distributing credits in the form of rubles which, not being a convertible currency, are good only for purchases in the USSR. In addition, since almost all Soviet credits are earmarked for specific projects, they constitute, in effect, "double-tied" aid, the consequences of which have been discussed in connection with strings on American aid.

Aid tied to purchases in the USSR is probably more confining than that tied to purchases in the United States, since in the latter instance the LDC can shop for an item on the basis of the best quality and lowest price offered from among many private suppliers. Purchases of the LDC in the Soviet Union are handled by monopolistic Soviet "trade corporations" which act as an intermediary between Soviet enterprises and the aid recipient; thus, the less developed countries have little choice in their selection of suppliers for the products desired.[47]

Another aspect of the Soviet program which might be considered to constitute strings on aid is the procedure by which exports from the recipient are used to repay Soviet credits. For the twelve years of the repayment period the USSR and the LDC conduct annual negotiations to determine the nature and prices of the goods to be delivered. This practice introduces a considerable factor of uncertainty in the actual terms upon which Soviet aid is being offered. To make such arrangements every year places the recipient in a position of having to face the USSR in a series of bilateral negotiatons, all of which afford the USSR an opportunity to affect significantly the economy of the less developed country. The de facto influence obtained by the Soviet Union through these contacts constitutes a string of low visibility; but perhaps because of its low visibility, and the fact that the Soviet Union has not forced harsh terms upon aid recipients as a result of the negotiations, this particular form of stipulation does not seem to concern most less developed countries.

The USSR appears, on the whole, to impose fewer strings than the United States on aid to the less developed countries. To be sure, there has been an impressive correlation between the anti-Western sentiment shown by a less developed country and the offer of Soviet economic assistance, but the USSR has carefully avoided imposing any explicit conditions on the behavior of its aid recipients. The strings which are attached to Soviet aid seem to be designed primarily to minimize the burden of giving aid (such as tying aid to purchases in the USSR) and to continue contacts with LDCs through the arrangement for annual negotiation of prices and products involved in the repayment of Soviet credits.

The Soviet Union has demonstrated a willingness to cancel credits abruptly or exert severe economic pressure on countries of importance to the USSR which adopt anti-Soviet policies. The withdrawal of Soviet assistance to Albania (1961),[48] China (1960),[49] and Yugoslavia (1957),[50] and the economic pressures exerted on Finland in 1958[51] are all vivid examples of this type of Soviet behavior. However, it should be noted that none of these cases involves less developed countries, with which the Soviet Union has tried to conduct relations with a minimum of the arbitrariness and high-handedness so often displayed in its relation with other Communist countries and Finland.

Aid recipients are generally well aware that strings of some type are inevitably a part of economic assistance; they seem most concerned about the visibility of the strings and the appearance of sacrificing their national sovereignty, independence, equality, and integrity to an aid donor. "Why we have all this talk of 'aid without strings' is because the United States made the strings too visible; all the recipients know that there are strings even though they hate to admit it."[52] The USSR recognizes this sensitivity and is more successful than the United States in limiting the number and lowering the visibility of strings which are attached to its aid.

Conclusions

In the American aid program one can clearly see more evolution in the financial terms accompanying aid than is visible in the Soviet program. This evolution has taken the form of a shift from grants to loans, increasing demands for repayment in dollars rather than in the local currencies of the recipients and increasing interest rates. These trends have resulted in a gradual hardening of the terms of U.S. aid.

As far as financial terms are concerned, the Soviet aid program has changed very little since its inception. Except for recent commercial credits to Latin America (whose significance is hard to assess at this time), gifts, and a few credits on easier terms, Soviet aid is distributed at 2.5 percent interest repayable in twelve years by exports of the recipient to the USSR. By contrast, the terms accompanying U.S. aid have changed considerably over the years and U.S. aid is distributed through a variety of aid mechanisms ranging from grants at one extreme to Export-Import Bank long-term loans (requiring repayment in dollars at from 5 to 6 percent interest) at the other.

The Soviet Union has been more successful than the United States in minimizing the number and visibility of strings on aid. This is particularly true regarding strings of a political nature, but there are also fewer explicit restrictions placed on Soviet aid for the purpose of improving the overall economic effectiveness of the aid. A major factor contributing to the imposition of numerous strings on American aid is the desire on the part of Congress to control the President in the use of aid and to affect directly the thrust of the aid program. The USSR has no comparable pressure from the Supreme Soviet or any other quarter.

Also, since the USSR seems less concerned than the United States with an attempt to combat systematically the problems of economic development in the less developed countries, there is less need for the Soviet Union to make aid conditional upon basic internal reforms and economic performance by the recipient. Thus, a difference in priorities concerning the objectives of aid contributes to the necessity for the United States to impose more restrictions on its aid than the USSR.

Hans Heymann notes this difference and gives the following advice on the use of strings in American economic assistance:

Often what may be an eminently successful tactic for Soviet purposes is altogether unsuitable for ours [U.S.]. For example, the notion of "aid without strings," whatever that means, . . . is a most fitting slogan for a Soviet policy concerned primarily with the political climate that it can create and with the unfavorable contrasts with Western imperialism that it can draw. Its appeal largely depends on its remaining aloof from the recipient's internal problems and on its ability to reduce its visible "strings" to a minimum. For us, however, "strings," in the sense of conditions concerning economic policies to be adopted by the recipient government, are indispensable to the success of the aid objectives we seek to attain.[53]

He goes on, however, to warn against imposing any strings which are not clearly relevant to the technical objectives of American aid and which serve to enforce compliance with U.S. ideological preferences.[54]

So, while there is a need for certain economic strings on American assistance, the Soviet Union has struck a responsive chord among aid recipients concerning the distribution of "aid without strings" and the tendency of the United States to overdefine the conditions accompanying its aid.

9

Support of United Nations Development Efforts

‡ So far our analysis has been confined to bilateral aid efforts of the United States and the Soviet Union. Both states have also given economic assistance to the less developed countries through the United Nations and the specialized agencies. This analysis will be confined to several multilateral programs which are indicative of the donors' responsiveness to the development needs of the third world.

Contributions to UN Programs

American and Soviet contributions to assistance programs under UN auspices provide a simple indication of their relative support of multilateral aid efforts. The real touchstone in this regard would be the contributions to the Expanded Program for Technical Assistance (EPTA) which began operations in 1950 and the Special Fund which began in 1959. These programs were combined to form the United Nations Development Program (UNDP) in January 1966. Through the EPTA component of the UNDP, technical assistance is extended to LDCs in the form of pilot projects, fellowships for LDC nationals, advice from experts, seminars, and other activities. The Special Fund component of the UNDP concentrates in preinvestment activities, involving surveys of resources, establishment of local research institutes, vocational and technical training, and other activities which are designed to establish the preconditions for attracting public and private investment capital to the less developed countries. The Soviet and American contributions to the UNDP are presented in Table 11.

TABLE 11

U.S. and USSR Contributions to EPTA and the Special Fund

Year	United States		USSR[a]		Total
	Millions of $	*% of Total*	*Millions of $*	*% of Total*	*Millions of $*
1960	$ 29.6	42	$ 2.4	3	$ 71.0
1961	37.3	42[e]	3.5	4	88.2
1962	43.6	42	3.5	3	103.4
1963	52.5	43	3.5	3	123.3
1964	59.1	43	3.5	3	137.2
1965	60.0	41	3.5	2	145.6
1966	63.0	41	3.5	2	153.5
1967[b]	70.0	41	3.5	2	170.3
1968[c]	75.0	41	3.5	2	181.7
Total	$490.1	42	$30.4	3	$1,174.2
Cumulative					
1950–1968[d]	$622.2	43	$39.8	3	$1,438.0

SOURCE: *Yearbooks of the United Nations, 1959–1965* (New York: United Nations, 1960–1967) except where noted otherwise.

a. USSR, Byelorussia SSR, and Ukraine SSR.
b. United Nations document DP/L.32.
c. UN document DP/L.62.
d. Derived from sources above plus figures for EPTA from UN document E/TAC/153/Rev. 1, Annex I, pp. 1–5.
e. After 1961 the U.S. share of total contributions to EPTA and the Special Fund was restricted by U.S. statute to no more than 40 percent. These data as presented in the *Yearbook of the United Nations* are projected estimates of a 40 percent share of total contributions, rather than actual U.S. contributions which are made only after the remaining 60 percent is paid in by other states.

From the table we see that the annual Soviet contributions to EPTA and the Special Fund have remained at $3.5 million since 1961, while annual U.S. contributions have doubled during the same period to produce a total of $75 million in 1968. As a result of the growth of these programs, the Soviet share of the total has decreased from 4 to 2 percent, compared to the steady U.S. figure of 40 percent.[1] It is interesting to compare these figures with the shares of the United States and the USSR in the regular assessed budget of the United Nations which are determined on criteria reflecting ability to pay. These shares are 32 percent for the United States and 17 percent for the Soviet Union (including Byelorussia and the Ukraine).

A more meaningful comparison of U.S. and Soviet multilateral aid through the United Nations can be seen in their annual voluntary contributions to all UN-related agencies involved in assisting less developed countries. In fiscal year 1968 the United States President requested $140.9 million for voluntary contributions to twelve international programs including the UNDP.[2] During calendar year 1967 the Soviet Union made voluntary contributions to only four of these programs in the amount of $4.8 million including the UNDP.[3] While the U.S. contribution is most impressive in relation to that of the USSR when expressed in terms of the total amounts, in both cases multilateral aid comprises a minute portion of total aid. These contributions represent just over 3 percent of total U.S. economic aid to the LDCs in fiscal year 1966 and about one-half of one percent of total Soviet economic aid commitments to the LDCs in 1966. Thus, both donors rely predominantly on bilateral economic assistance.[4]

These data are illustrative of the relative commitment of the United States and the Soviet Union to multilateral economic assistance through the United Nations and the specialized agencies. We have not even mentioned the capital subscriptions of the United States to the World Bank family which amount to over $1 billion. The USSR does not participate in these organizations. But, no matter what measure is adopted, it is evident that there is virtually no comparison between the American and Soviet contributions to multilateral aid programs within the UN family.

Substantial American financial support for programs such as EPTA, the Special Fund, the International Bank for Reconstruction and Development (IBRD) and its affiliates, the International Finance Corporation (IFC), and the International Development Association (IDA) is easily explained by the fact that all were created by U.S. initiative and shaped according to U.S. desires. American confidence in and support of these multilateral aid programs is sustained either by virtue of its power in formal weighted voting (IBRD, IFC, and IDA), the large share of its contributions (40 percent of the UNDP) affording leverage on the direction of the program, and/or the existence of a respected American as head of the organization (Robert McNamara as president of the IBRD and its affiliates, and Paul Hoffman as managing director of the Special Fund and later the UNDP).

The relative lack of Soviet support for these multilateral aid agencies is largely a consequence of the large American role in shaping and implementing the programs. The USSR attacked EPTA on the grounds that it was based on the Point Four program of President Truman and dominated by Washington, rather than being based on the charter of the United Nations and having a truly international character.[5] The USSR viewed the Special Fund as an American creation designed to do the spadework for private investors and to provide a deceptive and ineffective alternative for a capital development fund being demanded by the LDCs with Soviet verbal support.[6] Similarly, the USSR has attacked the IBRD family as an arm of American imperialism dominated by voting weighted to the advantage of the United States and engaged in promoting private enterprise at the expense of the state sector of the LDCs.[7]

The attacks of the USSR on these agencies are extreme, to be sure, but they reflect the reality of a predominant American role in shaping the programs. This American role, thus, explains at once American support for and Soviet opposition to the main aid agencies under UN auspices.

In spite of the influence the United States wields in the UN agencies receiving substantial American financial backing, U.S. support for these programs is not unqualified. The most celebrated incident casting doubt on the strength of the American commitment to even its preferred multilateral aid channels involves two Special Fund projects in Cuba. In May 1961 the governing council of the Special Fund approved an agricultural project for Cuba involving the study of tropical animal husbandry, soil classification, conservation, and crop diversification. The total cost to the Special Fund was to be $1,042,500.[8]

The United States opposed the project on political and economic grounds while it was under consideration by the governing council.[9] While economic reasons were necessarily relied upon in statements before the governing council, U.S. political opposition was succinctly stated by Richard Gardner, deputy assistant secretary of state for international organization affairs:

> Our policy toward Cuba involves opposition to any source of aid and comfort to the present regime. We pursue this policy in the United Nations and elsewhere by all means available to us. . . . We believe . . . that the Cuban government has so subordinated the economic and social welfare of the Cuban people to the narrow political aims of the present leadership that the minimum standards of efficiency and effectiveness which must guide the implementation of cooperative development projects—whether within the UN system or without—cannot possibly be met.[10]

In spite of American opposition to the project the United States found it impossible to break the tradition in the Special Fund of voting on the whole package of projects proposed by the managing director. No separate vote was taken on the Cuban project since the U.S. delegation was convinced it would be overruled by at least two-thirds of the other council members. Instead, the United States went on record as being opposed to the project while it was approved along with all the others.

When the Special Fund proceeded with the project in 1963 there was a bitter outcry from the U.S. Congress which precipitated an investigation of American participation in the Special Fund. During the hearings on this matter representatives of the administration pointed out: (1) that over 97 percent of Special Fund projects have gone to non-Communist countries; (2) that the Communist countries have donated more to the Special Fund than they have received in the form of projects; and (3) that Special Fund projects totaling $7.5 million in Korea, Taiwan, and Vietnam are being carried out over Soviet misgivings.

The response of this and other congressional committees has been not only to reprimand the administration for allowing the approval of Cuban projects, but also to question the American relationship with the Special Fund itself. The problem has been resurrected in every set of hearings on American foreign assistance through 1969, and it has been given new fuel by the approval in 1966 of a second Special Fund project to strengthen the faculty of technology at Havana University. One consequence of this congressional opposition to Special Fund projects for Cuba has been the addition of a clause in the statutory authority for voluntary U.S. contributions to international organizations stipulating that no U.S. contributions to the UNDP "shall be used for economic or technical assistance to the Government of Cuba, so long as Cuba is governed by the Castro regime."[11]

The degree of United States opposition to these Special Fund projects for Cuba casts doubt on the firmness of American support for multilateral aid agencies of the United Nations. The UN programs receiving most American support are ones in which the USSR either does not participate (IBRD, IDA, IFC) or in which the USSR finds itself in a permanent minority position (EPTA and the Special Fund). The Special Fund example suggests that when the United States finds itself in the minority, its support for UN aid agencies—even one whose director is a respected American citizen—is rather tenuous. This fact must be considered in evaluating the small size of Soviet contributions to UN agencies in which the USSR has been in a permanent minority.

The United Nations Capital Development Fund

Since 1951 the less developed countries have been proposing the creation of a UN agency to provide investment capital in the form of grants or long-term low interest loans for infrastructure type projects vital for economic growth but unable to earn a profit or pay for themselves—transportation, communication, and power systems, for example. This proposed Special United Nations Fund for Economic Development (SUNFED) was initially opposed by both the United States and the Soviet Union. American opposition was based primarily on the claim that it was not prepared to give financial support to such a fund while the burden of fighting a war in Korea was required. In 1951 the USSR was preoccupied with East European and Far Eastern problems, and at that time it engaged in no bilateral or multilateral aid efforts. The Soviet delegate to the Economic and Social Council (ECOSOC) emphasized that SUNFED overestimated the significance of foreign capital for economic development and tended to encourage intervention in domestic affairs of the LDCs through the channels of foreign capital. The program was viewed as a new means for the spread of American imperialism.

Throughout the 1950s the United States continued to oppose SUNFED by declarations and votes. As American opposition solidified, the Soviet Union gradually changed its position on the issue as part of a larger policy shift manifested in the announcement of 1953 that the USSR would begin to make contributions to EPTA. While continuing to express serious reservations and to counsel caution, in 1953 the USSR gave qualified support for the creation of SUNFED. By 1955 the Soviet Union had placed itself squarely on the side of the less developed countries in their demand for the creation of SUNFED and even committed itself to participate in the agency and to make contributions to it. This complete reversal of the Soviet position between 1951 and 1955 was an effort designed to demonstrate Soviet solidarity with the LDCs and to embarrass the United States which was unalterably opposed to the SUNFED concept.

Partially in compensation for its opposition to SUNFED in the late fifties, the United States promoted the creation of IFC in 1956, the Special Fund in 1959, and IDA in 1960. These programs did not meet LDC demands for capital investment funds, but they did provide an increase in the amount of money available to multilateral agencies for development purposes.[12]

The creation of these new aid channels had the temporary effect of slowing down the drive for SUNFED, but by 1960 pressure was again exerted for the establishment of a Capital Development Fund (the Special Fund's creation in 1959 preempted use of the SUNFED title for a capital investment program under UN auspices).

In December 1959 the General Assembly passed a resolution requesting the secretary general to solicit the views of the member states regarding the establishment of a Capital Development

Fund. The American response was a reassertion of its opposition to the program on the grounds that limited aid resources should not be wasted by multiplying administrative machinery for distributing them. The establishment of the IDA was viewed as the best way to accomplish the job at hand. "We [the United States] would see no merit in creating or even discussing additional machinery, when the real problem is to use effectively the machinery already in the process of being established [IDA]."[13] By contrast the Soviet response to the inquiry was that it "has consistently supported and continues to support the early establishment of a United Nations fund to finance industrial development in the economically underdeveloped countries. . . . The Soviet Union is ready to participate with other countries in contributing its material resources to SUNFED in the event of its establishment."[14]

With the support of the USSR and the other Communist states the less developed countries secured the passage of a resolution in December 1960 deciding "in principle" that a United Nations Capital Development Fund should be established. A committee of twenty-five states was to be designated by the president of the General Assembly to consider concrete preparatory measures including draft legislation necessary to that end.[15] The United States voted against this resolution, and even though it was a member of the committee on the establishment of a Capital Development Fund it did not participate in the work of drawing up a draft statute for the fund.

This draft statute was considered by the General Assembly in 1962. Although the less developed countries had the voting strength to actually create the Capital Development Fund, they refrained from doing so over the opposition of all the major donor nations of the West. This restraint was at least partly a consequence of the positive steps taken by the United States in expanding the flow of resources through multilateral agencies in the late fifties and early sixties.[16] Instead, a resolution was passed calling for the secretary general to obtain comments from the member states and members of the specialized agencies on the draft statute. The committee was instructed to study these comments on the draft statute and prepare practical measures to ensure the initiation of operation of the fund.[17]

The Soviet response to the secretary general's inquiry revealed that as the time approached for the actual creation of a Capital Development Fund, USSR support for the less developed countries on this issue deteriorated. The USSR argued that all contributions to the fund should be made on a voluntary basis, in national currencies or in kind (equipment, machinery, technical documents, drawings, and specifications). The principle of universal membership should be observed. In addition to an equitable geographic distribution on the policy-making organs a form of troika representation should also apply. Most importantly, the USSR insisted that the Capital Development Fund should be created by a gradual transformation of the Special Fund.[18]

Finally, on December 13, 1966, the United Nations Capital Development Fund was created as an autonomous organization within the United Nations as an organ of the General Assembly. Administrative expenses of the fund were to be financed through the regular budget, whereas expenses for operational activities were to be financed by voluntary contributions. The fund would extend grants and loans at low interest rates and long periods of amortization. A twenty-four member executive board would have final authority for approval of loans and grants submitted to it by the managing director. Members of the executive board would be elected on the basis of equitable distribution of the LDCs and the advanced countries, taking into account, also, the geographical distribution of the states.[19]

Consistent with its continued opposition to such a fund, the United States voted against its creation in 1966. It was pointed out that even existing UN organizations were operating well below their desired levels. Setting up a new program would imply (falsely, in the opinion of the United States) that resources of a suitable size and type would be available for investment. The United States vigorously opposed making administrative expenses of the Capital Development Fund payable through the regular, assessed budget of the United Nations as this "would set a very dangerous precedent. It would make those who had repeatedly disagreed with the establishment of the fund pay part of the cost of maintaining it."[20]

In spite of its earlier verbal support of the less developed countries in their quest for a Capital Development Fund, the USSR proved no more interested in making the enterprise operational than the United States. The Soviet Union and the other Communist states, not including Yugoslavia, abstained on the vote creating the fund in 1966. Thus, in the final instance the issue was resolved with the South lining up against the North, including the advanced countries of the East as well as the West. Soviet opposition to the creation of the Capital Development Fund was justified by the USSR on the grounds that the West and some LDCs yielding to Western pressure had turned their backs on the Soviet proposal to transform the Special Fund into a capital investment program. In place of a single managing director the Soviet Union desired a five-member directorate with two representatives each from the West and from the LDCs, and one from the socialist countries. The USSR, like the United States, was strongly opposed to financing the administrative expenses of the fund through the regular budget. Also, it deplored the fact that membership of the fund was not to be universal.[21]

At the first pledging conference held for the Capital Development Fund on October 31, 1967, neither the United States nor the USSR made any contribution to the program. Indeed, the equivalent of only $1.3 million was pledged by twenty-two less developed countries in local currencies—no advanced states of the East or West made a pledge.[22] The lack of response by the advanced countries resulted in the decision in December 1967 that on a provisional basis the administrator of the UNDP, Paul Hoffman, would be asked to administer the Capital Development Fund by performing the functions which had been envisioned for the fund's managing director. Similarly, the governing council of the UNDP would be asked to perform the functions foreseen for the Capital Development Fund's executive board.[23] Thus, it appears that the Capital Development Fund was stillborn.

This outline of the struggle by the less developed countries for a capital investment program reveals some interesting facets of American and Soviet responses to multilateral aid. The persistent opposition of the United States to the idea of a capital development fund stands in marked contrast to U.S. support of certain other UN aid programs mentioned in the first part of this chapter. This contrast suggests that U.S. interest in multilateral aid under UN auspices is largely confined to those particular programs which the United States has initiated and over which it exercises substantial control. Thus, the United States insisted that the IDA was the proper channel for a multilateral capital investment program. In that organization the major aid donors, and the United States in particular, possess the decisive voting power. In the Capital Development Fund, on the other hand, the recipients have an equal voice with the donors on the executive board.

In financial terms, the American response to the SUNFED idea which it would not support was in some measure offset by the creation at U.S. initiative of the IFC, the Special Fund, and the IDA. If these agencies fell short of LDC demands for capital investment, they have nevertheless expanded the flow of financial resources and U.S. contributions through the UN to the less developed countries.

As long as the United States and the major Western aid donors remained opposed to the SUNFED idea, and until serious negotiations were undertaken to operationalize such a program, the USSR expressed its complete solidarity with the less developed countries on this issue. However, when the time came for financial support of the fund, the Soviet Union was unwilling to participate in its operations.

If ever there was an occasion when the USSR could have molded a multilateral aid program to its liking, this was it. The United States was clearly unwilling to participate in the effort; indeed it even refused to work on drafting the statutory basis of a capital development fund. If the Soviet Union had been willing to make a substantial financial commitment during the critical phases of negotiating the creation of the fund after 1960, it may well have succeeded in getting the LDCs to meet enough of the Soviet demands on the nature of the fund to enable actual USSR support for the program. In this case the USSR would have been the major donor to a multilateral aid agency which was most closely identified with LDC interests. If the United States had later chosen to participate in the Capital Development Fund the USSR could justifiably have taken credit for the move. If the United States remained outside of the program the Soviet Union and the Communist states would have maintained the dominant donor influence over the operations of the fund.[24]

A truly effective program for capital investment in the less developed countries implies contributions on a scale which neither the United States nor the USSR is willing to sustain except on a bilateral basis. Their unwillingness to participate in the Capital Development Fund is a manifestation of this fact. On balance it appears that the United States is willing to give substantial support only to those UN aid efforts which it has sponsored. The Soviet Union, unlike the United States, has been unwilling to underwrite any UN aid programs and thus mold them to its liking. Instead, since 1953 it has made only minimal contributions to multilateral programs to which it is basically opposed.

The United Nations Conference on Trade and Development

The first United Nations Conference on Trade and Development (UNCTAD-I), held in 1964, was viewed by the less developed countries as the single most important event since the founding of the United Nations.[25] It represented a concerted effort of the LDCs to establish new principles for international trade which would guarantee increased capital flows necessary for economic development in the third world. Specifically, the LDCs demanded: (1) increased access and preferential treatment for their exports of manufactures and semimanufactures to industrially advanced states of the East and West; (2) commodity agreements designed to insure stable markets and remunerative (higher) prices for LDC exports of primary products; (3) increased flows of economic assistance on terms which would ameliorate the debt service burden faced by the LDCs; and (4) a permanent international organization within the framework of the United Nations which would promote LDC views on international economic problems and administer the restructuring of world trade on the basis of the principles being advanced at UNCTAD-I.

The conference was most significant as a manifestation of the LDCs' assertion that the North-South conflict should be afforded higher priority than that between the East and West. In the latter conflict the LDCs had played a peripheral role, whereas at UNCTAD-I these countries took the lead in mobilizing political demand for addressing development problems on an unprecedented scale.

This treatment of UNCTAD will not include an examination of the legitimacy or practicality of the LDCs' demands. Instead the analysis will focus on American and Soviet reactions to the idea of the conference and to LDC demands raised therein. The issues raised in UNCTAD precipitated U.S. and Soviet responses on the whole gamut of trade and aid problems as they relate to economic development of the LDCs. The conference and its continuing machinery have added a new dimension in the assessment of American and Soviet attitudes toward multilateral efforts to increase capital flows to the third world.

The United States was initially opposed to the convening of UNCTAD-I and went to the conference prepared to resist nearly all of the major proposals of the less developed countries. The American position was summarized by a State Department spokesman as follows: (1) An open, non-discriminatory, and liberal trade system remains the best hope for the LDCs—the principles of the General Agreement on Tariffs and Trade (GATT) were to be strongly defended. (2) There should be no use of trading devices as a disguised means of granting aid. (3) The responsibility for economic development is primarily that of the less developed countries. The United States will help and share responsibility with the LDCs and other advanced countries, but the LDCs must take steps to avoid inflation, to attract foreign capital, etc. (4) There is a North-South division, but the gap between the richer and poorer LDCs is just as significant.

Thus, there are few policies which would affect all LDCs alike. (5) The performance of the Western states in both trade and aid with the LDCs compares favorably with that of the Communist states. (6) Within the West, the United States has a creditable record with respect to trade and aid.[26]

The American delegation was sent to Geneva to conduct a spirited defense of existing international trade practices and institutions. American negativism at UNCTAD-I was reinforced by the instruction of its delegation not to abstain when it actually disagreed with specific proposals.[27] As a consequence, "the US became clearly identified as the least willing of the industrialized countries to even consider a 'new' international division of labor which would permit the developing countries to industrialize."[28] The American voting record on the General and Special Principles of the Final Act adopted at UNCTAD-I was the most negative at the conference.[29]

In distinct contrast with American opposition to the convening of UNCTAD-I, the USSR embraced the move. With some justification[30] USSR spokesmen claimed that UNCTAD was called as a result of Soviet efforts combined with those of other Communist states and the LDCs.[31] The conference was viewed by the Soviet Union as a means of (1) removing Western-imposed obstacles to East-West trade, (2) attacking the European Economic Community as a closed economic group negating the most-favored-nation concept and also as a mechanism for perpetuating European control over former African colonies, and (3) replacing the existing machinery for international trade—symbolized by GATT and operating in the basic interests of the United States—with an entirely new international organizational structure which had universal membership and which did not reflect Western concepts of world commerce and finance. Soviet and LDC preoccupations at UNCTAD were quite different, but the USSR hoped to ride the wave of LDC discontent with the existing international economic system and direct this force into channels supportive of Soviet and East European interests.

The cohesive bond between the USSR and the LDCs at UNCTAD-I was a common desire to alter international economic policies and institutions which they felt yielded primary benefits to the industrialized states of the West. The USSR voted with the LDCs on 26 of 28 General and Special Principles adopted in the Final Act of UNCTAD-I.[32] The difference in the Soviet and American voting records on the Final Act might suggest that the USSR was successful in isolating the United States and courting the less developed countries. In reality, however, the LDCs dominated the conference and the Soviet reaction to their specific demands was in many respects as rigid and as negative as that of the United States, in spite of the difference in voting performance.

Let us turn to an examination of American and Soviet responses to specific demands of the less developed countries as found in committee debates of UNCTAD-I. Only in this way can American and Soviet performance be compared meaningfully.

The demand by the LDCs for commodity agreements met with a cool reaction from both the United States and the USSR at UNCTAD-I. The United States expressed support of the major goal of ensuring growing markets and improved and stable prices for LDC exports of commodities. However, it warned that while commodity agreements might be practicable and essential for some products such as coffee, for others, they might be impractical or undesirable. Primary emphasis was placed on the need to consider underlying imbalances of supply and demand in various commodity markets through efforts to expand consumption and to shift production resources to other fields.[33] In essence, the American position rested on the assertion that the answer to the commodity problem lay in greater LDC efforts at diversification of their economies, both in agriculture and industry.[34]

The USSR insisted that the slow growth in demand for primary products was not a problem in LDC trade with the socialist countries. The deterioration in the terms of trade facing primary commodity exports and the fluctuations in import and export prices for LDC goods was a characteristic unique to the world capitalist market. The USSR considered, in light of these facts, that agreements to stabilize commodity prices and to eliminate the harmful effects of capitalist market forces could and should be concluded.[35] Such agreements, of course, would not in any way involve the Soviet Union. For its part, the USSR viewed long-term bilateral agreements "as its real contribution to the stabilization of commodity markets and prices."[36]

So, whereas the United States had claimed commodity problems were to be attacked fundamentally in the domestic economies of the LDCs, the USSR insisted that the world capitalist market of the West was the logical focus of attack. Each was saying that it should not be the focus of any concerted attempt to remedy the commodity problems faced by the less developed countries.

Demands were also made by the LDCs for increased access to markets of the industrially advanced countries and for nonreciprocal, preferential treatment of their manufactures and semimanufactures in these markets. The United States went to UNCTAD opposed to preferences on general principle. Throughout the conference the United States adopted the position that the principles of GATT ensured the greatest potential for LDC export expansion. At the core of these GATT principles was the gradual reduction of tariff and other barriers on manufactured goods on a reciprocal, most-favored-nation basis. These principles were regarded by the less developed countries as a means of ensuring equal competition among unequal partners, and their purpose at UNCTAD-I was to replace them with a trade system discriminating in favor of the less developed countries.

Nevertheless, the United States called attention to the GATT Action Program as a manifestation of the attention being devoted to LDC trade problems by the contracting parties.[37] The upcoming Kennedy Round of negotiations within GATT was viewed by the United States as the most efficient method for removing trade barriers and expanding the exports of LDC manufactures. In addition and irrespective of the results of the Kennedy Round, the United States promised to extend technical assistance in marketing to facilitate LDC exports of manufactures and semi-manufactures.[38] The United States made it quite clear that it was cool to preferential arrangements designed to benefit the LDCs which would result in a severe alteration of existing international trade principles and patterns.

The Soviet Union insisted that it never had and never would engage in any discriminatory practices directed against imports of manufactures and semimanufactures from the less developed countries. It promised to increase LDC access to the Soviet market by concluding long-term trade agreements providing for a steady rise in the mutual delivery of goods (including manufactures and semimanufactures), by initiating production-cooperation agreements, and by removing as of January 1, 1965 all customs duties on goods imported from and originating in the less developed countries.[39] In fact, these proposals represented only symbolic concessions to the LDCs. For reasons discussed in Chapter 7 the implementation of production-cooperation agreements on a significant scale seems to be a remote possibility. Also, Soviet customs duties on LDC goods prior to January 1, 1965 were minimal, and in a state trading system such as that of the USSR tariffs are not relied upon for the regulation of imports.

Indeed, in spite of these gestures, the USSR faced much criticism on the question of increased trade with the less developed countries. It was attacked most frequently for the difference in its import and domestic retail sales prices of goods purchased from the less developed countries. Spokesmen from the West and numerous LDCs suggested that the high level of Soviet domestic retail prices applied to goods imported from the LDCs at a much lower price level had the effect of depressing consumer demand for these goods and curtailing Soviet imports from these countries. Soviet spokesmen pointed out that the domestic sales prices of imported goods are fixed at the same level as those for domestically produced goods without discrimination as to origin. Also they insisted that the price difference in no way affected the volume of Soviet imports which were instead regulated by the state according to the planned needs of the economy. Moreover, the pricing issue was viewed as strictly a domestic affair of the Soviet Union.[40]

The Soviet response to this and other criticisms of its trade with the less developed countries (such as bilateralism, the meaningless nature of abolishing its tariffs on LDC goods, and the small size of Soviet-LDC trade) was unyielding. Since export earnings were the main source of foreign exchange for the USSR, it emphasized that the real guarantee of an expansion of Soviet imports from LDCs was for these states to buy more Soviet goods. "It would be unrealistic to expect of the Soviet Union unilateral commitments to purchase goods without an assured increase in its own exports."[41] The USSR considered it unjust to subject all states to the same rules in an attempt to facilitate export expansion of the third world countries. The Western states, which had for a long time enjoyed trading advantages in their colonies and obtained considerable profits through exploiting them, should grant favorable trading conditions to the LDCs *without expecting reciprocity*. For its part, the USSR, despite the fact that it had never had the same privileges, was willing to support the views of the LDCs and work for the creation of a trading system based on *equality* and *mutual advantage*.[42]

Thus, on the issues of trade in commodities and manufactures, the Soviet position was that the West is entirely responsible for all the real obstacles to LDC trade, including those which might exist between the USSR and the third world countries. It suggested that the conference should, therefore, attack Western practices rather than the imaginary problems that were alleged to exist in LDC-Soviet trade.[43] Any proposals to change Soviet trade or pricing policies were denounced as reflecting unfamiliarity with the socialist economic system and its differences from the capitalist system of the West.

LDC demands for increased aid on easier financial terms were met with less U.S. negativism than the other major issues raised at UNCTAD-I. The United States pointed to its bilateral aid program and to its role in financing and initiating multilateral aid efforts through the United Nations. It expressed pride in the fact that over 40 percent of all contributions to the various UN agencies promoting economic growth in the third world came from the United States. While expressing a preference for the expansion and improvement of existing multilateral programs to provide capital resources to the LDCs, the United States was willing to examine new programs such as supplementary and compensatory financing schemes.[44] The United States also endorsed the general proposition that all advanced nations should undertake to "spare a definite percentage of their gross national income for the economic and social development of the poor countries."[45]

The response of the USSR on the aid issue at UNCTAD-I made the lukewarm American position look enthusiastic by comparison. The Soviet Union argued that the large increase in aid required to meet the needs of the LDCs must come from the Western states since they alone bore the historical responsibility for the present economic situation of the third world. The less developed countries were warned not to expect equal aid contributions from the Communist states and the West.[46]

The Soviet position on compensatory financing is illustrative of its general approach to appeals for more aid. The USSR asserted that fluctuations in LDC export earnings and deterioration of their terms of trade were consequences of the capitalist economic system and the policies of monopolies. Soviet trade with the LDCs was free of such trends and policies, so, accordingly, the losses suffered by the less developed countries ought to be compensated by the countries responsible.[47] As with so many other issues the USSR supported LDC demands for a program from which it had exempted itself.

The less developed countries met with a very cool American response to their demands for a new international trade organization which would work towards the restructuring of world trade according to the principles being proposed by the LDCs at UNCTAD-I. The United States felt it would be better to rely on the solid foundations existing within the UN system than to establish a new organization.

Instead, the United States proposed the convening of periodic conferences with participation of all United Nations and specialized agencies' member states to meet every three years, or more frequently when necessary. These conferences should be convened by ECOSOC and would report to the General Assembly through ECOSOC. In addition, the United States proposed the establishment of a permanent commission of international trade under ECOSOC which would be empowered to establish sub-committees as might be required. The commission would be composed of thirty-four states elected to ensure equitable geographic distribution with equal representation for less developed and developed states, including the principal trading states. A secretariat would be created to service the periodic conferences and the permanent commission, but it should not be separate from the Secretariat of the United Nations.[48]

Through this proposal the United States sought to keep the institutionalization of UNCTAD within the confines of ECOSOC. Both the proposed permanent commission and ECOSOC assure the developed states equal voting powers with the less developed countries. The American approach would also preclude any real threat to the position of GATT, the IMF, and IBRD in the international economic system. Of course the American position was viewed as a totally inadequate response by the LDCs who were set on establishing a prestigious, powerful, autonomous organization within the United Nations which would operate under their control and in their interests.

The USSR was as anxious to challenge the preeminence of GATT, the World Bank family, and European regional economic groupings in the interests of increased influence of the socialist system in world economics as the LDCs were in the interests of increased development. Therefore it was much more supportive of LDC demands for the creation of an international trade organization than was the United States.

The Soviet Union submitted a memorandum at UNCTAD-I outlining its concept for an international trade organization. It argued that such an organization should have a wide field of competence in all matters of international trade and should ensure an equitable role for all countries regardless of their social and economic systems and level of economic development. The organization should be autonomous and universal, functioning under UN auspices. It should become a center for coordinating the activities of all subsidiary bodies in the field of world trade.

Some of these bodies, if they so agreed, might be incorporated as committees or departments under the proposed international trade organization. For example, GATT might become its committee on tariffs. The USSR called for equitable representation of the West, the LDCs, and the Communist states in all subsidiary bodies of the organization.[49]

The Soviet concept of an international trade organization was broader than that of the LDCs. The LDCs were interested exclusively in a permanent forum lobbying for increased capital flows to the third world through various forms of aid and the expansion of North-South trade. The USSR supported this function of the organization but wanted it to work actively on problems of East-West trade. As established, the continuing UNCTAD machinery basically reflects the LDCs' concept of the focus of the organization.

Several lessons emerged from UNCTAD-I regarding Soviet and American responsiveness to LDC demands that their development problems deserve top priority in international affairs. The stances adopted by the two superpowers on the issues outlined above clearly indicate that neither the United States nor the USSR was prepared to make significant concessions on issues which countries of the third world deem to be crucial to their development.

The United States was unwilling to accept the basic premise of the LDCs that the cause and cure of their development problems were largely external and systemic in nature. Instead, the American position was that domestic political, social, and economic reforms on the part of the less developed countries themselves provided the only hope for their developmental progress. The result was an almost completely negative American reaction to every proposal made by the LDCs at the conference. The United States viewed UNCTAD less as a mechanism for generating operational programs than as a conference for the purpose of exchanging and reconciling views on international economic problems as they affect the LDCs. Thus, the United States found itself in the unusual position of arguing for a restrictive interpretation of new UN action to be taken under the UNCTAD mandate.

On entirely different grounds the Soviet Union was as negative and rigid in the face of the LDCs demands as was the United States. It wholeheartedly endorsed the contention of the LDCs that their development problems were largely systemic in character. Indeed, it argued repeatedly that the LDCs themselves were taking too narrow a view of the systemic problems, because the East as well as the South was adversely affected by an essentially Western world economic system. The USSR deplored the failure of the LDCs at UNCTAD-I to press for reform in East-West trade as well as North-South trade. This placed the Soviet Union in an uncharacteristic position of championing a maximally expansionist view of the proper competence for UN action through UNCTAD.

In spite of this support for a systemic reform in international economics, the USSR refused to make any concrete commitments to facilitate the economic development of the third world. It held that the West was exclusively to blame for all the conditions precipitating LDC demands at UNCTAD; therefore, it was the West alone which must change its trade and aid policies toward the third world. The Soviet Union emphasized that it was entirely improper and unrealistic for the LDCs to expect the USSR and the Communist countries to enter into any commitments such as commodity agreements, meaningful nonreciprocal preferences, compensatory financing, or increased aid on a specified scale which the West was duty-bound to implement.

This lack of responsiveness by both the Soviet Union and the United States tends to corroborate Harry Johnson's contention that economic assistance is the soft option for policy towards the less developed countries.[50] Bilateral and multilateral aid can be given with little real effect on the internal and external economic policies of donors such as the United States and the Soviet Union. On the other hand, the transfer of increased capital to the LDCs through trade practices discriminating in favor of these countries raises a host of problems to the industrially advanced states.

At UNCTAD-I the United States was being asked to abandon the principles upon which its international trade was based and to open its domestic market to competition from third world products which threatened to replace some U.S. producers of similar goods. The American reaction was predictably negative. Whether or not such policy changes would be politically and economically efficacious for the United States is not at issue here. The point is that interests in the United States threatened by demands for trade reforms by LDCs make it difficult for the United States to accommodate LDC demands. It is in this sense that aid is a soft option for the United States if it wishes to increase the flow of capital for development to the less developed countries. Indeed, it was on aid issues that the United States was most responsive to LDC demands at UNCTAD-I.

Similarly the Soviet Union was unwilling to entertain any suggestions affecting existing Soviet policies such as reducing the gap between its domestic retail and import prices of LDC goods as a means of increasing Soviet imports from the third world. This was viewed by the Soviet Union as a strictly domestic affair. For the USSR as well as the United States, aid is a much easier means of increasing the flow of capital to the less developed countries. This fact has presented a critical stumbling block to the LDCs' attempt through UNCTAD to emphasize trade, not aid, as a source of external funds for economic development.

UNCTAD-I also demonstrated how little the USSR and the Communist states had to offer the less developed countries in comparison to the United States and the West. LDC exports to the advanced countries of the West were over twelve times their exports to Communist countries.[51] This statistic gives a rough indication of why the less developed countries largely ignored the Communist states and concentrated on the policies of the Western countries at UNCTAD-I. The USSR on several occasions at the conference noted that most of the recommendations being discussed were concerned only with Western-LDC relations, implying that the Communist states were being neglected, and it warned the LDCs not to compromise their interests in the West-South dialogue.[52] A Pakistani scholar, commenting on the UNCTAD proposal of the Communist states to enter into production-cooperation agreements with the LDCs, applauded the gesture but stated that the Communist countries at present can meet only the marginal requirements of the developing countries. "They as yet do not have enough goods, particularly capital goods, such as can satisfy the needs of the developing countries."[53]

Above all, the tone of the UNCTAD proceedings demonstrated as never before the solidification—at least as far as the LDCs were concerned—of a North-South confrontation on the issues of development. The countries of the East as well as the West were included in the South's attack on the North, even if the East was generally ignored at UNCTAD-I. Any cold-war polemics between the East and the West at the conference were roundly condemned and terminated by the LDCs who insisted that such debate was irrelevant to the problems of the third world being raised at Geneva.[54]

The Soviet Union bitterly opposed this development at the conference because it categorically refused to bear any responsibility for the existing economic position of the LDCs or for taking any concrete moves to improve that position. Since 1964 the Soviet Union has denied the validity of a North-South conflict, and Soviet spokesmen have suggested that the concept was advanced by imperialist ideologists and picked up by some statesmen of Asia, Africa, and Latin America along with the "Mao Tse-tung group."[55]

UNCTAD-I did result in precipitating some changes in the United States position on trade reforms demanded by the less developed countries. The most notable shift was manifested in President Johnson's expression of willingness to explore the possibility of granting temporary preferential tariff advantages to all LDCs in the markets of all industrialized countries. This statement, made during a conference of American heads of state at Punta del Este in April 1967, was cited by the secretary general of UNCTAD as an important change in U.S. trade policy—a change to be applauded by the LDCs.[56] Indeed, at the second meeting of UNCTAD in 1968 at New Delhi the U.S. undersecretary of state for political affairs stated that tariff preferences to all less developed countries without reciprocity on their part was accepted in principle by the United States and all states in

UNCTAD.[57] Thus, the United States had made a significant change in its position on this question between 1964 and 1968.

In addition, UNCTAD-I precipitated moves in other international organizations to afford higher priority to the economic problems of less developed countries. A new section was added to the General Agreement on Tariffs and Trade which for the first time gave formal recognition of the role of exports in economic development.[58] The International Monetary Fund enlarged its compensatory finance arrangements giving more liberal access to fund resources to LDCs placed in payments difficulties because of a decrease in export receipts from their primary commodities.[59] The Organization for Economic Cooperation and Development drafted a report submitted to UNCTAD-II on offering preferential or duty-free access to LDC exports of manufactures to OECD states.[60] Also, on the recommendation of UNCTAD-I, the staff of the IBRD drew up a report which was favorable to a proposed plan for long-term supplementary financing with the IBRD as administering agency.[61]

These are the very international organizations, strongly supported by the United States, which the LDCs were attacking in UNCTAD-I for being unresponsive to their needs. The activities of these American-supported institutions and the changed American view on the principle of tariff preferences since 1964 are only small steps toward the goals of the less developed countries in UNCTAD. Nevertheless, these steps represent an increased responsiveness by the United States and its preferred international economic organizations to the development demands of the third world. It should be noted, however, that their responsiveness has not yet found concrete action in the form of agreements to increase LDC export earnings.

The Soviet Union has taken some small practical steps consistent with the desires expressed by the LDCs at UNCTAD-I. As promised, the USSR did eliminate tariffs on its imports from less developed countries in January 1965, but the move was largely symbolic since it hardly affects the level of Soviet imports from these states. In a trade agreement concluded with Brazil in 1967 the Soviet Union agreed to use 25 percent of the actual receipts from its sales of machinery and equipment for purchases of Brazilian manufactured and semimanufactured goods. The USSR cited this agreement as a practical implementation of the recommendations of UNCTAD-I for the promotion of LDC exports in manufactures.[62] It also reported through the Council for Mutual Economic Assistance that studies were being made on extending the multilateral settlements system, established in 1963 for intra-CEMA transactions, to countries (LDCs) outside that organization.[63]

In spite of these steps, however, the Soviet position on most issues raised at UNCTAD-I has not changed since 1964. Most important, in 1968 the USSR still viewed the North-South confrontation formula as "utterly untenable," and it refused to abide by any recommendations for facilitating the development of the LDCs which hold the socialist and the Western states equally accountable for action.[64]

The materials were not yet available at the time of this writing to assess properly the roles of the United States and the USSR at UNCTAD-II; however, some general observations on that meeting are in order. The less developed countries went to UNCTAD-II with hopes of (1) arriving at a generalized system of tariff preferences for the exports of the LDCs and (2) securing action agreements to stabilize the prices and supply of basic commodities. There was also a successful attempt to redefine the target for aid donations as 1 percent of gross national product rather than of national income, the indicator used at UNCTAD-I. The GNP is usually about 20 percent higher than the figure for national income.

The debate on a generalized system of preferences centered on what products should be included. The LDCs wanted the agreement to cover semimanufactures (such as processed foods) along with manufactures. The developed states insisted that only manufactures should be covered. This prompted one LDC delegate to observe that the advanced states were willing to let the LDCs sell them jet aircraft and computers, but nothing the LDCs have any likelihood of being able to produce.[65] Also, the United States demanded that reverse preferences granted by some less developed countries to former metropoles be terminated as part of any general agreement.

The conference was unable to resolve these issues and finally passed a recommendation which did not even deal with them. There was simply a general call for the early conclusion of a general agreement on tariff preferences and the establishment of a special committee under the Trade and Development Board to deal with the problem. In light of the debate at UNCTAD-II the prospects for concrete results appear dim. The conference was no more successful on the question of commodity agreements.[66]

At UNCTAD-II America was preoccupied with a chronic balance-of-payments deficit, a gold crisis threatening the position of the dollar, and a huge budgetary deficit, all of which combined to blunt the urgency of LDC demands. Although by 1968 the United States was willing to agree on the general principle of nonreciprocal preferences for LDC exports in the markets of the industrialized countries, it was apparent at UNCTAD-II that the developed and less developed countries are far from ready to conclude concrete agreements to this end. The realization of this fact by the LDCs was largely responsible for the atmosphere of despair which pervaded and followed UNCTAD-II.[67]

Unlike UNCTAD-I, the conference in 1968 did adopt a resolution calling for a series of measures aimed at expanding East-West trade and trade between the developing and the socialist countries.[68] This resolution has been cited by Soviet spokesmen as a "big step forward as compared with Geneva."[69] It was viewed by the USSR as international corroboration of the Soviet contention that there is no solid North, that a sociopolitical demarcation line cuts across it, and that different criteria must be applied to socialist and Western states in UNCTAD recommendations for improving the economic position of less developed countries.

Conclusions

American and Soviet behavior in the various international organizations dealt with above would indicate that there are definite limitations to their willingness to entertain the demands of the less developed countries for meeting development needs through multilateral agencies of the United Nations.

The United States has provided substantial financial support for UN development programs which were initiated by the United States and/or operate on principles consistent with American development doctrines. On the other hand, congressional opposition to programs administered by the Special Fund in Cuba raises the question of the depth of American support for even these types of UN agencies. The United States has reacted with undisguised opposition to development programs (such as the UN Capital Development Fund and UNCTAD) which were proposed by the LDCs and call for massive flows of capital from donor nations according to criteria established by recipients. The United States is willing to concede that it and all developed countries of the East and the West have a responsibility to assist the development of the LDCs through multilateral and bilateral means, but securing agreement on precisely how this responsibility can best be discharged has become an intractable problem.

By any measure, the Soviet Union has made a very small financial commitment to UN development efforts. The lack of Soviet financial contributions is largely explained by the conviction of the USSR that all the operational programs are functioning in the basic interests of the United States. However, as the UN Capital Development Fund indicates, the Soviet Union is unwilling to make financial commitments to UN agencies in amounts which might result in shaping a program consistent with Soviet interests. Soviet behavior during the creation of the Capital Development Fund and UNCTAD suggests that the USSR will enthusiastically support LDC demands for development programs as long as these demands and programs are being discussed in general terms. As the time approaches when specific financial and other commitments are required of the USSR, its support of the less developed countries evaporates. The Soviet Union is willing to assist less developed countries in their development, but, unlike the United States, it will not admit to any responsibility for doing so, other than on the basis of largess.

10

Problems of Aid

ʄ A more complete understanding of Soviet and American assistance efforts requires an examination of some of the problems involved in the distribution of aid to less developed countries. The difficulties encountered by these two donors have been numerous, diverse, and of varying significance. The discussion which follows constitutes an effort to analyze and compare a few of the problems of Soviet and American aid which have been emphasized repeatedly in the literature on the two programs.

Detriments to Donor-Recipient Relations

There are several matters of a general nature which have served to make relations more difficult between the United States and the USSR and their aid recipients. The importance of these problems with regard to the aid programs lies primarily in the fact that they have created an atmosphere of distrust or misunderstanding exacerbating the operational difficulties which have arisen in connection with aid efforts. Let us examine these general problems as they relate to American and Soviet aid in turn.

In spite of American efforts to dismantle the colonial system following World War II, the moderation the United States demonstrated in an attempt to minimize the disruptive effect of the decolonization process served to compromise its image as a champion of anticolonialism. In direct contrast was the position adopted by the USSR—that of unqualified support for anticolonialism and its frequent concomitant, anti-Westernism. Many less developed countries were receptive to the argument that as an ally of the colonial powers the United States could never become wholly committed to anticolonialism. Moreover, the distribution of economic and military aid to newly independent countries was seen by some LDCs as merely a more subtle device employed by the United States and European powers to reimpose on the LDCs a semicolonial status, which would make them servants of the West once again. This atmosphere of distrust has presented an obstacle to smooth relations between the United States and its aid recipients.

Another factor adversely affecting U.S.-LDC aid relations is the frequently dated and parochial image each holds of the other's economic system. For their part, most less developed countries have an ideological preference and a practical need for significant government participation in economic activities. These countries are characteristically lacking in natural and human resources, in investment capital, in an entrepreneurial class, and they are vulnerable to external political and economic forces.[1] In light of these difficulties an emphasis upon the leading role of the state sector in the economy makes practical economic sense. In these countries there is often provision for, and sincere interest in, the parallel development of a private sector—albeit carefully controlled—in the attempt to harmonize private efforts with the overall design envisioned in national economic development plans.[2]

In addition to their pragmatic interest in socialism, however, there is an ideological preference for this system as opposed to capitalism. Socialism, in countries such as India, symbolizes a commitment to the inherent dignity of the individual, social welfare and security, less inequality, and improved opportunities for those masses of people who enjoy none of these things.[3]

The capitalist system, by contrast, is viewed by the less developed countries as being characterized by extreme acquisitiveness, a lack of social responsibility, extreme inequality, exploitation of human and natural resources for private interests, and chaos due to lack of social and economic planning in the national interest.[4] This image is fostered by the association of private foreign investment with the exploitation experienced by the LDCs while under colonial status, by reliance upon a nineteenth-century stereotyped view of capitalism, and by occasional (though less frequent) American assertions as to the inherent superiority of extreme laissez-faire capitalist economics which no longer resembles the operating American system (if, indeed, it ever did).[5]

The United States, on the other hand, harbors a profound distrust of socialism. Opposition to socialism rests upon the feeling that such a system inhibits private initiative, stifles economic growth, and places extraordinary power in the hands of the government, all of which result in the retardation of economic development and political development along lines compatible with American concepts of democracy. American ideological opposition to socialism in the less developed countries rests heavily upon a nineteenth-century view of Marxian socialism and upon an oversimplified association between the national socialisms espoused by the LDCs and that particular socialist model championed by the USSR.[6]

The result of the fundamentally different positions adopted by most LDCs and the United States concerning socialism and capitalism has been to introduce friction in the process of determining proper development strategies to be financed with the help of American economic assistance. While the tendency to oppose public sector projects on ideological grounds has been distinctly reduced since 1961, there are still cases, such as the Bokaro steel mill in India, in which the United States has refused to give aid primarily because the project was not to be located in the private sector.

The Marshall Plan experience has also contributed to problems in American economic assistance to the less developed countries. The distinction between recovery aid, such as that which went to Europe under the Marshall Plan, and development assistance to the less developed countries has been recognized since the inception of development assistance. However, while the differences were recognized, they were severely underestimated by Congress and particularly by the general public. The Marshall Plan became an ultimately dysfunctional prototype, because it prompted confidence, optimism, and expectations for relatively short-term success in connection with development assistance efforts, which by their very nature are frustrating and long-term propositions.

The basic difference between aid to Europe and aid to the less developed countries is obvious. In the case of the former, the transfer of capital from the United States was sufficient to precipitate a process of economic growth which within a few years resulted in self-sufficiency and the termination of aid. This phenomenal process of growth was made possible by the existence within European countries of technical skills, human resources, industrial experience, financial institutions, transportation and communication networks, and viable political systems. The physical economic plant had been destroyed by the war, but once reconstruction was accomplished all the ingredients necessary for growth were present. American economic assistance through the Marshall Plan was, therefore, primarily a pump-priming operation. Furthermore, the United States and its European Marshall aid recipients had relatively congruent perceptions of development priorities and of an external Soviet threat which forged strong cooperative bonds uncharacteristic of aid relations between the United States and the LDCs.

By contrast, the less developed countries have characteristically lacked all these factors which made European economic recovery possible, but the significance of this difference was underestimated. The result was a carry-over of the confidence generated by the success of the Marshall Plan to the aid program in the third world, and an overestimation of the ability to stimulate self-sustained economic growth through the use of economic assistance. Subsequent experience in the distribution of development assistance to the LDCs has proved that earlier expectations were not justified, and the optimism created by the Marshall Plan, in contrast with this experience, has contributed significantly to the growing disenchantment with economic assistance in Congress and to the erosion of political support for the aid program.[7]

Problems of a general nature have also detracted from the rapport attained between the USSR and its LDC aid recipients. The USSR initiated its aid program as a means of overcoming the legacy of distrust, hostility, and isolation in its relations with the less developed countries. This legacy constituted a problem for Soviet economic assistance, particularly in its earlier stages, because some LDCs were reluctant to accept aid offers from a country which had recently demonstrated hostility by supporting local Communist insurrections. Thus, Iran's refusal to accept Soviet economic assistance in 1959 was in part due to distrust of Soviet intentions sowed in the postwar period when the USSR supported a Communist-led separatist movement in Iranian Azerbaijan.

In addition to the distrust of Soviet intentions held by certain less developed countries, the fact that earlier policies had served to isolate the USSR from potential aid recipients created some practical difficulties in the initiation of the aid program. The LDCs generally had no familiarity with Soviet products, technology, markets, or purchasing techniques, which meant that the USSR had the problem of entering a new market or interesting the LDCs in the Soviet market. The problem gradually diminished in importance as the Soviet aid program developed momentum and acceptance in the third world. Frequently, the USSR overcame the reluctance of the LDCs to look toward the Soviet market by coming forth with trade and aid offers during a period when a less developed country faced marketing problems in the West (such as Burma in 1954)[8] or when it had been refused Western aid for an important project (such as the Bhilai steel mill of India in 1954).[9] Under these circumstances Soviet trade and aid were welcome in spite of a lack of familiarity with USSR practices and projects.

A more significant problem confronting the Soviet Union has been the necessity to reconcile the various roles it plays in international politics. The USSR is at once attempting to be the "authoritative center of the world Communist movement, leader of the Soviet bloc, friend, ally and mentor of the uncommitted, underdeveloped world, supporter of the peace and disarmament movement, and protagonist of the capitalist states."[10] The basic conflict involves the desire of the USSR to be identified as the leader of the Communist revolutionary movement while simultaneously serving as the champion of national bourgeois and revolutionary democratic governments in less developed countries. The difficulty in maintaining both stances is most conspicuously revealed in the constant Soviet denials that it is attempting to export revolution through aid,[11] while at the same time it also vigorously denies Chinese accusations that the USSR has lost its interest in and leadership of the world revolutionary process.[12]

The problem posed by the USSR's attempt to cement relations with LDC governments led by non-Communists, while still striking the pose of an ardent advocate of world revolution, is a detriment to the Soviet economic assistance effort. Insofar as the USSR seeks to be identified as a revolutionary leader through public statements or other means, some doubt must be generated among Soviet aid recipients as to the ultimate intentions of the USSR in the third world. Such doubts may have been a factor in Turkey's refusal to permit the establishment of a separate Soviet economic mission, like that which the United States maintains in Turkey, to implement a $200 million aid agreement signed in 1968.[13]

Another set of problems frequently referred to in connection with Soviet economic assistance involves the pricing of goods flowing to and from the LDCs as a result of aid, the quality of Soviet products distributed through the aid program, and re-exports of LDC commodities by the USSR.

There have been instances in which the USSR has reportedly overcharged aid recipients for Soviet exports (Egypt[14] and Burma[15]); on the other hand, there are reports from Yemen which state that the USSR constructed roads, ports, and factories at costs 30 percent below world market prices.[16] In spite of these cases, however, it appears that the prices of goods flowing to and from the less developed countries as a result of Soviet trade and economic assistance are generally consistent with prices prevailing in world markets. There is little evidence to suggest that the USSR has consciously or systematically attempted to extract economic advantages for itself through pricing practices on aid flows to third world countries or on goods sent as repayments by aid recipients to the USSR.

Insofar as pricing has constituted a real problem for relations between LDCs and the USSR, it has primarily been the result of imbalances or other difficulties arising in bilateral trade agreements. There have been several cases in which a less developed country has chosen to import Soviet or East European products at prices well above those on the world market in order to utilize balances accumulated through an export surplus to the USSR or an East European country, as when Argentina and Uruguay bought Polish coal in 1957.[17] The Burmese have indicated great dissatisfaction in bilateral trade operations with the Soviet Union, including the statement by U Nu in 1956 that, compared to trade prices in the world market at the time, Burma was losing 10 to 30 percent through bilateral arrangements.[18]

It should be noted that the cases mentioned above related to difficulties in trading through a bilateral framework and were not directly connected to goods flowing under Soviet economic assistance. Indeed, there have been occasions where countries have complained about overpricing and price-hiking after aid terms had been agreed upon (Afghanistan, Indonesia, and Iraq, for example), but such cases are rare, and the prices agreed upon by the USSR and its aid recipients for machinery, construction, and other goods appear to conform generally to those prevailing in the world market.[19] India, for example, maintains that in terms of price and quality its experience in purchases from the USSR has been satisfactory.[20]

The quality of goods supplied by the Soviet Union to the less developed countries under economic assistance programs has often been criticized by Western observers of Soviet aid.[21] There have been problems concerning the unsuitability of Soviet goods for tropical climates such as in Indonesia[22] and Guinea.[23] Civilian aircraft provided by the USSR to Guinea under the aid program proved inefficient and difficult to maintain.[24] In India, Argentina, and Egypt, Soviet drills have been of a quality far inferior to similar Western equipment.[25] In general, there is little question that Soviet equipment is in most cases below Western standards in terms of quality, tolerances, and finish; however, it has usually proved adequate for the jobs in less developed countries for which it has been supplied.[26] In certain cases, such as the Bhilai steel mill in India, the quality of the equipment and overall performance of the USSR in executing the project has been by all accounts good.

The Soviet Union is aware of and sensitive to criticism of the quality of its equipment, and it has taken steps to minimize problems of this nature. There are reports in the Soviet press of research and construction of equipment resistant to heat, humidity, corrosion, fungus, and termites for use in tropical areas.[27] There are, in addition, fewer complaints by aid recipients concerning the quality of Soviet merchandise than there were earlier in the Soviet aid effort.[28]

Accusations from less developed countries and the West have also arisen in connection with Soviet re-exports of commodities imported from the third world. Egyptian cotton and Burmese rice have been the most frequently cited examples of this practice, but charges of re-exporting have also been made in relation to cocoa from Ghana; Greek tobacco, cotton, sultanas, currants, and skins; Cambodian rice; and Indian cashew nuts, iron ore, raw hides, and yarn.[29] To the extent that the USSR or East European countries actually re-export LDC commodities obtained as repayment for aid or through regular trade channels, the LDC is itself deprived of sales from which it can earn foreign exchange.

In fact the meager evidence available to evaluate these charges suggests that whereas Communist countries have attempted to work out arrangements for re-exports, the actual volume of such sales has been quite limited.[30] Thus, it would appear that the problem of re-exports has been somewhat exaggerated in most non-Communist accounts.

The questions of pricing, quality, and re-exports which have arisen in Soviet-LDC relations have been discussed here because so much attention has been given them in Western literature on

Soviet economic assistance. At one time or another these factors have presented definite problems in USSR relations with certain aid recipients; but it is interesting to note that the specific cases most often cited in relation to these various problems date back to the 1950s during the earlier phase of Soviet economic assistance, and the same cases are usually brought up repeatedly as illustrations of the particular problems. These considerations, in addition to the facts presented above, lead to the conclusion that problems connected with Soviet pricing practices, the quality of equipment, and re-exports of LDC commodities by the USSR have most likely been exaggerated, and in any event they have become less serious as the Soviet Union has gained experience in its economic assistance program. To the extent that these problems have in fact existed, they do not seem to reflect a conscious policy on the part of the USSR to take economic advantage of less developed countries through its aid program.

Up to this point we have been discussing problems which are peculiar to either the United States or the USSR as aid donors. More decisive, however, are two problems faced by both donors in their relations with the less developed countries—the debt service burden and the political, social, and economic milieu of the LDCs within which any aid program must operate.

The less developed countries as a group are servicing an external public and publicly guaranteed debt of $43.6 billion.[31] In 1967 annual repayments of principal and interest were running at about $4 billion and were increasing at an average rate of 12 percent a year.[32] George Woods, former president of the World Bank, concluded that if present trends continue, in a little more than fifteen years gross capital inflow to the LDCs will be entirely offset by a capital outflow from the LDCs in the form of amortization, interest, and dividend payments on former debts.[33] The debt service problem in 1966 required that India, for example, use between 15 and 20 percent of her foreign exchange earned from exports to service external public debts.[34] In 1969, India's debt service was $547 million.[35]

The United States recognizes the difficulty of this burden on the LDCs and takes into account the ability of a recipient to service a debt when determining the interest rate, grace period, and maturity of a development loan. The terms are harder for recipients who are better able to finance an aid debt. Also, the decision as to what aid mechanism (Export-Import Bank loan, Development Loan, Development Grant, or Supporting Assistance) to use for a program is made, in part, on the basis of the recipient's ability to repay a loan.

The debt service burden is really only a reflection of the well-known fact that the less developed countries have incurred massive financial obligations to the United States, Europe, and the Communist countries in their quest for economic assistance. The real significance of the burden cannot be determined until we see the extent to which aid donors will convert loans to grants retroactively, extend repayment schedules, and declare moratoria on debt repayments in the face of such requests from LDCs in severe economic difficulties. The United States has shown its willingness to reschedule debts of India,[36] Indonesia,[37] and Poland,[38] for example. In rare cases the United States has also retroactively converted a loan to a grant.[39] Thus, the question of how serious the debt service problem will actually prove to be for the less developed countries depends upon the reaction of the donors. American officials have estimated, however, that about 30 percent of all new economic assistance distributed through AID is eaten up in maintaining the debt service of its recipients.[40]

The debt service burden of the LDCs presents the same difficulties for the USSR as it does for the United States. In 1964 the Soviet Union received $132 million in repayment for credits previously utilized by less developed countries.[41] During that year and in 1965, annual repayments on aid credits amounted to 40 percent of annual deliveries of Soviet economic aid.[42] These figures have remained about the same throughout the mid- and late sixties.

A more specific illustration of the magnitude of the debt service burden as it relates to Soviet aid can be seen in the case of India. As of March 31, 1965, India owed the USSR almost $500 million, and on the basis of Soviet credits extended as of December 1963, Indian repayments to the USSR in 1967 were scheduled at $57 million.[43] During 1965, for example, the debt service of India to the USSR was 47 percent of Soviet aid deliveries, as reflected in Category 16 exports to India.[44]

The USSR is sensitive to this problem and, like the United States, it has been faced with the inability of certain aid recipients to adhere to their repayment schedules. At various times economic difficulties have prompted Egypt, Ghana, Cuba, Guinea, and Indonesia to request postponements of debt repayments.[45] The reaction of the Soviet Union to debt postponement is indicated in the following statement by a Soviet official in Cairo referring to rumors of a new credit extension to Egypt for the purpose of financing repayments due on previous loans: "The Egyptians pay other countries back, why shouldn't they pay us as well? To do otherwise would establish a bad precedent for other developing countries which have had similar troubles."[46]

In spite of this attitude, however, the USSR has allowed aid recipients to postpone or reschedule debt payments. Two days before Nkrumah's fall from power it was announced that the Soviet Union had agreed to a moratorium on Ghana's repayment of credits.[47] It is believed that in September 1965 the USSR agreed to cancel $460 million of Egypt's military credit debt.[48] In 1966, following the turmoil in Indonesia, the Soviet Union apparently agreed to defer $40 million in debt repayments due during 1966 and 1967.[49]

This last example raises an interesting point concerning the mutuality of the debt service problem for the USSR and the United States. In 1966 Indonesia was simply unable to honor her financial obligations to any aid donors. Having received aid from the Soviet Union and the United States, an attempt was made by the new Indonesian government to reschedule her debt repayments to the East and the West. Difficulties arose because if the West granted concessions and the USSR did not, the West would find itself financing Indonesian debts to the Soviet Union—of course, the same held true if the USSR granted concessions without the West doing so. The result was a kind of tandem arrangement in which the USSR agreed to postpone repayments, whereupon the Western aid donors agreed to do so.[50] Neither the

United States nor the Soviet Union could have afforded to make concessions in the absence of a similar move by the other; yet neither country would have benefited by demanding scheduled payments, since the result would probably have been default.

Suzan Strange in a most perceptive analysis of the political implications of creditor-debtor relations for developing countries takes to task the popular mythology in rich and poor countries alike that "he who pays the piper calls the tune."[51] She points out that creditors such as the United States—and the USSR, I would suggest—by virtue of the economic leverage attained through aid have been unable to influence significantly the military, political, trade, and economic policies of LDCs on the verge of financial default. Indeed, the result of a confrontation precipitated by the threat of default on debt repayments as often results in the creditor providing more aid and/or more time for the LDC to repay as it does in reforms by the recipient demanded by its creditor.[52]

A factor contributing to all sorts of difficulties faced by the United States and the Soviet Union in their aid programs is the nature of the environment within which aid must operate. John K. Galbraith has outlined several factors prevailing in most less developed countries which seriously affect, if not determine, the results obtainable by the transfer of capital and technical assistance to the third world. They include: (1) the lack of education among the people and the lack of managerial and administrative skills among the elites in the third world; (2) the lack of social justice in the structure of taxes, for example, which makes workers and peasants feel they will not share in the fruits of harder work; (3) the lack of a clear view on the part of the LDC as to the difficulties and demands of the development process; and (4) the lack of an adequate government apparatus, public administration, and law and order.[53] All of these factors act as constraints limiting the contribution aid can make to a recipient; all combine to create a poor milieu for the achievement of significant economic development.

It is the existence of such inadequacies on the part of most aid recipients in the third world which makes economic development an inherently lengthy, difficult, and frustrating enterprise, bearing only faint resemblance to the expectations of self-sustained economic growth found in earlier development models for American aid. Unfinished or unsatisfactory aid projects are as often the result of the inability of the recipient to supply local human and material resources necessary for success, as they are the result of poor organization, planning, and personnel provided by the United States or other aid donors. The economic, political, and social milieu in which economic assistance must function and the uncertainty regarding the nature of the development process impose awesome difficulties for effective and efficient operation of American economic assistance efforts.

The Soviet Union, of course, faces the same situation in the LDCs as does the United States, and the results are similar. Let us examine some of the difficulties encountered by the USSR in this context as indicative of both Soviet and American aid experiences in the third world.

A major cause for the slowness with which Soviet aid commitments have actually been drawn upon is the existence of relatively primitive and chaotic political and economic conditions in the less developed countries which make it difficult to mobilize the local financial and human resources required for implementation of Soviet aid projects.[54] Since the USSR will not generally cover any local costs of aid projects, unlike the United States, the inability of many LDCs to generate local funds for Soviet projects often limits the pace of implementation. Leo Tansky points out that India, Egypt, and Afghanistan have been the LDCs in which Soviet aid has progressed most rapidly; he suggests that this is a reflection of India and Egypt's greater absorptive capacity in comparison to most countries in the third world. Afghanistan, on the other hand, is the only country for which the USSR has initiated a large commodity program to raise local funds and, thus, facilitate the execution of its aid projects.[55]

In addition to lack of local funds, Soviet aid has been hampered by the inability of some recipients to maintain a steady flow of local labor and materials to aid financed projects. This has resulted in numerous delays for which the USSR has been blamed. In order to overcome this problem in Guinea, for example, the Soviet Union made a most unusual agreement in 1963 whereby it assumed these responsibilities and established a special organization in Guinea to assure adequate local labor and material supplies for aid projects.[56]

The Soviet Union is understandably irritated by problems of this nature, and on occasion statements such as the following have appeared from Soviet sources pointing out that many delays in the aid program are not the fault of the USSR:

> It should also be noted that the success of cooperation depends on the accurate fulfillment of mutual obligations by both parties. Unfortunately, the experience of cooperation between the USSR and some of the developing countries shows that at times they do not provide all the conditions required for the timely installation of the equipment delivered. It also happens that raw materials, sales markets, requisite technical services, spare parts and the like are not always provided for the new enterprises in good time. Such shortcomings reduce the efficiency of these enterprises.[57]

The difficulties encountered by the LDCs in servicing their external public debts and in mobilizing internal resources for aid-financed projects certainly affect relations between donors and recipients. The United States and the USSR, particularly the former, have repeatedly taken steps to accommodate their recipients' needs in dealing with these problems. However, every time a debt must be rescheduled some friction is generated between donor and recipient; and every aid project which remains unfinished because of the lack of local currency or administration strains to some degree whatever rapport is established between these two donors and the less developed countries through economic assistance. These difficulties affect the operational performance of Soviet and American aid far more than the general factors peculiar to Soviet and American aid relations with less developed countries.

Factors Within the Donors

Numerous problems have been identified in the literature on Soviet and American aid which are felt to limit the effectiveness of the programs or to cast doubt upon the capacity or will of the donors to continue aid at present magnitudes. Let us examine several of these factors and their significance for the United States and the USSR.

The question of the burden imposed on the United States by economic assistance to the less developed countries has been raised repeatedly. In spite of the concern expressed over this issue, there is little evidence to suggest that America is economically incapable of sustaining aid donations at present levels. In the period 1961–1966 American economic aid to the LDCs averaged less than .6 percent of United States GNP. During 1965 the United States made aid disbursements in the amount of $19.47 per capita, when U.S. per capita GNP was $3,500.[58] If all types of economic and military assistance to all countries, even non-LDCs, are included, it was estimated that in 1965 U.S. aid was only .9 percent of GNP.[59] More significantly, the burden of aid has been decreasing steadily since the period between 1946 and 1948 when aid was 2.1 percent of GNP.[60]

These data are admittedly crude indicators of the economic burden placed on the United States as a consequence of its aid efforts. However, by any measure the conclusion is that, in relation to the overall economic position of the United States, aid represents a small burden, indeed.[61]

A much more significant problem, at least until recently, has involved the contribution of economic assistance to the deficit in the American balance of payments.

Until the economic recovery of Western Europe after World War II, the United States was the only major source of the capital goods required by the LDCs for their economic development. Further, the European countries had less foreign exchange than they desired for purchases in the United States. This meant that through the mid-fifties virtually all American aid dollars found their way back to the United States either through direct purchases of the LDCs in the United States, or through LDC purchases in Europe, which in turn used the dollars for imports from America. Therefore, even though aid funds were not tied to purchases in the United States, the result was an almost complete return of aid funds to the American market through direct or indirect means, and there was little concern about the effect of economic aid upon the American balance-of-payments position.

But, by the late fifties the European countries became effective competitors with the United States for supplying goods needed by the third world, and, in addition, they possessed more than enough dollars to finance their own import needs from the United States. Thus, more and more U.S. aid funds to the LDCs found their way to Europe; and these countries, rather than passing them back to America via imports, kept the funds and increased their foreign exchange reserve holdings. Then the real problem arose when the European states sought to exchange what they considered to be excess dollar reserves for gold.

Because of the general deterioration in the American balance-of-payments position in the late fifties, an attempt has been made since 1959 to minimize the contribution of economic aid to this problem by tying aid to purchases in the United States. Dramatic results have been achieved in this regard. In fiscal year 1961, 54 percent of AID funds were spent overseas which constituted a $980 million drain on the U.S. balance of payments.[62] In fiscal year 1968 over 90 percent of AID funds were spent in the United States, and repayments of principal and interest on past loans exceeded AID expenditures abroad. Thus by 1968 the aid program actually contributed favorably to the U.S. balance-of-payments position.[63] Moreover, in the coming years the ten-year grace periods on Development Loans which were disbursed in large amounts starting in 1961 begin to close. Thus, repayments of principal and interest from aid recipients to the United States should increase markedly. If aid continues to be tied to purchases in the United States, the 1970s should witness a significant positive contribution of aid efforts to the American balance-of-payments position.

There is, however, an indirect effect of tying aid which suggests that the effect on the balance of payments is much more severe than the figures cited above would indicate. It seems certain that the less developed countries use some tied aid to purchase goods in the United States which otherwise would have been bought out of the LDCs regular foreign exchange earnings. This practice results in a reduction of regular LDC imports from the United States. Jacob Kaplan estimates the magnitude of this reduction to be about $1.5 billion per year.[64] Of course, to the extent that such a substitution process actually occurs, it detracts in direct proportion from the positive contribution loan repayments and tied aid make to the American balance-of-payments position.

While there is little doubt as to the existence of this substitution effect, there is no widely accepted estimate of its magnitude. David Bell presented quite a different picture than Kaplan, suggesting that the amount of substitution is relatively small and by and large is offset by other indirect factors such as the return of aid dollars from U.S. contributions to UN aid activities.[65] It would appear that the $1.5 billion estimate of the substitution effect is definitely on the high side, and no precise estimate is available at present.

Because of these and other factors, the overall impact of economic assistance on the balance of payments is virtually impossible to determine in an exact sense. Clearly, U.S. AID officials found it in their interests to minimize the negative effects the program may have on the balance of payments. But the problem is certainly not what it was early in the 1960s, even if one is unwilling to concede the case made by AID since 1968 that economic assistance now helps the American payments position.

Another problem more directly influencing the efficacy of American aid efforts is the number of agencies involved in the program and the lack of meaningful coordination among them. A partial list of agencies connected with the administration of present U.S. aid efforts would include the departments of State, Defense, Agriculture, and the Treasury, AID, the Export-Import Bank, and the Peace Corps. This plethora of aid-related institutions exists in spite of efforts in 1961 to centralize the aid program under the direction of AID. The administrative fragmentation of American economic assistance is forcefully illustrated in the following description of the management of military and economic aid funds by various government agencies:

In 1964 only 40 per cent of new U.S. aid commitments to developing nations were made with funds directly controlled by the administrator of AID. The Department of Agriculture managed another 30 per cent and the Department of Defense about 15 per cent. The remaining 15 per cent of the program was divided between the Export-Import Bank, the Peace Corps, the Treasury controlled contribution to international financial agencies, and the State Department's contributions to international organizations.[66]

The existence of so many institutions directly involved in the distribution or control of economic assistance, with no single authority responsible for coordination among them, constitutes a problem of the first magnitude for the effective use of American aid. This administrative fragmentation is reinforced by the multitude of purposes for which aid has been given and the frequent creation of new agencies to administer new tacks in economic assistance. Thus, agricultural surplus commodity aid has existed apart from the primary economic aid agency since the inception of the program in 1954. As we have seen, particularly in the earlier phases of P.L. 480, this program had drives and purposes fundamentally different from economic aid per se; this fact, combined with its institutional separateness, exacerbates the difficulty of harmonizing various facets of the overall aid effort in the less developed countries.

The United States has also demonstrated a lack of coordination between trade and aid policies vis-à-vis the less developed countries. The aid program has tended to be viewed as a self-contained enterprise rather than one of several mechanisms employed to establish good relations between the United States and the third world. It has been noted that the impact on a less developed country of even the "most generous and best conceived program of foreign aid can be completely vitiated by a single ill-considered act of United States commercial policy, such as raising a protective tariff against the principal export commodity of the aided country."[67] Thus, the success of economic assistance in forging positive relationships with the LDCs depends largely upon the existence of commercial and other policies which reinforce rather than undercut the benefits of aid.

In practice, the United States, as well as other advanced countries of the West, have maintained commercial policies which place significant restrictions on the ability of the less developed countries to sell products in the markets of the West. In addition to quantitative barriers in commodity trade,[68] existing tariff structures affect exports of manufactures by the LDCs. Tariff structures in the United States and the West are usually escalated by stage of production, with duty rates rising from raw materials to semimanufactures and from semimanufactures to finished goods. Also, these rates are generally set lower on capital goods than on consumer goods. This escalation process gives effective protection at rising rates (and at rates higher than nominal tariff rates on the goods) to goods at successive stages of the production process; and it also gives greater effective protection to consumer goods than to capital goods.[69] The result of these tariff structures, is, therefore, "to impose especially heavy barriers to the goods [manufactures] that the less developed countries are most likely to be able to produce for export, namely consumer goods that are relatively labor intensive and employ a relatively unsophisticated technology."[70]

These commercial policies of the United States and the West severely restrict the ability of the LDCs to earn foreign exchange through exports of commodities and manufactures. They work at cross purposes with the use of economic assistance to transfer capital necessary for the development of third world countries. There is an obvious incongruity in the American attempt to pose as champion of LDC development aspirations through aid and its uncompromising opposition to trade reforms (admittedly extreme and discriminatory in favor of the third world) being demanded by the LDCs in UNCTAD which would eliminate some of these barriers to LDC trade with the advanced countries of the West.

In 1969 the Nixon administration took an important step to these ends. In a proposal to OECD the United States invited the other industrialized countries to join it in granting special tariff preferences to all less developed countries. Moreover, it was asserted that if the other industrialized nations did not agree to the proposal, the United States would move on its own toward preferential treatment for Latin American products alone.[71] It should be noted, however, that implementation of these proposals will require congressional approval; the true implications will be impossible to assess until the precise nature of congressional approval is revealed.

Congress has also contributed certain difficulties to the exercise of the U.S. aid program. The stance taken by Congress on the question of economic aid to the less developed countries has characteristically been one of distrust of the administration's execution of the program and lack of enthusiasm for the instrument itself.

Congressional distrust of the manner in which the executive branch has handled economic assistance is manifested in the stipulations which are attached to aid legislation and the extent of annual committee hearings on the program. The nature of the strings which Congress has attached to the distribution of aid (such as the 50/50 shipping clause, no trade with North Vietnam, and others) has been described earlier, as well as the fact that these conditions largely represent congressional desire to place restrictions on the executive branch in its implementation of the program.

Every year the aid program must pass through extensive examination by four congressional committees before it reaches the voting stage. These hearings, in each of the committees, range from inquiries and admonitions concerning specific aid projects to consideration of general foreign policy objectives of the United States. In 1968 the statements and testimony on the Foreign Assistance Act occupied over 4,800 pages of text. To be sure, this process has shed a great deal of light on the aid program, exposed many inadequacies, resulted in substantial reductions in aid expenditures, and yielded other positive results. Nevertheless, the fact that aid operations must be authorized anew each year amid acrimonious debate questioning even the need for the program casts doubt on the American commitment to aid and results in an immense drain on the time and attention of aid personnel. It has been estimated that from April through September "one fourth to one third of the time of the senior executives responsible for administering overseas economic and military assistance programs is devoted to the Congressional hearings."[72]

In addition to congressional behavior reflective of a general distrust of the executive branch in its administration of aid, there are indications of significant legislative antipathy to the value of an aid program directed toward the less developed countries. In fiscal year 1968 the House passed the bill authorizing the aid program by only eight votes.[73] During the period 1955–1965 annual congressional reductions of appropriations requests for aid have averaged 20 percent,[74] and in 1969 and 1970 the reductions in economic assistance will probably average 33 percent. All government programs face budgetary cuts in Congress, but foreign aid requests have characteristically suffered more severe reductions than most "permanent" programs.[75] Particularly in times of financial difficulties the foreign aid program proves to be a poor competitor in the struggle for resource allocation within the U.S. budget. The drastic cuts in aid appropriations in recent years are certainly a reflection of AID's inability to compete for funds with military and domestic political programs during a period of inflationary economic difficulties and foreign and domestic political malaise.

The various factors mentioned in this discussion of congressional attitudes and behavior toward economic assistance to the less developed countries in no way constitute a balanced appraisal of the contributions of the legislature to the American aid program. The record is certainly not as completely negative as it appears here. However, the points made above are indicative of certain problems posed for the U.S. aid effort by Congress. The imposition of strings on aid has often created friction in a basically sound U.S.–LDC aid relationship. The marathon of committee hearings severely taxes the energy and efficiency of aid officials for a substantial portion of every year. Congressional reluctance to grant long-term authorization for the aid program, heavy budgetary cuts, insistence on higher interest rates accompanying aid, and appeals for termination of economic assistance to the less developed countries all serve to undermine the confidence of the third world in the seriousness of the American commitment to development interests which they regard as fundamentally important.

It should be noted, on the other hand, that AID and its predecessor agencies have contributed to these factors in congressional behavior. The economic development rationale for aid has generated expectations of self-sufficient economic growth and the termination of the aid program. Economic assistance has frequently been oversold to Congress with regard to the results (for the recipients as well as the United States) obtainable from it. The expectation of budgetary cuts from Congress has prompted the executive branch to "pad" authorization and appropriation requests. Because of such behavior on the part of the administration at various times since the inception of the aid program, Congress has had some justification for raising the obstacles mentioned above.

An examination of some internal factors affecting the aid program of the Soviet Union reveals similar problems. Of particular interest in this regard is the burden of the program on the Soviet economy and domestic opposition to aid to less developed countries.

In terms of the size of the program, at least, economic assistance to the less developed countries poses little strain on the Soviet economy. Over the period 1960–1964 Soviet economic aid deliveries, as estimated by Category 16 exports to LDCs, averaged about 0.1 percent of Soviet GNP.[76] A comparable average for Soviet aid commitments during this period is not very useful since 1962 and 1963 were abnormally low years in terms of new credit extensions. In 1964, however, new commitments totaled $998 million[77] or 0.3 percent of Soviet GNP.[78] This remains the record for new credit extensions, so the 1964 figure of aid commitments as a percentage of GNP must be considered as maximal. By such measures the burden of aid on the Soviet economy is less than that imposed on the American economy (U.S. economic aid deliveries averaged 0.6 percent of the American GNP over the 1961–1965 period).

Per capita figures yield similar results. During 1964 USSR aid commitments amounted to $4.42 per capita, and actual deliveries of Category 16 exports to less developed countries came to $1.30 per capita.[79] U.S. aid deliveries per capita in 1965 were $19.47, and even considering the fact that Soviet per capita GNP for 1964 was $1,295 (just over one-third that of the United States for 1965), it seems apparent that by this criterion, also, the economic assistance program constitutes less of a burden on the USSR than it does on the United States—particularly if aid deliveries rather than aid commitments are the focus of analysis.

Insofar as the aid program poses a problem for the economy of the USSR, it would most likely be in the form of increased LDC requests for certain types of industrial equipment, such as steel-rolling mills and chemical equipment, which are still in great demand for meeting the domestic needs of the Soviet Union. Even if this situation should arise, the practice of making commitments well in advance of deliveries would allow such items to be integrated into future Soviet economic planning,[80] thus minimizing the burden or consequences of such requests. In fact, the requests of Soviet aid recipients have been broad enough to allow the USSR to select project or commodity commitments which are most compatible with its current and planned availabilities. Indeed the USSR has shown great interest in giving aid for purposes closely aligned to particular Soviet capabilities—such as petroleum exploration and production, construction of hydroelectric facilities, provision of standardized machine tools, and agreements to construct small or medium-sized, fully equipped manufacturing plants.[81]

Thus, economic assistance at present levels is well within the economic capacity of the USSR, and the burden imposed by the program appears to be less than that of the United States. In spite of this fact, however, there is concern in the USSR about the aid burden, as is the case in the United States. This concern is manifested in the practice of distributing virtually all aid as loans rather than grants. Also the concern over the burden of giving aid to the LDCs seems to be a factor in the ambiguity characterizing domestic press coverage of the terms and amounts of Soviet aid, and in the frequent attempt in Soviet literature directed at the domestic audience to place USSR aid in the context of total aid efforts by all the Communist countries.

There are definite indications that the Soviet aid program has its detractors among certain officials and the public at large. Through the manner in which the aid program is described in Soviet publications as well as by statements of high Soviet officials, it is apparent that there is some domestic opposition to economic assistance efforts in the third world. The significance of this opposition should not be overestimated, but there is little doubt that anti-aid feelings constitute a problem for the program.

Literature on Soviet economic assistance for domestic audiences demonstrates a reluctance on the part of the USSR to indicate the magnitude of the program in any detail, an emphasis on trade with the LDCs as distinct from aid to them, a stress on the greater amount of aid that has gone to other Communist countries in comparison to Soviet aid to the less developed countries, and a linkage of Soviet and East European aid emphasizing the contribution of the latter to an overall Communist effort in the third world.

The data available to Soviet citizens on economic assistance has characteristically consisted of an aggregate ruble figure for cumulative Soviet aid to the LDCs, accompanied by figures on the number and output of various types of industrial enterprises being constructed with the help of Soviet aid.[82] The manner in which the aid program is presented in Soviet literature makes it almost impossible to gain from such sources alone any precise rundown of the ruble amounts of specific aid projects and total country programs for each of the Soviet aid recipients in the third world. Thus, it would appear from Soviet academic and press coverage that the USSR is reluctant to reveal the actual extent of its aid operations to the less developed countries, except in very general terms.

Nadia Derkach made the interesting observation, as a result of comparing a Soviet work as published in Russian and in English, that the Russian text emphasized trade, as opposed to aid, to the LDCs, while the reverse was true in the English text. The most significant difference in this regard was the fact that the English text contains a statistical table covering Soviet credits to LDCs from 1955 to 1960, whereas the Russian text excludes this table and contains a table not found in the English text on the foreign trade turnover of the USSR with the LDCs between 1938 and the period 1955–1960.[83] This is perhaps the best example of a tendency in Soviet literature for domestic consumption to stress trade rather than aid as the primary component of Soviet-LDC economic relations.

It is also quite common in Russian language presentations of Soviet economic assistance to emphasize the amount of aid that has gone to other Communist countries in discussions of the overall aid program. For example, in A. Smirnov's article on Soviet technical assistance in constructing plants abroad the thrust of the piece is clearly on aid to other socialist countries rather than on aid to the third world. Smirnov points out that 80 percent of Soviet aid from 1947 to 1959 went to countries in the socialist camp.[84] Not all articles on Soviet aid for domestic readers stress aid to other Communist states to this extent, but references to such assistance can usually be found in articles on economic assistance to the third world. A major reason for these references could be to counter criticism by nationals of the USSR and other Communist states that the Soviet aid program unduly rewards LDCs when some Communist states could put similar funds to good use.

Finally, literature for domestic consumption on Soviet economic assistance often links USSR and East European aid as one program.[85] The result stresses East European contributions to Communist aid efforts and minimizes the appearance of aid's constituting a burden on the USSR alone.

This discussion may have overstated the defensiveness of the presentation of the aid program to Soviet audiences. Nevertheless, all of these aspects in the coverage of Soviet aid to the third world are manifestations of a sensitivity to domestic opposition to the program. Milton Kovner has made similar observations with regard to Soviet efforts to "sell" the aid program in the face of lagging public and other support.[86]

In addition to such evidence of misgivings on the part of the general public, there are also reasons to believe that Soviet economic assistance to less developed countries has opponents among public officials. It is to be expected that conservative elements in the Soviet bureaucracy who give utmost priority to domestic capital formation and economic growth would question the value of exporting capital goods to the third world under the aid program.[87] In addition, the aid program is known to have been a factor in the "anti-Party" group's opposition to Khrushchev and his policies. A member of this group, A. M. Saburov, stated in a speech before the Twenty-first Congress of the Communist Party of the Soviet Union that they "opposed the Central Committee's policy in such important problems as the necessity of developing our economic ties with the Peoples Democracies and extending aid to these countries, to say nothing of our aiding the poorly developed and dependent countries of Asia and the Near East."[88]

The evidence presented here is inferential, to be sure, but it is sufficient to demonstrate that there is opposition to the Soviet aid program by some public officials as well as elements of the general public in the USSR. It is doubtful that the treatment of Soviet economic assistance to the less developed countries would take the form it does if domestic misgivings about the program did not constitute a problem for the Soviet leadership.

In spite of evidence of the existence of domestic opposition to Soviet aid, it is very difficult to demonstrate in any direct sense how this opposition affects the magnitude and content of the program itself. We simply do not have detailed information on the manner in which the aggregate size of new aid commitments are determined each year in the Soviet Union, much less how the final program differs from original proposals generated in the Soviet bureaucracy. It appears, nevertheless, that critics of Soviet aid among public officials have wielded nowhere near the influence that congressional critics of U.S. aid do, and whatever opposition there is among the general public of the USSR probably resembles that found among the mass of American people who are by and large passive except for a certain amount of grumbling about the extension of aid to other countries when the funds could be used at home.

The coordination of trade and aid policies poses less of a problem for the Soviet Union than it does for the United States. The Soviet state trading system is much more susceptible to manipulation in concert with aid for registering short-term impact on less developed countries than the market system of the United States. The USSR has had much success as a buyer of last resort for LDC goods facing poor market conditions in the West.

However, UNCTAD made it clear that the Soviet Union is even less willing than the United States to entertain basic reforms in its trade policy which would regularize trade relations with the LDCs in a manner resulting in much larger flows of capital to the third world. Thus, in contrast to its short-term coordination of trade and aid on a country-by-country basis, the USSR manifests much less ability to forge a long-term generalized trade policy which would supplement aid in giving the LDCs access to large amounts of Soviet resources. It is likely that this problem of harmonizing aid and general trade policies will affect Soviet relations with the LDCs more than it did prior to UNCTAD.

American and Soviet Relations with Allies

Economic assistance to less developed countries has introduced friction between the United States and the USSR and at least certain of the members of their respective alliance systems. The friction in the U.S. alliance has focused primarily on the issue of burden-sharing, whereas the USSR has faced the more serious problem of direct conflict with the Chinese over aid policies.

Over the years Congress has demonstrated substantial opposition to the economic aid program on grounds, valid or not, that the United States is carrying more than its fair share of the aid burden. Largely because of this opposition the United States has stressed the burden-sharing issue with its European allies through the Development Assistance Committee (DAC) of the Organization for Economic Cooperation and Development. The burden-sharing problem is difficult to analyze with precision because of the differences in the form and terms of aid given by the various Western nations, the methodological problems involved in comparing GNP data from many countries, and the absence of widely accepted norms concerning the proper magnitude of economic assistance to be expected from donors having different levels of national income or GNP. Notwithstanding these obstacles, some general conclusions can be reached on the burden-sharing issue.

One measure of the relative burden of aid among the various Western donors is aid as a percentage of GNP. In 1962 the United States ranked third among DAC members on this measure with aid constituting 0.62 percent of GNP—only Portugal and France bore a heavier burden of aid by this criterion. By 1967, however, U.S. aid was only 0.47 percent of GNP and five Western donors carried greater aid burdens in this regard—Portugal, France, Australia, Belgium, and the Netherlands.[89] This trend is likely to continue due to decreases in American aid appropriations and commitments made by some DAC members to achieve the UNCTAD-II aid target of one percent of GNP.

Another factor in assessing the distribution of the aid burden involves aggregate aid shares in comparison to relative proportions of U.S. and other DAC members' GNP as a percent of the combined GNP of the Western donors. In 1962 the United States' share of the total GNP of the DAC countries was 53 percent, whereas it provided 60 percent of total DAC aid.[90] In 1970 it is estimated that America's share of the total DAC members' GNP will be 53 percent, whereas its share of total DAC members' aid will drop to only 48 percent.[91] This is expected to happen even though the per capita GNP of the United States is approximately $4,000 in comparison to an average per capita GNP of only $1,700 for the other Western donors.[92] In light of these data it is difficult to see how the United States can continue to manifest concern over the burden it bears in the Western economic assistance effort.

Most critics coming to the conclusion that America is giving more than its fair share of aid do so on the basis of including domestic and foreign defense expenditures along with economic assistance efforts in evaluating a total burden.[93] If economic assistance is considered to be an inherent part of an overall mutual security program for an Atlantic community, then the total burden approach is justified, and the United States is clearly carrying more than its fair share. On the other hand, as far as economic assistance itself is concerned, "there is . . . no strong justification for a U.S. complaint of inequitable burden sharing."[94]

Before leaving this discussion on burden-sharing there are some qualifications which ought to be mentioned. The idea of burden-sharing implies an identity of interests among the United States and other Western donors in the distribution of economic assistance which may not be entirely reflective of reality. The long-term general goal of a third world sympathetic to Western ideals, economically developed, politically stable, and engaging in vigorous economic relations with the West is undoubtedly shared by all the members of DAC. However, within this general consensus there is a good deal of diversity in interest among the Western donors. Germany gives aid to promote its commerce in the third world vis-à-vis that of the United States and other DAC countries. France focuses aid upon its former colonies in an attempt to retain in the LDCs a political and cultural influence which is not always compatible with U.S. policies. The United States has used "presence aid" in some former European colonies as a counterbalance to the influence of their former metropoles.[95] In these and other instances it is evident that the goals and interests of the United States and other Western countries are not entirely mutually reinforcing. Therefore, to think in terms of burden-sharing may be to exaggerate the consensus of the interests and goals among the Western powers as aid donors.

There has never been a public debate about the problem of burden-sharing between the USSR and East Europe as dominant as that between the United States and West European countries; nevertheless, it is interesting to note some figures relating to this question. In 1964 the GNP of East Europe[96] as a portion of combined USSR and East European GNP was 26 percent.[97] In the same year these countries' aid commitments of $340 million[98] to non-Communist LDCs amounted to 25 percent of total Soviet and East European extensions; so if the GNP ratio is taken as a norm for adequate aid commitments, East Europe is carrying its proper share of combined Soviet and East European aid. For purposes of comparison with the USSR, East European per capita aid commitments for 1964 amounted to $3.40, and total aid constituted 0.3 percent of the GNP of the six East European countries. These figures are similar to those for the USSR.

Whereas there does not appear to be a problem relating specifically to burden-sharing between the USSR and Eastern Europe, there are indications of discontent with the burden of aid in some East European countries. In Poland, Hungary, and particularly in Czechoslovakia (whose aid commitments on a per capita basis or as a percentage of GNP are the highest among the Communist states), there are persistent press reports of public resentment against aid.[99]

If the primary aid issue causing friction among the countries of the West has been the burden-sharing problem, the most significant aid issue in the East involves Sino-Soviet aid competition. The United States like the USSR has recently been able to command less deference from its once dependent allies, and certain differences in the aid goals of various Western states have been noted. But on no occasion and from no quarter in aid to the LDCs has the United States faced a confrontation from a Western power which approaches the intensity of Sino-Soviet rivalry in aid.

In terms of overall magnitude and scope of aid operations, China's program is dwarfed by that of the USSR. Through 1968 Chinese aid commitments to the less developed countries amounted to $949 million in contrast to the Soviet aid figure of $6.3 billion.[100] Actual aid disbursements to LDCs from China have totaled only about $200 million,[101] or 20 percent of aid commitments, as opposed to Soviet disbursements of approximately $3 billion (over 47 percent of total commitments). Chinese aid has been concentrated in Asia and Africa and has been extended to twenty-three less developed countries in all.[102]

In East Africa and Asia particularly, it is clear that both

Chinese and Soviet aid efforts are directed at least as much against each other as they are against U.S. and Western aid. Sino-Soviet aid competition is apparent in certain data on commitments, in behavior by USSR and Chinese officials in the field, and in press attacks on each other's programs.

Perhaps the most impressive indication of head-to-head competition between the USSR and China in assistance to the less developed countries can be found in aid extensions just prior to the Afro-Asian Conference scheduled to take place in Algeria in June 1965. The Chinese were actively and openly opposing Soviet participation in the conference, and the USSR and China used aid offers in an attempt to gain support for their respective positions on the issue. Marshall Goldman has compiled an interesting table on the dates and size of Soviet and Chinese aid offers to LDCs prior to the Algerian conference which clearly indicates an intense aid competition on a country-by-country basis.[103]

Not only is competition between the Soviet Union and China revealed in the timing and direction of aid commitments, but it is also evident in the terms accompanying aid packages. The terms of Chinese economic assistance have been conspicuously more lenient than the standard Soviet terms of credits given at 2.5 percent interest repayable in twelve years beginning one year after delivery of the aid. The Chinese have usually offered aid on the basis of loans with no interest, repayable in ten years following a grace period of ten years. In addition, China has extended about 20 percent of its aid on a grant basis, while grants account for only 5 percent of Soviet aid offers.[104]

There is no question that the use of such terms in Chinese economic assistance is designed primarily to provide a favorable comparison between its aid and that offered by the Soviet Union and East European countries. For example, in 1960 most Communist countries came forward with an aid package to Cuba for the first time. Soviet and East European aid proposals were offered at terms characteristic of their aid to countries of the third world, whereas China made quite an impression on Cuban officials by the comparative leniency of repayment terms:

We were told by an official of the [Cuban] revolutionary government, who had an active part in the credit operation with Cuba, that it was hard to believe the conditions offered by China. When the date for amortization was brought up, the decision was left to Cuba, but was finally fixed for 1966, five years after the delivery of the machinery and when this machinery will be in production. . . . If Cuba could not begin to service the debt on the date specified, there would be no trouble about postponement.[105]

Since at the time of the offer the only aid competition to China was coming from other Communist states, this display of generosity in Cuba was clearly meant to place Chinese aid in a favorable light as compared with the East European and Soviet offers.

Several incidents involving Chinese and Soviet behavior in the third world reveal the extent to which the intensity of their aid competition has progressed. In 1964 a Soviet technician in Nepal was reported in a local paper to have accused the Chinese of trying to undermine the Panauti hydroelectric project being built with Soviet aid by removing stones from and damaging the only road over which supplies were carried to the job site.[106] Also, in Nepal, the economic counselor of the USSR eagerly sought information about a Chinese leather and shoe factory from an American who had visited the project, because the Chinese would not allow any Russian to come near the plant.[107]

A still more striking example of the intensity of Sino-Soviet aid rivalry is the following incident which occurred on Chou En-lai's goodwill tour of Africa in early 1964:

When Chou landed at the Bamako [Mali] airport Soviet leaflets entitled "Friends and Comrades in Africa" were being distributed among the crowd gathered to meet the Chinese Premier. The leaflets contained a recitation of the extensive aid given Africa by the Russians and a vitriolic attack upon the Chinese for their attempts to disrupt proletarian internationalism for their own ends.[108]

The Chinese have attacked the operational methods employed by the Soviet Union in the distribution of economic aid, the intentions of the USSR as an aid donor, and the consequences of Soviet aid to less developed countries ruled by non-Communist leaders. This constant barrage of criticism has forced the USSR to defend its program and make countercharges against Chinese aid. The essence of this Sino-Soviet dialogue over economic assistance will be outlined briefly to illustrate more fully the nature of the competition explained above and to show the verbal overlay of the conflict.

The most publicized Chinese statement on aid contains the Eight Principles of foreign aid outlined by Chou En-lai during his visit to Africa in early 1964.[109] Ostensibly these principles relate to the rules governing Chinese aid to the less developed countries, but they also constitute a thinly veiled attack on the nature of Soviet economic assistance. Included in the Eight Principles are assertions that in the extension of aid China "never attaches any conditions or asks for any privileges, . . . extends the time limit for the repayment when necessary so as to lighten the burden of the recipient countries as far as possible, . . . help[s] the LDC's embark step by step on the road of self-reliance and independent economic development," and sends experts to recipient countries who "will have the same standard of living as the experts of those countries."[110]

The significance of these principles ostensibly governing Chinese aid efforts can be more fully appreciated when juxtaposed with more or less simultaneous remarks about the nature of Soviet aid made at the second Asian Economic Seminar held in Pyongyang, North Korea, and attended by representatives of most Afro-Asian nations. At this gathering the Chinese delegate noted that not unlike the "imperialists" of the West, "the modern revisionists [USSR] also talk about 'economic cooperation and economic aid.' But they have no sincere desire to help the Asian and African countries to develop their independent national economies." In dealing with the developing countries, the Chinese delegate warned that the modern revisionists "sometimes provide equipment while withholding technical knowledge, trying all they can to make the Asian and African countries dependent on them." Also, the Chinese warned about the experience they had with Soviet aid by pointing out that "they [USSR] have even gone so far as to cancel aid, withdraw experts, and tear up contracts as a means of applying pressure."[111]

In the light of these remarks on Soviet economic assistance, it is clear that the Eight Principles are as much a Chinese view of what Soviet aid is not, as they are a description of the nature of Chinese aid.

The response of the USSR to Chinese attempts to discredit the Soviet aid program is most clearly seen in an *Izvestia* article with the title, "Fact and Fancy about Aid to Developing Countries." In this article the Eight Principles are attacked as having an "obviously demagogic character" in pursuit of the goal "to discredit the disinterested aid of the Soviet Union and other socialist countries to the young national states." Further, it is pointed out that only 18 LDCs are receiving Chinese aid whereas the USSR and East European countries have given aid to 45 countries, and that heavy industrial projects account for 50 percent of Soviet aid, compared to only 20 percent of Chinese aid. China is also chided for a record of "extremely slow" rates for the implementation of aid agreements. The USSR states that China has actually constructed only about 10 projects out of 100 promised to various less developed countries. The article refers, in addition, to the poor quality of equipment delivered by China to the aid recipients and the relatively small size of Chinese aid in terms of monetary value.[112]

The tone of this dialogue bears remarkable similarity to that of the aid debate between the USSR and the United States during the 1950s. Only in the case of the Sino-Soviet debate, the Soviet Union has adopted the position taken by the United States a decade ago.

On a more general level, the Chinese have attempted to portray the Soviet Union as a status-quo country preferring accommodation with the West and at best giving only second priority to the revolutionary movement and the complete liberation of colonial peoples. They have refused to recognize any basic distinction between the U.S. and Soviet aid programs, and see the USSR as employing typically "imperialist" methods in dealing with small states—interfering in internal affairs and producing dependency upon the aid donor as a means for obtaining special concessions.[113] Peking has sought to portray the Soviet Union, along with the United States, as a great power intent primarily upon preserving its interests and status in the international arena at the expense of the less developed world, including China. The Chinese stress the developmental gap between the USSR and the third world and have tried to force the Soviet Union out of Afro-Asian organizations as a means of identifying it with the advanced countries of the West. The Chinese maintain that the USSR does not understand the problems and revolutionary aspirations of the LDCs as do the Chinese.[114]

Within the Communist world the Chinese have disagreed with the strategy of Soviet aid to the less developed countries. They emphasize that Communist leadership of the economic development process is the essential ingredient for domestic progress and the transition to socialism by the LDCs. Non-Communist leaders in the third world are believed by the Chinese to be most unreliable allies.[115] Thus, Soviet aid to governments with national bourgeois leaders or even to national democratic states with non-Communist leadership is not expected by Peking to result in the transition to socialism. Instead it is felt that such aid serves only to strengthen non-Communist leaders at the expense of local Communists in the less developed countries.

It is also felt that the promotion of the state sector in a country ruled by non-Communist leaders will not lead to socialism, but will only lay the foundations for "bureaucratic capitalism" which the Chinese understand to be the "use of the economic power of the state for the accumulation of private fortunes and privileged economic position by political office-holders and their families."[116] Economic assistance to the state sector of countries ruled by non-Communist leaders is, of course, the essence of the Soviet aid program.

The Soviet interpretation of the consequences of Chinese policies for the third world are no less harsh than the Chinese views of Soviet policies outlined above.[117] Soviet spokesmen admit that there is a natural tendency for LDCs to look toward China's revolutionary and developmental experiences as a guide to action. The similarities in terms of backwardness of economic structures, a large peasant population, and a recent colonial or semicolonial past are compelling, on the surface at least. However, the LDCs are warned of the "catastrophic consequences" in store for them if they follow Peking's policy prescriptions. The Chinese are criticized for their failure to recognize the "diversity of revolutions" and for their dogmatic insistence that all peoples on all continents must follow without objection or modification the model of Chinese revolutionary experience. The LDCs are warned against excessive haste in agricultural collectivization and industrialization which ignore "objective laws of economic development" and can result in economic collapse which throws these countries back into the embraces of the imperialists.

Moreover, the Chinese appeal for revolutionary action on the part of LDCs is condemned for ignoring the length of time necessary to achieve the transition to socialism, even in those cases where countries have taken the noncapitalist path of development. In the case of LDCs "proceeding along the capitalist path," the Chinese appeal for revolutionary action is considered "irresponsible adventurism" because of the weak position of those social elements within those countries which favor alignment with the Communist camp. Finally, the Chinese attempt to structure world revolution in terms of the countryside (LDCs and China) versus the cities (imperialist powers and the USSR) is ridiculed as being divisive of the revolutionary front and depriving the LDCs of much needed assistance (political and economic) from the USSR, Eastern Europe, and working class elements within the advanced Western states.

Chinese attacks on the Soviet aid program, on the interests of the USSR as a world power, on the relatively low priority given by the Soviet Union to the promotion of revolution, as well as the timing and direction of Chinese aid offers and the behavior of Soviet and Chinese officials in the field—all indicate the nature and extent to which Sino-Soviet conflict is reflected in the question of economic assistance to the third world. In its aid efforts the Soviet Union finds itself continually harassed by the Chinese, who are attempting to discredit Soviet intentions in the eyes of the less developed countries and to undermine any Soviet gains in the third world obtained as a result of the aid program. These activities by China unquestionably constitute a problem of major significance for Soviet economic assistance.

Conclusions

Of the problems examined in this chapter the debt service burdens of the LDCs and the economic, political, and social environment within which aid must operate seem to pose the greatest challenge to the United States and the USSR as aid donors. The debt service burden is becoming increasingly serious and is facing more and more LDCs. The United States and the Soviet Union can continue to reschedule payments on a country-by-country basis, but every such incident exacerbates relations between donor and recipient or gives rise to increasing opposition to aid from elements within the donor nations.

The difficulties experienced by LDCs in financing local costs, providing services, and mobilizing adequate supplies of materials and labor necessary for the support of Soviet and American economic assistance projects explain a significant portion of the delays, unsatisfactory enterprises, and unfinished projects which have occurred frequently in both programs. Unless the donor is willing to take responsibility for these aspects of an aid program, such problems will continue to plague any economic assistance program on the scale of those being carried out by the United States and by the USSR. On the other hand, to take on this responsibility as a general practice would be extremely costly for the donor and detract from the development of such skills on the part of the recipients. Through country programming, large commodity import programs, program assistance, and attempts at institutional development the United Sates has made greater strides in combatting these problems than the USSR.

It is very difficult to evaluate the significance of factors within the donors which detract from aid performance. Relative to the Soviet Union the United States seems to have more problems of interagency orchestration, more serious incongruencies between aid and other foreign economic policies, and more significant domestic opposition to the aid program. However, in the case of the USSR, concrete information on these factors is very difficult to obtain.

While domestic opposition to Soviet aid exists, there is nothing in the USSR analogous to the U.S. Congress which amid great publicity annually questions the utility and performance of the program. Also, in Soviet literature on aid one does not find comparable detailed descriptions of aid blunders (real or imagined), candid criticism of the aid instrument, or explicit questions as to the usefulness of aid as a device to extract concessions or influence policies of the LDCs—the stock-in-trade of American literature on the U.S. program. The visibility and frankness of such debate in the United States makes it much more difficult for America to present the image of a positive, selfless aid program to the third world than it is for the Soviet Union where domestic opposition to aid and debates on aid issues are muted.

On the other hand, visible congressional and public opposition to the American aid program affords AID some leverage in its negotiations with the less developed countries. American insistence on a reduction in aid or upon locating a project in the private sector of the recipient, for example, can be justified in terms of an intransigent congressional stance on these issues.[118]

The Sino-Soviet conflict certainly poses a problem for the Soviet program unparalleled by any factor in American aid experience. Aid-related issues have created differences between the United States and its West European allies, but at no time has there been a conflict between Western aid programs with the persistent intensity found in Sino-Soviet aid competition.

This discussion by no means constitutes an exhaustive catalogue of problems facing the United States and the USSR as large aid donors. Other difficulties which have occurred in the United States and the USSR alike would include domestic opposition to aiding LDCs when aid resources could be usefully applied at home, resentment from allies over the amount of aid going to uncommitted countries in the third world, resentment among aid recipients engaged in regional disputes for aid given to their rivals (India-Pakistan and Ethiopia-Somali Republic are examples of this problem which have arisen in U.S. and Soviet aid), the occurrence of aid "blunders," and distrust by aid recipients of the intentions of the United States and the USSR as great powers operating in the third world through the aid instrument. These difficulties, as well as most of those mentioned above, are apparently characteristic of any aid program operating on a large scale; and, thus, they constitute the nature of the aid business itself, more than inadequacies peculiar to a specific aid donor.

While both the United States and the Soviet Union have certain problems which are not shared, the number and nature of the difficulties which both face are impressive, indeed. It seems apparent that the problems most affecting the operational aspects of the two programs are quite similar, and determined at least as much by the nature of the aid environment as by the policies and practices of the donors themselves.

11

American and Soviet Aid Appraised

⁑ The basic economic strength and position of the United States in the world market relative to the Soviet Union, or any other country, give it a fundamental advantage over the USSR in the distribution of aid. The size of the American economy gives the United States a capability to distribute aid on a scale which dwarfs the Soviet program with little real strain domestically in terms of availability of resources. Perhaps the most salient manifestation of U.S. economic strength is the ability to produce staple agricultural commodities in amounts far in excess of domestic needs. This capability has enabled the United States to distribute massive quantities of food aid to less developed countries whose populations threaten to outrun indigenous agricultural output. The Soviet Union is simply unable to engage in this form of economic assistance on a sustained basis.

In the international economy the United States enjoys a dominant position vis-à-vis the USSR. It accounts for a larger percentage of trade than does the Soviet Union in all but a few countries in the third world. The same applies to aid commitments and aid deliveries in particular. The quality of American goods in comparison to Soviet products flowing through trade and aid channels is widely respected. Through UNCTAD the less developed countries are presently clamoring for access to the U.S. market in addition to, or in lieu of, more aid. Similar demands on the USSR are not as intense primarily because the Soviet Union is generally believed by the LDCs to be less willing and less capable than the West of mobilizing more capital for use in the development of the third world. Thus, the basic strength of the American economy gives the United States a significant advantage relative to the Soviet Union in the forging of economic ties with the less developed countries through trade and aid mechanisms.

The fact that the United States has engaged in economic assistance efforts to the third world for a longer period of time, in a larger number of countries, and with a wider diversity of aid mechanisms than the Soviet Union must also yield some advantages. To be sure, the uncertainties of economic assistance continue to outweigh knowledge concerning its effective use and probable results. But the contacts forged with LDC nationals, the economic and political information on third world countries obtained through aid efforts, the handling of a wide array of financial arrangements, and the experience over two decades derived from a virtually endless number of diverse aid projects—all have served to give the United States an unparalleled exposure to the needs and problems of less developed countries. This experience makes the United States better equipped than the USSR or any other donor nation to deal with development problems through economic assistance. The question remains, however, whether or not the United States has the political will and interest necessary to employ the experience to maximal advantage for itself and the LDCs.

Finally, the more active posture which the United States has assumed in the distribution of its aid gives it more influence at the earlier stages of project and program preparation by recipients than is the case for the Soviet Union. The United States has made a practice of encouraging and assisting the less developed countries to draw up development plans which can be used to establish priority needs and serve as a basis for determining projects to be financed with the help of American aid. The USSR, by contrast, usually responds to specific project requests of the less developed countries without regard to the existence of a national development plan or the role of the particular project in such a plan. The result is that the United States is more often in the position of influencing the nature and priority of development plans and projects as they are conceived by aid recipients than is the Soviet Union.

Thus, for example, after a long period of close contact of the United States with Indian economic officials through the aid program, there appears to be a gradually increasing acceptance of a larger role for the private sector in the Indian economy. This shift in attitude is observable in the relaxation of marketing and price controls over private fertilizer companies which discouraged private investment in fertilizer.[1] India's present interest in increasing fertilizer output through private production is primarily a result of inadequate production levels under previous state controls, but there can be little question that recent emphasis on the agricultural sector and increased investment in fertilizers is at least partially a result of American prompting. The United States urged India to increase import allocations for fertilizer in 1965[2] and provided a $50 million loan to help finance such imports.[3] These changes in Indian policies are a manifestation of the consequences derivable from an activist U.S. aid stance. The importance of this difference in U.S. and Soviet aid should not be overestimated, but over the years this type of influence could substantially affect the options chosen by LDCs in a manner consistent with what the United States feels to be desirable paths of economic growth.

The Soviet Union possesses advantages in the distribution of its economic assistance which to some degree offset the aid assets of the United States. Some of these advantages center around the administration of the Soviet aid program and the existence of a centralized political system in the USSR.

There is a natural tendency to mistake the lack of information on inter- and intra-agency relations in the Soviet Union for genuine harmony and complete coordination of all government activities, thus exaggerating the efficiency of its centralized political system. Nevertheless, it is quite certain that the administration of Soviet economic assistance suffers far less from organizational fragmentation and lack of coordination than its American counterpart. The State Committee for Foreign Economic Relations seems to be the single agency primarily responsible for Soviet aid activities, in marked contrast to the situation in the United States where AID, Food-For-Peace, and the Export-Import Bank constitute three separate, large aid channels which have different fundamental purposes and are insufficiently coordinated. The advantages in terms of administrative efficiency and policy coordination are obvious.

In addition, the administrators of Soviet economic assistance are not required to face a separate repository of governmental power, to present publicly, and to defend Soviet aid goals and operations in minute detail. Nor is there a separate repository of power in the Soviet Union which can amend the statutory basis of the aid program to impose severe restrictions on the prerogatives of the Politburo, the USSR Council of Ministers, and the State Committee for Foreign Economic Relations in their conduct of the aid program.

The lack of an equivalent to the role played by the U.S. Congress in the administration of Soviet aid has allowed the Soviet program to achieve an organizational cohesiveness and stability unknown to American economic assistance. Moreover, the centralized political system accounts for the conspicuous absence of candid criticism of aid from various political figures and interests within Soviet society.

However, the greater administrative cohesion and more benign image of Soviet aid afforded by the lack of a body such as the U.S. Congress by no means constitutes an unmitigated asset to the USSR program. If the U.S. Congress has introduced bothersome constraints on the prerogatives of the executive, it has also prevented much waste, given AID and its predecessor agencies some bargaining power vis-à-vis the LDCs, and precipitated serious reevaluations of the overall performance and purposes of American aid from time to time.

A more significant Soviet advantage is afforded by the fact that the United States preceded the USSR in establishing aid programs in most less developed countries. In the absence of experience with Soviet aid the LDCs tended to attribute the various operational problems arising in connection with American aid as peculiar to aid relations with the United States, and Soviet aid suggested itself as an alternative with fewer difficulties. In addition, these countries feared becoming overly dependent upon the United States and the West through aid and other economic relationships; so Soviet trade and aid was attractive as a means of countering Western influence.

A notable exception to this general rule was Guinea, which received Soviet aid before an American or any Western program was initiated. The problems encountered with Soviet aid (machinery ill suited to climatic conditions and enterprises of too large a scale), as well as the fear of overdependence on the USSR and other Communist countries, prompted Sékou Touré to solicit American aid as a counterweight to Communist presence, and as a source of aid free from difficulties of the nature of those arising in connection with Soviet assistance.[4]

This particular case in which the United States benefited from being the second aid donor points to the advantage held by the Soviet Union as the more frequently untried aid alternative. It should be noted, however, that this advantage is vitiated once an aid program is established in a country, because operational difficulties encountered in economic assistance will probably arise regardless of the aid donor. Thus, expectations of substantially less trouble in assistance from untried donors are seldom realized, and the extent of the Soviet aid program today is such that this advantage will continue to decrease in importance since experience will temper expectations of Soviet performance (as has been the case with the United States).

Of the advantages peculiar to the United States and the USSR as aid donors, one stands above all in importance. Regardless of the relative attractiveness and administrative cohesion of aid packages, only the United States and Western Europe are perceived by most less developed countries as possessing the economic capacity to expand the flow of capital and other resources to the third world on a scale necessary to meet the demands for economic growth. This fact was made abundantly clear at the first and second meetings of UNCTAD, and it gives the United

States an opportunity, denied the USSR, to make great political inroads in the third world through imaginative trade and aid policies. Given its economic capacity, the problem facing the United States is the extent to which it can or is willing to take advantage of this unique opportunity.

In a fundamental sense the less developed countries are likely to suffer as much from becoming economically irrelevant to the rich states as from being exploited.[5] American preoccupation with the Kennedy Round and its relative disinterest in UNCTAD is symptomatic of the fact that, in terms of U.S. economic interests, the advanced states of Western Europe and Japan are much more important than the LDCs. Because of this situation, it is problematical whether or not the United States will take advantage of its unique economic capacity to forge meaningful relationships with the less developed countries as a group.

From the perspective of the late sixties the limitations of Soviet and American aid as instruments of foreign policy seem every bit as impressive as their utility. There are no cases where aid has changed the allegiance of a less developed country in the cold war, and there are few cases where even a dominant aid presence has assured a rapport between recipient and donor on major issues of foreign policy. This lack of readily observable political return on economic assistance investments in the LDCs by the United States and the Soviet Union prompted the following assessment from a student of Soviet foreign affairs:

At least it can be said that Soviet policy makers and planners are now almost as confused as Western ones with respect to the purposes and effects of development assistance programs. No country has become Communist because of Soviet aid. No country has adopted a pro-Soviet political posture primarily because of Soviet aid. The Soviet leaders are discovering that the effects of external aid are slow, diffuse, complex, and unpredictable and that once begun, an aid program cannot be cast off without cancelling out any accumulated gratitude for sacrifices previously made by the donor.[6]

The inability of the United States or the Soviet Union to elicit decisive political influence in the third world through the use of aid is primarily a consequence of the neutralizing effect each program exercises on the other. As long as both countries maintain aid programs on approximately their present scales, it is doubtful that either will be able to reduce a less developed country to unwilling dependence through trade and aid ties. Under present circumstances all LDCs are confident they can obtain aid and other support from the rival power if one donor attains the actual, or even the potential, position of being able to apply unacceptable leverage on economic and political decisions of the recipient. Because of the willingness of both the United States and the USSR to respond enthusiastically to requests for aid from virtually any LDC which feels threatened by overdependence upon the rival country, no economic indicator such as a certain percentage of trade turnover with the donor or a certain level of aid as a percentage of a recipient's GNP can be used to gauge the degree of political dependency afforded by such economic ties.

The marginal political influence derived as a consequence of economic assistance to the LDCs is becoming an increasingly recognized fact of international politics. It has strongly conditioned the dynamics of Soviet and American aid in the sixties. With a decrease in the conviction that aid generates dependence, both the United States and the USSR manifest little interest in pursuing the preemptive aid policies characteristic of the fifties. Less developed countries can exercise less leverage in playing the Soviet Union and the United States against each other in aid competition as preemptive aid policies of the donors give way to tolerance of a mutual aid presence in many LDCs.

Indeed, in countries like Afghanistan and India where both the United States and the USSR have conducted sizable aid programs, there is today even a type of de facto, though not open, cooperation in aid efforts. In Afghanistan "highways built by the United States and the Soviet Union 'happen' to meet, experts consult on mutual problems and information about local conditions is exchanged."[7] It has also been reported that Soviet advisors in Afghanistan suggested that the government take United States advice and expand private enterprise.[8] Both donors have pressed for Afghanistan to do more for itself, as 80 percent of its outlay for development in 1967 was derived from foreign sources.[9]

It is interesting to note that in cases such as Afghanistan where the two donors have established a continued aid presence, the smaller program seems to reap disproportionate benefits. The larger donor winds up financing most of the bills and constitutes more of a threat to the LDCs' jealously guarded sovereignty and independence. The smaller program tends to be solicited by the recipient as a mechanism for balancing the aid presence and pressures of the larger donor. Some American aid personnel feel this is precisely what is occurring in Afghanistan with a smaller American program yielding disproportionate benefits to the United States.[10]

Even in cases where one of the superpowers has an aid dominance or monopoly, the fear of enforced dependence on the donor has probably been exaggerated. In spite of a major aid effort by the Soviet Union in Algeria, qualified Algerian and foreign sources feel that "Moscow's influence on [Algerian] policy has so far been almost nonexistent."[11] Indeed, it may be wise for the United States or the USSR to avoid becoming the only major aid donor in a particular less developed country. It leaves such a donor in the position of paying the foreign exchange costs of development with marginal influence on the domestic and foreign policy decisions of the recipient. The recipient may even feel threatened by a pervasive aid presence. Moreover, a monopoly donor tends to become a prime target for an LDC leader venting frustration over development and domestic political problems. The political vulnerability accompanying such an aid position was demonstrated by Sékou Touré's diplomatic attack of the Soviet Union during the Guinean teachers strike of 1961.

The less developed countries are preoccupied with their own interests, as opposed to the interests of the United States and the USSR in the conduct of the cold war. This fact has led one scholar to suggest that "these states look at the world from their own angle. They treat both East and West according to their merits or failing as they see them. They will be militant in their own interests, and they will accept the militancy [and aid] of others on their behalf. But they are perfectly capable of seeing where others' interests depart from their own."[12] With these facts in mind, neither the United States nor the USSR needs to "write off" an LDC merely because of a dominant aid presence and a coincidence of views on certain policy questions. Such circumstances do not necessarily denote dependency. As Herbert Dinerstein suggests, it seems that at best LDC leaders can be rented through aid; they cannot be bought.[13]

Whereas the Soviet Union and the United States may be frustrated by the lack of highly visible political returns from aid, certain benefits have been derived from economic assistance activities in the third world.

Economic assistance has proven to be a useful instrument for establishing political entree, maintaining a presence, and gaining access to decision-makers in less developed countries. The United States and the USSR have found economic assistance to be in many cases a prerequisite for creating the political atmosphere within which meaningful diplomatic relationships can be forged in the third world.

Aid is also useful for prompting a recipient to opt for political and economic solutions to its problems in a manner most consistent with what the donor feels to be advantageous to the interests of both countries. Through economic assistance the United States had prompted local LDC efforts in tax reform, land redistribution, inflationary control, and stabilization of exchange rates by giving program assistance. It has also promoted LDC private-sector capabilities through Cooley loans, commodity import programs, and the creation of local financial institutions. Similarly, the USSR has encouraged the development of the state sector in LDCs by financing large public projects. Its increased economic intercourse with the third world has also led to the creation of state trading agencies in countries such as India to facilitate exchanges with the USSR and Eastern Europe.

Soviet and American economic assistance has contributed substantially to the development performance of LDCs receiving aid in large amounts. In a recent comparative study of U.S. and Soviet aid in Turkey, the United Arab Republic, and India, it was concluded that, in the absence of Soviet and U.S. aid (particularly the latter), none of these states would have experienced any significant increase in per capita income. United States and Soviet aid were found to have contributed substantially to capital formation through investment expenditures and increased domestic savings.[14]

If aid has proven to yield only limited political influence over LDC recipients, the neutralization effect of the two programs has meant that aid has been successfully employed by both the United States and the USSR as part of a policy of denial in the third world. Since this policy of denial plays such an important role in the motivations underlying Soviet and American aid, on these grounds alone both donors can and do claim success for their aid efforts.

Thus, economic assistance has proven to be a most useful instrument for both the United States and the USSR in achieving a political entree and maintaining a presence facilitating access to decision-makers in newly independent countries, in exerting limited but cherished influence on the direction and speed of development in the third world, and in providing an alternative to dependence of less developed countries on one of the superpowers. Both countries have succeeded to some extent in demonstrating their interest in the problems and aspirations of the less developed countries through the distribution of aid even though their behavior in UNCTAD and other UN agencies casts doubt on the depth of their commitment to development goals of the LDCs.

It might be noted that all of these factors can be considered necessary, but not sufficient, conditions for the accomplishment of the long-term motivations for aid—cultural influence and system maintenance or conversion. So, while it is too soon to tell the extent to which these long-term goals of aid will actually be realized, the accomplishments of the programs have probably been impressive enough to convince both the United States and the USSR that their long-range goals of aid are still attainable. The types of gains attributable to aid are unobtrusive, but their importance to the two superpowers as leaders of camps competing for the allegiance of the third world should not be underestimated.

It now seems clear, however, that the results attainable from aid are not commensurate with the expectations which generated the Soviet and American aid programs. Foreign aid, particularly in the case of the United States, has tended to be a substitute for a foreign policy vis-à-vis the third world, rather than a facet of a carefully conceived program to establish durable positive relationships with the LDCs. Both countries are presently confronted with the tasks of justifying the continuation of their economic assistance programs at current levels and in substantially the same form while recognizing that the gains for the donor attributable to aid are much less predictable and manifest than they were once felt to be.

It has been pointed out that "the route from the present to the future world is unfortunately not discernible in useful detail, and the notion that expenditures on aid, necessarily modest in relation to the immensity of problems, can establish the United States in the role of history's midwife is disturbingly utopian."[15] This statement would apply as well to the Soviet Union whose aid program is but a fraction of the size of that of the United States. Both donors have come to realize the validity of this proposition and as a consequence it has become increasingly more difficult to mobilize domestic political support for foreign economic assistance activities. This situation combined with the obvious reluctance of the United States or the USSR to meet the demands of the LDCs in the field of trade suggests that the prospects are poor for a meaningful increase in the flow of development capital to the LDCs from the two superpowers.

There are, indeed, differences in the administration, programming, implementation, and financial terms of Soviet and American economic assistance to the third world. There is a direct conflict in the goals of Soviet and American aid. However, basic similarities in the types of expectations underlying the programs, in the difficulties encountered in the distribution of aid, and in the nature of the relationships forged between the recipients and the United States and USSR as aid donors suggest that the determining factors in economic assistance do not necessarily lie in the political and economic systems of the donors. Certainly there is little concrete evidence to indicate that the Soviet system is inherently more capable of managing a successful aid effort than the U.S. system. Instead, the programs seem to be shaped primarily by the roles of the United States and the Soviet Union as leaders of competing camps in the international system and by the environment of the third world in which both aid programs must operate.

Epilogue

‡ Since the completion of this manuscript, a number of important reports have been produced on the problems and prospects of American and international aid efforts.[1] Among these, the Peterson Report to the President of the United States necessitates a brief epilogue since it relates so directly and importantly to one of the aid programs outlined in this book.

The Peterson Report "recommends a new focus for US aid programs, a new emphasis on multilateral organizations, and a new institutional framework."[2] The report suggests that AID be abolished and that development assistance be divorced completely from military aid and from economic aid given for essentially political purposes. Thus, aid in the form of Supporting Assistance and the Contingency Fund would be administered by the Department of State, military aid would be administered by the Department of Defense, and development assistance would be administered by several newly created institutions replacing AID.

A U.S. International Development Bank would be created as an independent government corporation with a board of directors composed of government officials and private members. The bank would operate with a minimum of field representatives and without country programming of the sort characteristic of AID. It would disburse capital and technical assistance loans in selected countries and for selected programs of special interest to the United States.[3]

A U.S. International Development Institute would also be created as an independent government agency to concentrate on research, training, population problems, and social development. The report suggests that the United States should seek to operate these technical assistance efforts more as a private foundation would, with the abandonment of the current practice in U.S. aid of employing large numbers of technicians and advisory personnel in many fields and in many countries.[4]

These two proposed institutions would operate alongside of the recently authorized Overseas Private Investment Corporation which was established in 1969 to mobilize and facilitate the participation of U.S. private capital and business skills in international development.

The final component of the new edifice to replace AID would be a U.S. Development Council designed to assure consistency among U.S. development programs, the positions taken in international agencies and forums, and the actions taken on trade and financial issues relating to developing countries. The council would also see to it that international development received greater emphasis in U.S. trade, investment, financial, agricultural, and export-promotion policies. The chairman of the council would be a full-time official appointed by the President and located in the White House. The council would consist of the secretaries of state, the treasury, and agriculture, the President's special trade representative, the president of the Export-Import Bank, the director of the Peace Corps, the president of the U.S. International Development Bank, the director of the U.S. International Development Institute, and the president of the Overseas Private Investment Corporation.[5]

At the time of this writing it is not yet clear exactly what parts of the report will be included in President Nixon's proposals for the aid program. Also, even if Nixon should embrace the Peterson Report in its entirety, it is not clear how receptive Congress would be toward it. For example, in the light of congressional efforts to maintain close scrutiny and control over aid practices, there may be some reluctance to view with favor the creation of a U.S.

International Development Bank and a U.S. International Development Institute as independent government agencies which would be consulting Congress only intermittently after their initial capitalization. Because of the uncertainty as to the real influence the Peterson Report will have on the shape of future American aid efforts, it is possible at this time merely to point out the relationship between the report and some of the observations raised in our discussion of the Soviet and American aid programs.

We have noted how early optimism in the political and economic developmental results generated by aid gave way to a degree of frustration and disillusionment with the aid instrument in the cases of both the United States and the USSR. In the United States this frustration has been reflected in severe budgetary cuts in the aid program in each of the past several years. The proposals of the Peterson Report reflect how serious the lag in domestic political support for the aid program has become in the United States. The dismantling of AID, the dispersion of various components of AID's programs to various existing departments and newly created semipublic institutions, and the emphasis on minimizing the visibility of the U.S. aid presence abroad can be interpreted as conscious steps to lower the profile of a politically vulnerable program now administered by AID.[6] The fact that a task force on American aid would make these types of proposals tends to corroborate the extent of the malaise surrounding aid noted in the concluding chapter.

It is also worth mentioning that the recommendations of the Peterson Report regarding organizational reform are typical of past attempts to restore confidence in and support for the American aid program. The existing agency associated with whatever faults are attributed to aid efforts is to be abolished and replaced by one or more new agencies with a clean slate. As has been the case in the past, there is an assumption that institutional changes of this sort have the benefit of making it easier to execute and dramatize a shift in aid focus as well as to generate more political support for the "new" program. But there are also costs in terms of a loss of morale among U.S. aid personnel and in the danger of raising expectations of drastic improvements in aid performance as a consequence of administrative adjustments which may not be met in fact. The point is that in terms of organizational reform as a means of placing aid on a firmer foundation, the proposals of the Peterson Report are in many ways more consistent with past aid practices than a departure from them.

In spite of the attention given to the new institutional setting for U.S. aid prescribed in the Peterson Report, the most significant proposal is the abandonment of the reliance upon field missions, country programming, and an active aid stance vis-à-vis the LDCs. Throughout the report the suggestion is made that the United States should alter its basic aid stance from one of direction and leadership of Western bilateral and multilateral development assistance efforts to one of support. It is asserted that this change in the United States' approach to aid is made possible by the increased capacities of LDCs to establish their own development priorities, the expansion of aid activities by other Western nations, and the increased capacities of international organizations such as the IBRD in coordinating and directing aid flows from many donors.[7]

With the United States still providing the lion's share of development assistance through bilateral as well as multilateral aid channels,[8] it is difficult to see how it could successfully abdicate its directive role in favor of a supporting one—notwithstanding changes in the aid environment noted above. It is also hard to determine what states or international institutions would have the capacity to take up the slack left by such a move on the part of the United States. However, should the recommendations of the Peterson Report be implemented on this point it would mark a profound change in American aid practice and in the entire international aid picture.

This is far from a comprehensive analysis of the Peterson Report's contents or its potential impact on the American aid program. That would be an impossible task at this juncture anyway, since it will be some time before it is clear just how much and which parts of the proposal will be accepted by the President and Congress. However, it is likely that the report will provide the focus for a vigorous public debate on American aid in the coming months.

Appendixes
Notes
Bibliographical Essay
Index

Appendix A

Regional Definitions in U.S. Aid Data

‡ The following list indicates the countries included in the regional areas used in the presentation of United States aid data:

AFRICA

Algeria	Guinea	Rwanda
Botswana	Ivory Coast	Senegal
Burundi	Kenya	Sierra Leone
Cameroon	Lesotho	Somali Republic
Central African Republic	Liberia	Southern Rhodesia
	Libya	Sudan
Chad	Malagasy Republic	Swaziland
Congo (Brazzaville)	Malawi	Tanzania
Congo (Kinshasa)	Republic of Mali	Togo
Dahomey	Mauritania	Tunisia
Ethiopia	Mauritius	Uganda
Gabon	Morocco	Upper Volta
Gambia	Niger	Zambia
Ghana	Nigeria	

NEAR EAST AND SOUTH ASIA

Afghanistan	Iraq	Saudi Arabia
Ceylon	Jordan	Syrian Arab Republic
Cyprus	Kuwait	Turkey
Greece	Lebanon	United Arab Republic
India	Nepal	(Egypt)
Iran	Pakistan	Yemen

Far East

Burma	Indonesia	Ryukyu Islands
Cambodia	Korea	Singapore
Republic of China	Laos	Thailand
Hong Kong	Malaysia	Vietnam
Indochina	Philippines	Western Samoa

Latin America

Argentina	Cuba	Mexico
Bahamas	Dominican Republic	Nicaragua
Barbados	Ecuador	Panama
Bolivia	El Salvador	Paraguay
Brazil	Guatemala	Peru
British Honduras	Guyana	Surinam
Chile	Haiti	Trinidad and Tobago
Colombia	Honduras	Uruguay
Costa Rica	Jamaica	Venezuela

Soviet Aid Deliveries to LDCs

‡ The best estimate of Soviet economic aid deliveries to the less developed countries is found in Category 16 of official Soviet trade statistics. The chief of the Economic Planning Administration of the Ministry of Foreign Trade, D. F. Tokin, reaffirmed this in an interview with Marshall Goldman in 1964.[1]

Category 16 consists of equipment and materials for complete plants and represents the value of technical services as well as material goods supplied by the USSR to aid-receiving countries.[2] This type of export is unique in Soviet trade statistics as an indicator of aid deliveries to less developed countries, because unlike exports such as machinery or foodstuffs the only way the LDCs can afford to purchase the expensive plants in Category 16 is through credit. Thus, we can assume, along with corroboration from the USSR, that all exports of Category 16 goods to less developed countries are flowing under Soviet credits.

Table A presents a country-by-country summary of Category 16 exports to all the less developed countries which have received Soviet aid. No LDCs which have not concluded an aid agreement with the USSR have received Category 16 exports. Since goods other than equipment and material for complete plants are exported to less developed countries under aid agreements, Category 16 does not represent total aid deliveries. However, these data give us the most reliable minimum estimate of drawings on Soviet economic assistance commitments.

In addition, Soviet economic aid commitments to the less developed countries have been presented to provide a contrast between aid agreements and actual deliveries.

1. Marshall I. Goldman, *Soviet Foreign Aid* (New York: Frederick A. Praeger, 1967), p. 27.
2. Ibid.

TABLE A

Category 16 Commitments and Deliveries of Soviet Exports to the Less Developed Countries
(In Millions of U.S. Dollars)

Recipients	1955	1956	1957	1958	1959	1960	1961	1962	1963	1964	1965	1966	1967	Total
Africa	$ 0.1						$ 9.7	$ 12.7	$ 21.7	$ 25.7	$ 34.1	$ 18.9	$ 13.9	$ 136.8
Algeria									0.6	2.0	5.8	1.7	2.9	13.0
Congo (Brazzaville)											1.0	0.9	0.6	2.5
Ethiopia										2.2	6.1	2.9	0.4	11.6
Ghana							0.1	2.6	4.5		8.0	2.9		20.5
Guinea							9.0	7.4	7.3	4.5	1.9	0.7	1.1	34.0
Mali							0.6	2.6	3.3	3.9	2.5	3.4	5.2	22.0
Somalia									2.8	4.1	5.6	3.7	2.2	18.1
Sudan									2.5	5.3	1.0	2.3	0.4	11.6
Tunisia								0.1	0.7	3.7	2.2	0.4	0.9	6.7
Uganda													0.2	0.2
Asia	$ 1.1	$ 7.6	$ 46.6	$ 107.5	$ 48.4	40.2	66.7	95.0	121.9	186.6	150.8	118.5	123.5	1,114.4
Afghanistan	1.0	1.8	3.3	9.7	14.5	17.3	18.4	19.1	23.7	27.6	29.7	44.6	28.3	238.9
Burma									1.0	2.2	0.4	0.2		3.8
Cambodia				0.6						0.4				1.0
Ceylon								0.9	2.9	7.0	4.2	0.9	1.1	17.5
India	0.1	5.8	43.3	97.2	33.9	17.9	39.2	64.1	80.5	128.4	99.9	63.7	89.6	763.8
Indonesia						5.0	8.9	7.4	9.6	17.8	13.1	3.7	0.3	65.7
Pakistan							0.2	3.5	4.3	3.0	3.3	5.2	4.2	23.7

Recipients	1955	1956	1957	1958	1959	1960	1961	1962	1963	1964	1965	1966	1967	Total
Middle East														
Iran			0.4	3.9	20.1	27.7	60.6	73.1	75.0	80.7	96.4	104.9	133.5	676.3
												4.7	22.2	27.1
Iraq					0.2	4.2	15.7	29.5	25.6	18.2	5.3	4.3	4.5	107.5
Syria				1.9	1.0	2.0	8.5	2.2	1.7	1.0	4.3	5.8	20.8	49.0
Turkey				0.2	1.2	3.6	1.4	0.2	0.1			0.1		6.9
UAR (Egypt)		0.1	0.4	1.2	15.5	15.7	34.9	41.1	47.6	61.3	85.3	84.6	79.9	467.6
Yemen				0.6	2.0	2.2	0.1	0.1			1.5	5.4	6.1	18.2
Total Deliveries	$ 1.1	$ 7.6	$ 47.1	$111.3	$ 68.5	$ 68.0	$137.0	$180.8	$218.6	$293.0	$281.3	$242.3	$270.9	$1,927.5
Total Commitments[a]	$126.0	$243.0	$310.0	$415.0	$855.0	$594.0	$547.0	$ 53.0	$236.0	$998.0	$653.0	$974.0[b]	$269.0[c]	$6,273.0[d]

SOURCES: Information on aid deliveries from USSR, Ministerstvo Vneshnei Torgovli, *Vneshnyaya torgovlya v 1956–67 godakh* (Moscow: Vneshtorgizdat, 1957–1968). Information on aid commitments, except where noted, from Leo Tansky, "Soviet Foreign Aid to the Less Developed Countries," in U.S., Joint Economic Committee, *New Directions in the Soviet Economy*, pt. 4, 89th Cong, 2d sess, 1966, p. 951.

NOTE: Rubles converted to dollars at official exchange rates: 1 r = $1.11 for data since 1961, and 1 r = $0.25 for figures prior to 1961.

a. Includes aid commitments to Argentina in the amount of $115 million.
b. U.S., Department of State, Bureau of Intelligence and Research, *Communist Governments and Developing Nations: Economic Aid and Trade*, RSB-80, July 21, 1967, p. 2.
c. U.S. Department of State, Bureau of Intelligence and Research, *Communist Governments and Developing Nations: Aid and Trade in 1968*, RSE-65, September 5, 1969, p. 2.
d. Sum of yearly totals. Due to revision in estimates of past Soviet aid commitments the source cited in the previous footnote places cumulative commitments through 1967 at $5,989 million.

Appendix C

Soviet Aid as Percentage of Gross National Product

‡ There are two basic approaches to calculating Soviet aid deliveries and/or commitments as a percentage of Soviet GNP: (1) the aid and GNP figures both must be expressed in domestic rubles; or (2) the aid and GNP figures both must be expressed in dollars. The second method is the one adopted here.

The conventional practice would be to use the first approach in which the Soviet GNP is expressed in rubles. However, goods flowing under Soviet aid agreements are not expressed in domestic rubles; instead, they are priced at world market prices expressed in Soviet foreign-trade rubles.[1] Thus, one runs into the serious difficulty of obtaining an aid figure in domestic rubles. The process of arriving at such a figure involves the determination of a ruble value for aid goods in terms of Soviet internal prices, rather than the world market prices in which they are actually expressed.

Because of these difficulties, the second alternative seems preferable for our purposes. Soviet GNP expressed in dollar values has been calculated by Stanley Cohn for various years since 1950.[2] His data for the years 1960, 1962, 1963, and 1964 have been used in these calculations of Soviet aid as a percentage of Soviet GNP. Soviet aid figures are expressed in dollars converted at the official exchange rate of 1 ruble (foreign-trade) = 1.11 dollars. This conversion is possible because the USSR, itself, expresses aid figures in dollars (or some other convertible currency) and then converts them to rubles at the official exchange rate.

1. For an explanation of the difference in domestic and foreign-trade rubles, see note 33, Chapter 8.
2. Cohn, "Soviet Growth Retardation: Trends in Resource Availability and Efficiency," in U.S. Congress, Joint Economic Committee, *New Directions in the Soviet Economy*, 89th Cong., 2d sess., 1966, pt. 2a, p. 109.

Notes

Notes to Chapter 1

1. The terms *less developed countries, LDCs,* and *countries of the third world* will be used interchangeably throughout this study to mean the non-Communist nations of Asia (excluding Japan), Africa (excluding the Republic of South Africa), the Near East (excluding Israel and including Greece), and Latin America.

2. Military assistance has frequently been a concomitant of, or a substitute for, economic aid. However, except for occasional reference to military assistance and its relationship to economic aid, our attention will be focused exclusively upon the economic component of the Soviet and American foreign aid programs. This emphasis on economic assistance implies a conviction that economic aid is a complex phenomenon worthy of inquiry on its own, and does not necessarily suggest that military aid to LDCs is less consequential in determining relations between aid donors and their recipients.

3. U.S., Congress, House, Committee on Foreign Affairs, *Hearings, Foreign Assistance Act of 1969,* 91st Cong., 1st sess., 1969, pp. 99 and 128.

4. Max Millikan, "Perspectives on Postwar Aid," in *U.S. Foreign Aid,* ed. Grant S. McClellan (New York: H. W. Wilson Co., 1957), p. 18.

5. U.S., Congress, House, Committee on Foreign Affairs, *Hearings, Mutual Security Act of 1959,* 86th Cong., 1st sess., 1959, p. 791. For a more recent statement to the same effect by William S. Gaud, see U.S., Congress, House, Committee on Appropriations, *Hearings, Foreign Assistance and Related Agencies, Appropriations for 1969,* pt. 2, 90th Cong., 2d sess., 1968, p. 391.

6. John D. Montgomery, *The Politics of Foreign Aid* (New York: Frederick A. Praeger, 1962); Edward Mason, *Foreign Aid and Foreign Policy* (New York: Harper & Row, 1964); Herbert Feis, *Foreign Aid and Foreign Policy* (New York: St. Martin's Press, 1964); and Hans Morgenthau, "Preface to a Political Theory of Foreign Aid," in *Why Foreign Aid?,* ed. Robert Goldwin (Chicago: Rand McNally and Co., 1962).

7. *The Mutual Security Act of 1951,* Public Law 165, 82d Cong., 1st sess., section 2, in *Documents on American Foreign Relations* 13 (1951): 128.

Notes to Chapter 2

1. Phillip W. Bell, "Colonialism as a Problem in American Foreign Policy," *World Politics* 5, no. 1 (October 1952): 86.

2. Russell H. Fifield, *Southeast Asia in United States Policy* (New York: Frederick A. Praeger, 1963), p. 17.

3. Ibid., p. 16.

4. For a discussion of the American approach to neutralism in the third world, see Cecil V. Crabb, Jr., "The United States and the Neutralists: A Decade in Perspective," *The Annals of the American Academy of Political and Social Science* 362 (November 1965): 92–101.

5. Harold K. Jacobson, *America's Foreign Policy,* rev. ed. (New York: Random House, 1965), Foreword.

6. For an excellent discussion of the implications involved in the choice of the actor and the level of analysis in international relations studies, see "The Actors in International Politics," in Arnold Wolfers, *Discord and Collaboration* (Baltimore: John Hopkins Press, 1962), pp. 3–24; and J. David Singer, "The Level of Analysis Problem in International Relations," in *The International System,* ed. Klaus Knorr and Sidney Verba (Princeton: Princeton University Press, 1961), pp. 77–92.

7. U.S., Congress, Senate, Committee on Foreign Relations, *Hearings, Mutual Security Act of 1951,* 82d Cong., 1st sess., 1951, p. 413.

8. U.S., Congress, Senate, Committee on Foreign Relations, *Hearings, Foreign Assistance, 1965,* 89th Cong., 1st sess., 1965, p. 584.

9. *New York Times,* January 23, 1967, p. 6.

10. Ibid., p. 1.

11. See Robert A. Packenham, "Political Development Doctrines in the American Foreign Aid Program," *World Politics* 18, no. 2 (January 1966): 194–235.

12. For an excellent discussion of the ways in which U.S. aid has been employed for the purpose of influencing the short-run internal political situation of the recipient nations, see Joan Nelson, *Aid, Influence and Foreign Policy* (New York: Macmillan Co., 1968), pp. 93–103.

13. Quoted in V. Rimalov, "Economic Competition of the Two Systems and the Problem of Aid to Underdeveloped Countries," *Mirovaya ekonomika i mezhdunarodnye otnoshenia* [World Economics and International Relations], no. 2 (1960), trans. in *Problems of Economics* 3, no. 8 (December 1960): 45.

14. These countries in order of the magnitude of such aid received through FY 1968 are South Vietnam, South Korea, Pakistan, Turkey, Taiwan, Greece, Iran, Thailand, and the Philippines. Data from U.S., Agency for International Development, *U.S. Overseas Loans and Grants and Assistance from International Organizations, Obligations and Loan Authorizations July 1, 1945–June 30, 1968,* May 1969.

15. See U.S., Agency for International Development, *Principles of Foreign Economic Assistance,* 1965, p. 20.

16. U.S., Congress, Senate, Committee on Foreign Relations, *Hearings, Mutual Security Act of 1951*, 82d Cong., 1st sess., 1951, p. 3.

17. U.S., Library of Congress, Legislative Reference Service, *U.S. Foreign Aid: Its Purposes, Scope, Administration and Related Information*, 86th Cong., 1st sess., House doc. no. 116, 1959, p. 68.

18. John Pincus, *Trade, Aid and Development* (New York: McGraw-Hill Book Co., 1967), p. 54.

19. U.S., Congress, House, Committee on Appropriations, *Hearings, Foreign Assistance and Related Agencies, Appropriations for 1969*, 90th Cong., 2d sess., 1968, pt. 2, p. 58.

20. U.S., Congress, House, Committee on Foreign Affairs, *Hearings, Mutual Security Act of 1958*, 85th Cong., 2d sess., 1958, pp. 910–11.

21. See Gunnar Myrdal, *An International Economy* (New York: Harper and Brothers, 1956), p. 123. Also by the same author *Beyond the Welfare State* (New Haven: Yale University Press, 1960).

22. For a concise summary of this argument, see Max Millikan and W. W. Rostow, *A Proposal: Key to an Effective Foreign Policy* (New York: Harper and Brothers: 1957), pp. 141–42.

23. U.S., Department of Defense, Office of Assistant Secretary of Defense (Public Affairs), *News Release*, no. 422–66, May 18, 1966, p. 5 (cited hereafter as Dept. of Defense, *News Release*).

24. Myrdal, *An International Economy*, p. 134.

25. I. L. Claude, "Economic Development Aid and International Political Stability" (Paper delivered before the Seventh World Congress of the International Political Science Association, Brussels, Belgium, 1967), pp. 9–13.

26. Dept. of Defense, *News Release*, p. 8. Emphasis in original.

27. For an example of the multiplicity of motivations behind the economic assistance program at a given time, see U.S., Congress, Senate, Committee on Foreign Relations, *Hearings, Mutual Security Act of 1952*, 82d Cong., 2d sess., 1952, pp. 616–17.

Notes to Chapter 3

1. Henry A. Kissinger, *Nuclear Weapons and Foreign Policy* (New York: Harper and Brothers, 1957), pp. 370–71.

2. Ibid., p. 383.

3. For an excellent brief discussion of peaceful coexistence, see Milton Kovner, *The Challenge of Coexistence* (Washington, D.C.: Public Affairs Press, 1961), chap. 2, pp. 4–20.

4. For a typical Soviet statement on the "zone of peace," see *The USSR and Developing Countries* (Moscow: Novosti Press Agency Publishing House, 1966), p. 84.

5. Alvin Z. Rubinstein, *The Soviets in International Organizations* (Princeton: Princeton University Press, 1964), pp. 32–33.

6. *Pravda*, Feb. 15, 1956, trans. in *Current Digest of the Soviet Press* (cited hereafter as *CDSP*) 8, no. 4 (March 7, 1956): 7.

7. See Robert S. Walters, "Soviet Economic Aid to Cuba," *International Affairs* (London) 42, no. 1 (January 1966): 74–75.

8. Robert L. Allen, "The Soviet and East European Foreign Credit Program," *American Slavic and East European Review* 16, no. 4 (December 1957): 449.

9. Ibid., p. 439.

10. William B. Ballis, "Soviet-Iranian Relations During the Decade 1953–64," *Bulletin, Institute for the Study of the USSR* 12, no. 11 (November 1965): 13–14.

11. Marshall I. Goldman, *Soviet Foreign Aid* (New York: Frederick A. Praeger, 1967), pp. 168–69.

12. For a good example of Soviet writing contrasting Soviet and U.S. aid, see R. G. Iskandarov, *K voprosu o pomoshchi slaborazvitym stranam* [The Problem of Aid to Developing Countries] (Moscow: Publishing House of the Higher Party School and the Academy of Social Sciences attached to the Central Committee CPSU, 1960), trans. in Joint Publications Research Service, no. 16141, November 13, 1962.

13. U.S., Department of State, Bureau of Intelligence and Research, *Communist Governments and Developing Nations: Aid and Trade in 1965*, RSB-50, June 17, 1966, p. 3.

14. *New York Times*, February 20, 1967, p. 1.

15. See Khrushchev's statement cited by V. Vanin, "Economic Cooperation of the USSR with countries of the Arab East and Africa," *Mirovaya ekonomika i mezhdunarodnye otnoshenia* [World Economics and International Relations], no. 11 (1961), trans. in *Problems of Economics* 4, no. 12 (April 1962): 54.

16. V. Rimalov, "Soviet Assistance to Underdeveloped Countries," *International Affairs* (Moscow), no. 9, (1959), p. 24.

17. John Pincus, *Trade, Aid and Development* (New York: McGraw-Hill, 1967), p. 13.

18. Ibid.

19. Goldman, *Soviet Foreign Aid*, p. 186.

20. Western analysts of the Soviet economy have concluded that this is indeed the case, as well as that the history of Soviet prices tends to confirm the proposition on relative costs. Robert L. Allen, "Economic Motives in Soviet Foreign Trade Policy," *Southern Economic Journal* 25, no. 2 (October 1958): 193–96; and Stanley J. Zyzniewski, "The Soviet Bloc and the Underdeveloped Countries," *World Politics* 11, no. 3 (April 1959): 384–85.

21. Allen, "Economic Motives," pp. 198–99.

22. Ibid., p. 191.

23. See Carole A. Sawyer, *Communist Trade with Developing Countries 1955–1965* (New York: Frederick A. Praeger, 1966), p. 42.

24. I. Kapranov, "The USSR and Industrial Development in the Newly Free States," *International Affairs* (Moscow), no. 6 (1966), p. 35.

25. For a discussion on how deficiencies in cost-price data impede Soviet foreign trade calculations, see Frederic L. Pryor, "Foreign Trade Theory in the Communist Bloc," *Soviet Studies* 14, no. 1 (July 1962): 40–61.

26. *Pravda*, July 13, 1958, p. 4, cited in Kovner, "Soviet Aid Strategy in Developing Countries," *Orbis* 8, no. 3 (Fall 1964): 634. The same theme was sounded in 1958 when it was asserted that USSR aid to Yugoslavia was exclusively to the advantage of the recipient from the commercial point of view. It was

pointed out that it would be of greater advantage to the USSR to use the aid funds for the construction of factories in the USSR and then export the finished products to Yugoslavia than to build plants in Yugoslavia. *Pravda,* July 1, 1958, p. 2, trans. in *CDSP* 10, no. 26 (August 6, 1958): 9.

27. *New York Times,* September 13, 1955, p. 2.

28. Leo Tansky, *U.S. and U.S.S.R. Aid to Developing Countries: A Comparative Study of India, Turkey and the U.A.R.* (New York: Frederick A. Praeger, 1967), p. 9.

29. See *Pravda,* August 7, 1963, pp. 4–5, trans. in *CDSP* 15, no. 32 (September 4, 1963): 3.

30. Ibid., p. 4.

31. Tansky, *U.S. and U.S.S.R. Aid,* p. 11.

32. Herbert S. Dinerstein, "Soviet Doctrines on Developing Countries: Some Divergent Views," in *New Nations in a Divided World,* ed. Kurt London (New York: Frederick A. Praeger, 1963), p. 78.

33. Kovner, *Coexistence,* p. 107.

34. Sawyer, *Communist Trade,* p. 17.

35. Erwin D. Canham, "Introduction," in Robert L. Allen, *Soviet Economic Warfare* (Washington, D.C.: Public Affairs Press, 1960), p. v.

36. John D. Montgomery, *The Politics of Foreign Aid* (New York: Frederick A. Praeger, 1962), p. 11.

37. Henry E. Aubrey, "Sino-Soviet Aid to South and Southeast Asia," *World Politics* 12, no. 1 (October 1959): 67–69.

38. "Milieu goal" as used here is a concept of Arnold Wolfers presented in *Discord and Collaboration* (Baltimore: Johns Hopkins Press, 1962), pp. 73–74. For a further elaboration, see I. L. Claude, "National Interests and the Global Environment," *Journal of Conflict Resolution* 8, no. 3 (September 1964): 294–95.

Notes to Chapter 4

1. U.S., Congress, Senate, Committee on Foreign Relations, *Hearings, Mutual Security Act of 1951,* 82d Cong., 1st sess., 1951, p. 413.

2. Millikan and Rostow, *A Proposal: Key to an Effective Foreign Policy* (New York: Harper and Brothers, 1957).

3. U.S., Congress, Senate, Special Committee to Study the Foreign Aid Program, *Foreign Aid Program, Compilation of Studies and Surveys,* 85th Cong., 1st sess., 1957 (cited hereafter as U.S., Senate, *Foreign Aid Program,* 1957).

4. Center for International Studies, Massachusetts Institute of Technology, *The Objectives of United States Economic Assistance Programs,* January 1957, in U.S., Senate, *Foreign Aid Program,* 1957, p. 20.

5. For a more detailed discussion of assumptions underlying American developmental aid, see ibid., pp. 16–25; and Millikan and Rostow, *A Proposal.*

6. U.S., Department of Defense, Office of Assistant Secretary of Defense (Public Affairs), *News Release,* no. 422–66, May 18, 1966 (cited hereafter as Dept. of Defense, *News Release*). See Chapter 2.

7. U.S., Congress, House Committee on Foreign Affairs, *Hearings, Foreign Assistance Act of 1963,* 88th Cong., 1st sess., 1963, p. 188.

8. Robert A. Packenham, "Political Development Doctrines in the American Foreign Aid Program," *World Politics* 18, no. 2 (January 1966): 231.

9. This point is pursued in Lucien Pye, "The Soviet and American Styles in Foreign Aid," *Orbis* 4, no. 2 (July 1961): 165–66.

10. U.S., Agency for International Development, *Principles of Foreign Economic Assistance,* 1965, p. 4.

11. Ibid.

12. U.S., Congress, House, Committee on Foreign Affairs, *Hearings, Foreign Assistance Act of 1963,* 88th Cong., 1st sess., 1963, p. 187.

13. James S. Coleman, "The Political Systems of the Developing Areas," in *The Politics of the Developing Areas,* ed. Gabriel Almond and James S. Coleman (Princeton: Princeton University Press, 1960), pp. 538–44; Everett E. Hagen, "A Framework for Analyzing Economic and Political Change," in Robert Asher et al., *Development of the Emerging Countries: An Agenda for Research* (Washington, D.C.: Brookings Institution, 1962), pp. 2–6; and Bruce Russett, *Trends in World Politics* (New York: Macmillan Co., 1965), p. 140.

14. Russett, *Trends,* p. 137; and Dept. of Defense, *News Release,* p. 5.

15. Charles Wolf, Jr., *United States Policy in the Third World* (Boston: Little, Brown and Co., 1967), pp. 31–32.

16. Russett, *Trends,* pp. 136–37.

17. Samuel P. Huntington, "Political Development and Decay," *World Politics* 8, no. 3 (April 1965): 395. See also idem, *Political Order in Changing Societies* (New Haven: Yale University Press, 1968).

18. Ibid., p. 386.

19. Packenham, "Political Development Doctrines," pp. 220–23.

20. Ibid., pp. 215–20.

21. Ibid., p. 226.

22. U.S., Congress, Senate, Committee on Foreign Relations, *Legislation on Foreign Relations,* 90th Cong., 2d sess., 1969, pp. 23–24.

23. U.S., Congress, House, Committee on Foreign Affairs, *Hearings, Foreign Assistance Act of 1969,* 91st Cong., 1st sess., 1969, pp. 90–91.

24. See Albert O. Hirschman, *The Strategy of Economic Development* (New Haven: Yale University Press, 1959), and idem, *Journeys Toward Progress* (New York: Twentieth Century Fund, 1963).

25. See Walt W. Rostow, *The Stages of Economic Growth* (London: Cambridge University Press, 1960).

26. Packenham, "Political Development Doctrines," pp. 228–29.

27. This is the standard evaluation of Soviet aid in the 1950s. See Philip E. Mosely, "Communist Policy in the Third World," *Review of Politics* 28, no. 2 (April 1966): 217; and Joseph S. Berliner, *Soviet Economic Aid* (New York: Frederick A. Praeger, 1958), p. 24.

28. S. Ogurtsov, "The Developing Countries and Social Progress," *Azia i Afrika segodnya,* no. 7 (July 1963), trans. in *Current Digest of the Soviet Press* 15, no. 37 (October 9, 1963): 11.

29. Ibid.

30. Ibid.

31. See I. Potekhin, "On African Socialism," *International Affairs* (Moscow), no. 1 (1963), pp. 73–74.

32. Ibid.

33. For further elaboration on national democracy, see: D. S. Carlisle, "The Changing Soviet Perception of the Development Process in the Afro-Asian World," *Midwest Journal of Political Science* 8, no. 4 (November 1964): 385–407; William T. Shinn, Jr., "The 'National Democratic State,' A Communist Program for Less Developed Areas," *World Politics* 15, no. 3 (April 1963): 377–89; and Richard Lowenthal, "On 'National Democracy': Its Function in Communist Policy," *Survey*, no. 47 (April 1963), pp. 119–33.

34. Shinn, "National Democratic State," p. 378.

35. Lowenthal, "On 'National Democracy,'" p. 131.

36. For an excellent analysis of the issues and the parties in this debate, see Uri Ra'anan, "Moscow and the 'Third World,'" *Problems of Communism* 14, no. 1 (January–February 1965): 22–31.

37. Richard Lowenthal, "Russia, The One Party System, and the Third World," *Survey*, no. 58 (January 1966), pp. 44–45.

38. G. Mirsky, "The Proletariat and National Liberation," *New Times*, no. 18 (May 1, 1964), pp. 6–9; see also K. Brutents, "Integral Part of the World Revolutionary Process," *International Affairs* (Moscow), no. 2 (1964), pp. 30–37.

39. Ra'anan, "Moscow and the 'Third World,'" p. 25.

40. Ibid., p. 26.

41. Ibid.

42. R. A. Yellon, "The Winds of Change," *MIZAN* 9, no. 4 (July–August 1967): 158.

43. G. Kim and A. Kaufman, "Non-Capitalist Development: Achievements and Difficulties," *International Affairs* (Moscow), no. 12 (1967), p. 73.

44. Y. M. Zhukov, "Contemporary Pace of Development of National Liberation Revolutions," *International Affairs* (Moscow), no. 5 (1967), p. 52.

45. N. A. Simoniya, "On the Character of National Liberation Revolutions," *Narody Azii i Afrika*, no. 6 (1966), trans. in *MIZAN* 9, no. 2 (March–April 1967): 44–45; and V. L. Tyagunenko, "Capitalist and Non-Capitalist Development," *International Affairs* (Moscow), no. 5 (1967), p. 58.

46. Kim and Kaufman, "Non-Capitalist Development," p. 74. For further examples in Soviet literature of the extremely cautious assessments of the prospects for rapid transformation of the LDCs into socialist states, see David Morison, "Africa and Asia: Some Trends in Soviet Thinking," *MIZAN* 10, no. 5 (September–October 1968): 167–84; and William Zimmerman, *Soviet Perspectives on International Relations* (Princeton: Princeton University Press, 1969), p. 210.

47. Zimmerman, *Soviet Perspectives*, p. 282.

48. See Yellon, "The Winds of Change," p. 168.

49. "Socialism, Capitalism and the Underdeveloped Countries," *Mirovaya ekonomika i mezhdunarodnye otnoshenia* [World Economics and International Relations], no. 4 (1964), pp. 116–31, and no. 6 (1964), pp. 62–81, trans. in "The USSR and the Developing Countries," *MIZAN* 6, no. 10 (November 1964): 4–5.

50. Ibid., p. 7.

51. Mosely, "Communist Policy," p. 230.

52. Ibid., p. 231; and Herbert S. Dinerstein, "Soviet Doctrines on Developing

Countries: Some Divergent Views," in *New Nations in a Divided World,* ed. Kurt London (New York: Frederick A. Praeger, 1963), p. 82.

53. Marshall I. Goldman, *Soviet Foreign Aid* (New York: Frederick A. Praeger, 1967), p. 68.

54. Donald Zagoria, *The Sino-Soviet Conflict, 1956–1961* (Princeton: Princeton University Press, 1962), p. 252.

55. Ibid.

56. See particularly Simoniya, "National Liberation Revolutions"; and Morison, "Africa and Asia."

57. Dankwart Rustow, *A World of Nations* (Washington, D.C.: Brookings Institution, 1967), p. 275.

58. Jacob Kaplan, *The Challenge of Foreign Aid* (New York: Frederick A. Praeger, 1967), p. 84.

Notes to Chapter 5

1. This is the definition of aid offered by David Bell as administrator of AID. U.S., Senate, Committee on Foreign Relations, *Foreign Assistance Hearings,* 1965, p. 144.

2. Leo Tansky, *U.S. and U.S.S.R. Aid to Developing Countries: A Comparative Study of India, Turkey, and the U.A.R.* (New York: Frederick A. Praeger, 1967), pp. vii–viii.

3. U.S., Agency for International Development, *U.S. Overseas Loans and Grants and Assistance from International Organizations, Obligations and Loan Authorizations July 1, 1945–June 30, 1968,* May 1969, p. 6 (cited hereafter as *Overseas Loans and Grants,* 1969).

4. Throughout this study P.L. 480, Food-For-Peace, and Food-For-Freedom will be used interchangeably to denote the U.S. program for distributing surplus agricultural commodities.

5. Derived from U.S., Agency for International Development, *Operations Report, Data as of June 30, 1968,* 1968, p. 68 (cited hereafter as *Operations Report,* 1968).

6. U.S., Agency for International Development, *Principles of Foreign Economic Assistance,* 1965, p. 20.

7. Ibid.

8. *Operations Report,* 1968, p. 68.

9. Ibid.

10. Ibid., pp. 98–99.

11. See *The Agricultural Trade Development and Assistance Act of 1954,* P.L. 480, 83rd Cong., 2d sess., sect. 2, in U.S., Congress, House, Committee on Foreign Affairs, *Legislation on Foreign Relations,* 89th Cong., 2d sess., 1966, p. 200.

12. U.S., Library of Congress, Legislative Reference Service, *U.S. Foreign Aid: Its Purposes, Scope, Administration and Related Information,* 86th Cong., 1st sess., House doc. no. 116, 1959, p. 75.

13. Derived from *Operations Report,* 1968, pp. 68–69.

14. Derived from U.S., Department of Commerce, Office of Business Economics, *Foreign Grants and Credits by the United States Government,* no. 79, 1965, pp. S-7–S-10.

15. The 12 countries are Greece, Turkey, Iran, Afghanistan, Pakistan, India, Nepal, Burma, Laos, South Vietnam, Taiwan, and South Korea.

16. This figure was derived from *Overseas Loans and Grants,* 1969. In an interesting attempt through regression analysis to assess the relative salience of numerous goals motivating U.S. economic aid to the third world, geographical proximity to the socialist camp was found to be the best predictor of U.S. aid; see Masakatsu Kato, "A Model of U.S. Foreign Aid Allocation: An Application of a Decision Making Scheme," in *Approaches to Measurement in International Relations,* ed. John Mueller (New York: Appleton-Century-Crofts, 1969), pp. 198–215.

17. The 28 countries are the 19 signatories of the Rio Pact (excluding Cuba), Greece, Turkey, Thailand, Pakistan, the Philippines, Iran, Korea, Taiwan, and South Vietnam, which is included even though it is not a formal ally of the United States.

18. Population data found in U.S., Agency for International Development, *Proposed Foreign Aid Program FY 1967,* 1966, pp. 232–36. Assistance figures from U.S., Agency for International Development, *U.S. Overseas Loans and Grants and Assistance from International Organizations, Obligations and Loan Authorizations July 1, 1945–June 30, 1967,* March 1968.

19. A. Alexeyev and Yu. Shiryayev, "Sovyetsky soyuz v ekonomike sovremennovo mira" [The Soviet Union in the Economy of the World Today], *Mirovaya ekonomika i mezhdunarodnye otnoshenia,* no. 3, 1966, p. 27. This figure was still being cited by Soviet sources in 1968. See M. Lavrichenko, "Who is Responsible for Third World Economic Backwardness?", *International Affairs* (Moscow), no. 8 (1968), p. 46.

20. U.S., Department of State, Bureau of Intelligence and Research, *Communist Governments and Developing Nations: Aid and Trade in 1965,* RSB-50, June 17, 1966, p. 2 (cited hereafter as Dept. of State, RSB-50).

21. United Nations, Department of Economic and Social Affairs, *International Flow of Long-Term Capital and Official Donations 1961–1965* (E/4170), 1966, p. 22.

22. Derived from Dept. of State, RSB-50, p. 6; ibid., *Communist Governments and Developing Nations: Aid and Trade in 1967,* RSE-120, August 14, 1968, p. 8 (cited hereafter as Dept. of State, RSE-120); and ibid., *Communist Governments and Developing Nations: Aid and Trade in 1968,* RSE-65, September 5, 1969, p. 4 (cited hereafter as Dept. of State, RSE-65).

23. Leo Tansky, "Soviet Foreign Aid to the Less Developed Countries," in U.S., Congress, Joint Economic Committee, *New Directions in the Soviet Economy,* 89th Cong., 2d sess., 1966, pt. 4 (cited hereafter as Joint Economic Committee, *New Directions*).

24. Ibid.

25. Dept. of State, RSE-120, p. 7.

26. Tansky, *U.S. and U.S.S.R. Aid,* p. 17.

27. Maurice Ernst, "Postwar Economic Growth in Eastern Europe," in Joint Economic Committee, *New Directions,* pt. 4, p. 900.

28. Statement of Robert McNamara in U.S., Congress, Senate Committee on

Foreign Relations, *Hearings, Foreign Assistance Act of 1963*, 88th Cong., 1st sess., 1963, p. 220.

29. Hertha W. Heiss, "The Soviet Union in the World Market," in Joint Economic Committee, *New Directions*, pt. 4, p. 923.

30. Ibid., pp. 924–25.

31. Carole A. Sawyer, *Communist Trade with Developing Countries 1955–1965* (New York: Frederick A. Praeger, 1966), p. 9.

32. Ibid., pp. 11–12.

33. Dept. of State, RSB-50, p. 6.

34. Sawyer, *Communist Trade*, pp. 50–51.

35. I. Kapranov, "The USSR and Industrial Development in the Newly Free States," *International Affairs* (Moscow), no. 6 (1966), p. 35.

36. Sawyer, *Communist Trade*, p. 51.

37. Ibid., pp. 28–31.

38. Ibid., p. 31.

39. Ibid., p. 20, and United Nations, Department of Social Affairs, *Yearbook of International Trade Statistics, 1964* (ST/STAT/SER.G/15), 1966, p. 28.

40. Ibid., p. 34.

41. Soviet GNP in 1964 was calculated to be \$293 billion (Stanley Cohn, "Soviet Growth Retardation: Trends in Resource Availability and Efficiency," in Joint Economic Committee, *New Directions*, pt. 2-A, p. 108). The U.S. GNP figure of \$643 billion in 1964 is from U.S., Agency for International Development, *Gross National Product, Growth Rates and Trend Data*, RC-W-138, March 31, 1967, p. 13.

42. Dept. of State, RSE-65, September 5, 1969, pp. 22–23.

43. Alexander Eckstein, *Communist China's Economic Growth and Foreign Trade* (New York: McGraw-Hill Book Co., 1966), p. 98.

44. Heiss, "The Soviet Union in the World Market," p. 923.

Notes to Chapter 6

1. For a description of this organizational evolution in American aid through 1959, see U.S., Library of Congress, Legislative Reference Service, *U.S. Foreign Aid: Its Purposes, Scope, Administration and Related Information*, 86th Cong., 1st sess., House doc. no. 116, 1959, pp. 69–70 (cited hereafter as Legislative Reference Service, *U.S. Foreign Aid*).

2. C. Tyler Wood, "Problems of Foreign Aid Viewed from the Inside," *American Economic Review: Papers and Proceedings* 49, no. 2 (May 1959): 204.

3. Legislative Reference Service, *U.S. Foreign Aid*, p. 70.

4. U.S., Congress, Senate, Special Committee to Study the Foreign Aid Program, *Foreign Aid Program, Compilation of Studies and Surveys*, 85th Cong., 1st sess., 1957, p. 426 (cited hereafter as U.S., Senate, *Foreign Aid Program*, 1957).

5. Legislative Reference Service, *U.S. Foreign Aid*, p. 70.

6. Ibid.

7. These results are vividly presented in a press release of a former deputy-director of U.S. economic assistance: D. A. Fitzgerald, "Musical Chairs in the

Foreign-Assistance Program," in *Foreign Aid and American Foreign Policy,* ed. David A. Baldwin (New York: Frederick A. Praeger, 1966), pp. 134–38.

8. Ibid., p. 135.

9. Ibid., p. 136.

10. U.S., General Services Administration, National Archives and Records Service, Office of the Federal Register, *United States Government Organization Manual, 1967–1968,* June 1, 1967, p. 91.

11. Ibid., p. 92.

12. Ibid.

13. Ibid.

14. U.S., Congress, Senate, Committee on Foreign Relations, *Hearings, International Development and Security,* 87th Cong., 1st sess., 1961, p. 328.

15. This discussion was taken largely from an AID memorandum submitted to Congress—U.S., Congress, Senate, Committee on Foreign Relations, *Hearings, Foreign Assistance, 1965,* 89th Cong., 1st sess., 1965, pp. 585–87. At present the programming process is being altered to implement the "Planning-Programming-Budgeting System" (PPBS) approach to programming which is being introduced to many government agencies. In essence, the PPBS involves an agency's stating broad objectives, then proceeding to outline specific program goals required to achieve these objectives, and, finally, determining what resource and other inputs are needed to carry out the program goals. However, these changes do not significantly alter the basic thrust of existing AID programming. Also, see U.S., Agency for International Development, *Principles of Foreign Economic Assistance,* 1965, p. 45 (cited hereafter as AID, *Principles,* 1965); statement of William S. Gaud before the Subcommittee on National Security and International Operations of the Senate Government Operations Committee, July 11, 1968, mimeographed; and U.S., Congress, House, Committee on Foreign Affairs, *Hearings, Foreign Assistance Act of 1968,* 90th Cong., 2d sess., 1968, pp. 455–58.

16. AID, *Principles,* 1965, p. 45.

17. U.S., Congress, Senate, Committee on Foreign Relations, *Legislation on Foreign Relations,* Joint Committee Print, 90th Cong., 1st sess., 1967, p. 216.

18. AID, *Principles,* 1965, p. 24.

19. U.S., Congress, Senate, Committee on Foreign Relations, Subcommittee on Technical Assistance Programs, *Soviet Technical Assistance,* Staff Study no. 7, 85th Cong., 2d sess., 1956, p. 6.

20. Marshall I. Goldman, *Soviet Foreign Aid* (New York: Frederick A. Praeger, 1967), p. 75.

21. Ibid., p. 76.

22. Ibid.

23. Waldemar Nielson and Z. S. Hodjera, "Sino-Soviet Bloc Technical Assistance," *The Annals of the American Academy of Political and Social Science* 323 (May 1959), p. 45.

24. See George S. Carnett and Morris H. Crawford, "The Scope and Distribution of Soviet Economic Aid," in U.S., Congress, Joint Economic Committee, *Hearings, Dimensions of Soviet Economic Power,* 87th Cong., 2d sess., December 11, 1962, p. 466.

25. Goldman, *Soviet Foreign Aid,* p. 76. See Figure 2.

26. U.S., Department of State, *The Sino-Soviet Economic Offensive in the Less*

Developed Countries, Department of State Publication, no. 6632, May 1958, p. 28.

27. Goldman, *Soviet Foreign Aid,* p. 76.

28. Council for Economic Research, Inc., "Foreign Assistance Activities of the Communist Bloc and their Implications for the United States," Study no. 8, in U.S., Senate, *Foreign Aid Program,* 1957, p. 629.

29. Goldman, *Soviet Foreign Aid,* p. 76.

30. Some of the foregoing was derived from a personal interview with Milton Kovner, U.S. Department of State, Bureau of Intelligence and Research, Chief of Bloc International Economic Activities Division, May 9, 1967.

31. Skachkov, for example, led the Soviet delegation in the talks with India resulting in the Soviet offer of $330 million for the fourth Indian five-year plan, *New York Times,* December 11, 1966, p. 11.

32. Nielson and Hodjera, "Sino-Soviet Bloc Technical Assistance," p. 46.

33. Ibid., and Leo Tansky, "Soviet Foreign Aid to the Less Developed Countries," in U.S., Congress, Joint Economic Committee, *New Directions in the Soviet Economy,* 89th Cong., 2d sess., 1966, pt. 4, p. 955.

34. Tansky, "Soviet Foreign Aid to the Less Developed Countries," p. 955. In recent years the USSR has begun to place more emphasis on the relevance of its experience in economic planning for LDC development, and Gosplan personnel have been sent to help the United Arab Republic, Afghanistan, Algeria, and other LDCs in drawing up plans. See R. Andreasyan, "Soviet Experience and the Developing Countries," *International Affairs* (Moscow), no. 8 (1967), pp. 17–22.

35. I. Kapranov, "The USSR and Industrial Development in the Newly Free States," *International Affairs* (Moscow), no. 6 (1966), p. 34.

36. Klaus Billerbeck, *Soviet Bloc Foreign Aid to the Underdeveloped Countries* (Hamburg, Germany: Verlag Weltarchiv GMBH, 1960), p. 55.

37. Tansky, "Soviet Foreign Aid to the Less Developed Countries," p. 953.

38. Charles Wolf, *Foreign Aid: Theory and Practice in Southern Asia* (Princeton: Princeton University Press, 1960), p. 394.

39. Nielson and Hodjera, "Sino-Soviet Bloc Technical Assistance," p. 46.

Notes to Chapter 7

1. U.S., Agency for International Development, *Principles of Foreign Economic Assistance,* 1965, p. 36 (cited hereafter as AID, Principles, 1965).

2. Robert Asher, *Grants, Loans, and Local Currencies* (Washington, D.C.: Brookings Institution, 1961), p. 90.

3. John P. Lewis, *Quiet Crisis in India* (Washington, D.C.: Brookings Institution, 1962), p. 276.

4. U.S., Congress, Senate, Committee on Foreign Relations, *Hearings, Foreign Assistance Act, 1965,* 89th Cong., 1st sess., 1965, p. 436.

5. U.S., Congress, House, Committee on Foreign Affairs, *Hearings, Foreign Assistance Act of 1965,* 89th Cong., 1st sess., 1965, p. 1123.

6. Ibid.

7. Ibid., p. 1124. See also U.S., Agency for International Development, *Proposed Foreign Aid Program FY 1968,* 1967, pp. 248–49.

8. Joan Nelson, *Aid, Influence and Foreign Policy* (New York: Macmillan Co., 1968), p. 78.

9. AID, *Principles*, 1965, p. 35.

10. U.S., Congress, House, Committee on Foreign Affairs, *Hearings, Foreign Assistance Act of 1965*, 89th Cong., 1st sess., 1965, p. 1124.

11. AID, *Principles*, 1965, p. 36.

12. U.S., Agency for International Development, *Operations Report*, data as of June 30, 1963, 1964, 1965, 1966, 1967, and 1968.

13. Since 1968 a good deal of emphasis has been placed on sector loans as a new type of disbursement mechanism lying somewhere between program and project assistance. Sector loans resemble program loans except that they are confined to use within a particular sector of the economy such as agriculture, education, or health. For example, sector loans have been disbursed to Ecuador, Brazil, and Chile for the development of education. See U.S., Congress, House, Committee on Appropriations, *Hearings, Foreign Assistance and Related Agencies, Appropriations for 1969*, pt. 2, 90th Cong., 2d sess., 1968, p. 68; and U.S., Agency for International Development, *U.S. Foreign Aid and the Alliance for Progress*, 1968.

14. U.S., Congress, Senate, Committee on Foreign Relations, *Hearings, Foreign Assistance Act of 1962*, 87th Cong., 2d sess., 1962, p. 106.

15. U.S., Agency for International Development, *Operations Report, Data as of June 30, 1967*, 1967, p. 19 (cited hereafter as *Operations Report, 1967*), and *Operations Report, Data as of June 30, 1968*, 1968, p. 21 (cited hereafter as *Operations Report, 1968*).

16. AID, *Principles*, 1965, p. 21.

17. U.S., Congress, Senate, Committee on Foreign Relations, *Hearings, Foreign Assistance Act of 1967*, 90th Cong., 1st sess., 1967, p. 195.

18. AID, *Principles*, 1965, p. 20.

19. AID, *Operations Report*, 1968, p. 120.

20. Ibid., pp. 123 and 125.

21. Ibid., p. 123.

22. Ibid., p. 125.

23. Organization for Economic Cooperation and Development, Development Assistance Committee, *Development Assistance, 1968 Review*, 1968, pp. 276–77 (cited hereafter as OECD, *Development Assistance, 1968*).

24. For a summary of the main fields of study for LDC nationals in the United States who are publicly financed, see Organization for Economic Cooperation and Development, Development Assistance Committee, *Development Assistance Efforts and Policies, 1967 Review*, 1967, pp. 198–201.

25. AID, *Principles*, 1965, p. 44.

26. Ibid., pp. 44–45.

27. AID, *Operations Report*, 1968, p. 98.

28. AID, *Operations Report*, 1967, p. 100.

29. AID, *Principles*, 1965, p. 4.

30. Andrew F. Westwood, *Foreign Aid in a Foreign Policy Framework* (Washington, D.C.: Brookings Institution, 1966), p. 89.

31. See Max Millikan and W. W. Rostow, *A Proposal: Key to an Effective Foreign Policy* (New York: Harper and Brothers, 1957), pp. 52–53.

32. AID, *Principles*, 1965, p. 45.

33. For a discussion of changes in U.S. policy concerning the use of soft loans, grants, and commercial transfers to the less developed countries, see David Baldwin, *Economic Development and American Foreign Policy* (Chicago: University of Chicago Press, 1966).

34. AID, *Principles*, 1965, pp. 22–23; and U.S., Agency for International Development, *Program Guidance Manual*, Order no. 1012.7, pp. 1–7.

35. Ibid.

36. Leo Tansky, *U.S. and U.S.S.R. Aid to Developing Countries: A Comparative Study of India, Turkey, and the U.A.R.* (New York: Frederick A. Praeger, 1967), p. 170.

37. AID, *Program Guidance Manual*, Order no. 1011.2, p. 2.

38. See U.S., Congress, House, Committee on Foreign Affairs, *Hearings, Foreign Assistance Act of 1966*, 89th Cong., 2d sess., 1966, pp. 33–34.

39. This line of argument is presented in Charles Wolf, Jr., "Economic Aid Reconsidered," *Yale Review* 50, no. 4 (June 1961): 520.

40. James Schlesinger, *The Political Economy of National Security* (New York: Frederick A. Praeger, 1960), p. 235.

41. Leo Tansky, "Soviet Foreign Aid to Less Developed Countries," in U.S., Congress, Joint Economic Committee, *New Directions in the Soviet Economy*, 89th Cong., 2d sess., 1966, pt. 4, p. 953.

42. Ibid., p. 961.

43. Ibid.

44. Ibid., p. 954.

45. Ibid., p. 955.

46. Tansky, *U.S. and U.S.S.R. Aid*, 1967, p. 30.

47. Ibid., pp. 29–30.

48. "The USSR and the Developing Countries," *MIZAN* 6, no. 10 (November 1964): 4–5.

49. Tansky, "Soviet Foreign Aid to the Less Developed Countries," p. 955.

50. Ibid., pp. 955–56.

51. I. Kapranov, "The USSR and Industrial Development in the Newly Free States," *International Affairs* (Moscow), no. 6 (1966), p. 35.

52. U.S., Congress, Senate, Committee on Foreign Relations, *Hearings, Foreign Assistance Act of 1962*, 87th Cong., 2d sess., 1962, p. 267.

53. Tansky, "Soviet Foreign Aid to the Less Developed Countries," p. 960.

54. Ibid., and estimates for 1966 to 1968 from U.S., Department of State, Bureau of Intelligence and Research, *Communist Governments and Developing Nations: Economic Aid and Trade*, Research Memorandum, RSB-80, 1967, p. 6 (cited hereafter as Dept. of State, RSB-80); ibid., *Communist Governments and Developing Nations: Aid and Trade in 1967*, Research Memorandum, RSE-120, August 1968, p. 11; and ibid., *Communist Governments and Developing Nations: Aid and Trade in 1968*, Research Memorandum, RSE-65, September 5, 1969, p. 10 (cited hereafter as Dept. of State, RSE-65).

55. Dept. of State, RSE-65, p. 10.

56. Janos Horvath, "Moscow's Aid Program: The Performance So Far," *East Europe* 12, no. 11 (November 1963): 15.

57. Ibid.

58. Waldemar Nielson and Z. S. Hodjera, "Sino-Soviet Bloc Technical Assistance," *The Annals of the American Academy of Political and Social Science* 323 (May 1959): 47.

59. Tansky, "Soviet Foreign Aid to the Less Developed Countries," p. 961.

60. U.S., Congress, House, Committee on Foreign Affairs, *Hearings, Mutual Security Act, 1957*, 85th Cong., 1st sess., 1957, p. 1620.

61. U.S., Congress, Senate, Committee on Foreign Relations, *Hearings, Foreign Assistance Act of 1962*, 87th Cong., 2d sess., 1962, p. 269.

62. *New York Times*, May 13, 1966, p. 10.

63. U.S., Congress, Senate, Committee on Foreign Relations, *Hearings, Foreign Assistance Act of 1962*, 87th Cong., 2d sess., p. 269.

64. *Izvestia*, July 6, 1960, trans. in *Current Digest of the Soviet Press*, 12, no. 27 (August 3, 1960): 18.

65. U.S., Congress, Senate, Committee on Foreign Relations, *Hearings, Foreign Assistance Act of 1962*, 87th Cong., 2d sess., 1962, p. 269.

66. See U.S., Congress, Senate, Committee on Foreign Relations, *Hearings, Foreign Assistance Act of 1965*, 89th Cong., 1st sess., 1965, p. 589.

67. Table 9.

68. Ibid.

69. Dept. of State, RSB-80, p. 9.

70. Dept. of State, RSE-65, p. 11.

71. See I. Kapranov, "The USSR's Technical Assistance to Foreign Countries," *Vneshnyaya torgovlya* [Foreign Trade], no. 6, 1961, trans. in *Problems of Economics* 4, no. 12 (April 1962): 49.

72. Tansky, "Soviet Foreign Aid to the Less Developed Countries," p. 957.

73. L. Zevin, "The Mutual Advantage of Economic Cooperation Between the Socialist and Developing Countries," *Voprosi ekonomiki* [Problems of Economics] no. 2, 1965, trans. in *American Review of Soviet and East European Foreign Trade* 1, no. 4 (July–August 1965): 37.

74. Ibid.

75. Ibid., p. 38.

76. Ibid., p. 45.

77. United Nations, *Proceedings of the United Nations Conference on Trade and Development*, vol. 5, 1964, p. 358.

78. United Nations, *World Economic Survey, 1965*, 1966, p. 114.

79. Zevin, "Mutual Advantage," p. 49.

80. See Henry Aubrey, *Coexistence: Economic Challenge and Response* (Washington, D.C.: National Planning Association, 1961), p. 270.

Notes to Chapter 8

1. U.S., Agency or International Development, *Program Guidance Manual*, Order no. 1011.6, p. 3.

2. U.S., Agency for International Development, *Overseas Loans and Grants and Assistance from International Organizations, Obligations and Authorizations July*

1, 1945–June 30, 1968, May 1969, p. 6 (cited hereafter as *Overseas Loans and Grants,* 1969).

3. U.S., Senate, Committee on Foreign Relations, *Hearings, Mutual Security Act of 1954,* 83rd Cong., 2d sess., 1954, p. 68.

4. John P. Lewis, *Quiet Crisis in India* (Washington, D.C.: Brookings Institution, 1962), p. 307.

5. U.S., Senate, Committee on Foreign Relations, *Hearings, Mutual Security Act of 1954,* 83rd Cong., 2d sess., 1954, pp. 68–69.

6. L. Stepanov, "Soviet Aid and its Critics," *International Affairs* (Moscow), no. 6 (1960), p. 24; and Joseph S. Berliner, *Soviet Economic Aid* (New York: Frederick A. Praeger, 1958), p. 147.

7. Upon the resumption of U.S. aid to Burma in 1957, the premier is reported to have expressed a distinct preference for loans over grants, because the former created a more solid basis for friendship and mutual respect (Berliner, *Soviet Economic Aid,* p. 148).

8. U.S., Congress, Senate, Committee on Foreign Relations, *Hearings, Foreign Assistance, 1966,* 89th Cong., 1st sess., 1965, p. 90.

9. Organization for Economic Cooperation and Development, Development Assistance Committee, *Development Assistance, 1968 Review,* 1968, p. 62 (cited hereafter as OECD, *Development Assistance,* 1968).

10. Ibid., and OECD, *Development Assistance Efforts and Policies, 1967 Review,* 1967, p. 76 (cited hereafter as OECD, *Development Assistance,* 1967).

11. *The Agricultural Trade Development and Assistance Act of 1954, as Amended,* Title I, sec. 103, in U.S., Senate, Committee on Foreign Relations, *Legislation on Foreign Relations,* 90th Cong., 1st sess., 1967, p. 203.

12. See OECD, *Development Assistance,* 1967, p. 76; and ibid., 1968, p. 62.

13. *Overseas Loans and Grants,* 1969, p. 6.

14. *The Foreign Assistance Act of 1961, as Amended,* pt. 3, chap. 1, sec. 620, in U.S., Congress, Senate, Committee on Foreign Relations, *Legislation on Foreign Relations,* 90th Cong., 1st sess., 1967, p. 46.

15. Ibid., sec. 603, p. 37.

16. *New York Times,* January 23, 1967, p. 1.

17. See George Liska, *The New Statecraft* (Chicago: University of Chicago Press, 1960), p. 103.

18. See David E. Bell, "The Quality of Aid," *Foreign Affairs* 44, no. 4 (July 1966): 602.

19. *The Foreign Assistance Act of 1961, as Amended,* pt. 3, chap. 1, sec. 603, in U.S., Congress, Senate, Committee on Foreign Relations, *Legislation on Foreign Relations,* 90th Cong., 1st sess., 1967, p. 37.

20. Ibid., sec. 602, p. 37.

21. David Wrightman, "Food Aid and Economic Development," *International Conciliation,* no. 567 (March 1968), pp. 42–43.

22. U.S., Congress, House, Committee on Appropriations, *Hearings, Foreign Assistance and Related Agencies, Appropriations for 1969,* pt. 2, 90th Cong., 2d sess., 1968, p. 381.

23. *New York Times,* February 6, 1969, p. 9.

24. UN document TD/7/Sup.8, p. 15. John Pincus, on the other hand, reports that one study of twenty aid projects showed that "bids from tied sources have

been around 50 per cent more expensive than the lowest competitive worldwide bids on the same projects." See *Trade, Aid and Development* (New York: McGraw-Hill Book Co., 1967), p. 311.

25. The concept of "double tying" and its consequences are developed more completely in Lewis, *Quiet Crisis*, pp. 278–85.

26. I. Kapranov, "The USSR's Technical Assistance to Foreign Countries," *Vneshnyaya torgovlya* [Foreign Trade], no. 6, 1961, trans. in *Problems of Economics* 4, no. 12 (April 1962): 49.

27. Leo Tansky, "Soviet Foreign Aid to the Less Developed Countries," in U.S., Congress, Joint Economic Committee, *New Directions in the Soviet Economy*, 89th Cong., 2d sess., 1966, pt. 4, pp. 953–54.

28. Marshall I. Goldman, *Soviet Foreign Aid* (New York: Frederick A. Praeger, 1967), p. 117.

29. Ibid., p. 206.

30. E. Glovinsky, "Soviet Economic Expansion in the Developing Countries," *Studies on the Soviet Union* 1 (n.s.), no. 2 (November 1961): 189.

31. V. Rimalov, *Economic Cooperation Between the USSR and Underdeveloped Countries* (Moscow: Foreign Language Publishing House, 1961), p. 50.

32. For a good discussion of the Soviet preference for credit over grant assistance in which many of these same points are made, see Berliner, *Soviet Economic Aid*, pp. 144–50.

33. These are foreign trade rubles valued at 1r = $1.11. They are not the same as domestic rubles because of the revaluation in 1961 in which a new domestic ruble equals ten old rubles and a foreign trade ruble equals 4.44 old rubles. All goods exported from the Soviet Union under trade and aid agreements are sold at world market prices expressed in foreign trade rubles calculated at the official exchange rate from the prices in convertible currency (such as U.S. dollars). These prices in foreign trade rubles have no relation to Soviet internal prices expressed in domestic rubles.

34. U.S., Department of State, Bureau of Intelligence and Research, *The Sino-Soviet Economic Offensive Through June 30, 1962*, p. 24.

35. U.S., Dept. of State, Bureau of Intelligence and Research, *The Communist Economic Offensive through 1963*, RSB-43, p. 21 (cited hereafter as Dept. of State, RSB-43).

36. U.S., House, Committee on Foreign Affairs, *Hearings, Foreign Assistance Act of 1967*, 90th Cong., 1st sess., 1967, p. 97. See also Franklyn Holzman, "Soviet Trade and Aid Policies," *Proceedings, The American Academy of Political Science* 29, no. 3 (1969): 111.

37. For example, see "The Agreement on Economic and Technical Cooperation Between the Union of Soviet socialist Republics and the Republic of Egypt," in Goldman, *Soviet Foreign Aid*, p. 225.

38. Leo Tansky, *U.S. and U.S.S.R. Aid to Developing Countries: A Comparative Study of India, Turkey, and the U.A.R.* (New York: Frederick A. Praeger, 1967), p. 109.

39. Derived from U.S., Agency for International Development, *Overseas Loans and Grants and Assistance from International Organizations, Obligations and Authorizations, July 1, 1945–June 30, 1966*, March 1967.

40. OECD, *Development Assistance*, 1967, p. 76; and ibid., 1968, p. 62.

41. Ibid.

42. U.S., Department of State, Bureau of Intelligence and Research, *Communist Governments and Developing Nations: Aid and Trade in 1967*, RSE-120, 1968, p. 7; and Franklyn D. Holzman, "Soviet Trade," p. 111.

43. See Dept. of State, RSB-43, p. 11.

44. For an example of technical assistance financed by a Development Loan, see U.S., Agency for International Development, *Tunisia, Country Assistance Program, FY 1967*, pt. II, October 1965, p. 141 (unclassified).

45. See Robert L. Allen, "The Soviet and East European Foreign Credit Program," *American Slavic and East European Review* 16, no. 4 (December 1957): 439; and William B. Ballis, "Soviet-Iranian Relations During the Decade 1953–1964," *Bulletin, Institute for the Study of the USSR* 12, no. 11 (November 1965): 13–14.

46. A. B. Scott, "Soviet Economic Relations with the Underdeveloped Countries," *Soviet Studies* 10, no. 1 (July 1958): 51.

47. See Harry Schwartz, *Russia's Soviet Economy*, 2d ed. (Englewood Cliffs, N.J.: Prentice-Hall, 1954), pp. 478–80.

48. Janos Horvath, "Moscow's Aid Program: The Performance So Far," *East Europe* 12, no. 11 (November 1963): 17.

49. Alexander Eckstein, *Communist China's Economic Growth and Foreign Trade* (New York: McGraw-Hill Book Co., 1966), pp. 144–45.

50. Milton Kovner, *The Challenge of Coexistence*, (Washington, D.C.: Public Affairs Press, 1961), p. 74.

51. Ibid., pp. 61–68.

52. *Capital*, Calcutta, November 14, 1957, in Henry Aubrey, *Coexistence Economic Challenge and Response* (Washington, D.C.: National Planning Association, 1961), p. 232.

53. Hans Heymann, Jr., "Soviet Foreign Aid as a Problem for U.S. Policy," *World Politics* 7, no. 4 (July 1960): 532.

54. Ibid.

Notes to Chapter 9

1. U.S. figures as reported in the *Yearbook of the United Nations* (New York: United Nations, various years) are projected estimates based on 40 percent of the total pledged contributions each year. This is the maximum percentage possible for actual contributions to the UNDP since 1961.

2. U.S., Congress, House Committee on Appropriations, Subcommittee on Foreign Operations and Related Agencies, *Hearings, Foreign Assistance and Related Agencies, Appropriations for 1968*, 90th Cong., 1st sess., 1967, pt. 2, p. 1610.

3. Ibid., p. 1701. The difference in the figures cited in the text and those from this source is a result of adding the figures for Byelorussia SSR and Ukraine SSR to those for the USSR given on p. 1701.

4. For a different assessment of U.S. and USSR aid to multilateral agencies vs. bilateral aid, see A. Z. Rubinstein, "Soviet and American Policies in International

Economic Organizations," *International Organization* 18, no. 1 (Winter 1964): 34–35.

5. Alvin Z. Rubinstein, *The Soviets in International Organizations* (Princeton: Princeton University Press, 1964), p. 25.

6. Harold K. Jacobson, *The USSR and the UN's Economic and Social Activities* (Notre Dame, Ind.: University of Notre Dame Press, 1963), pp. 248–50.

7. See I. Oleshchenko, "The Export of Capital to South-East Asia," *International Affairs* (Moscow), no. 8 (1958), pp. 47–68.

8. John G. Stoessinger, *The United Nations and the Superpowers* (New York: Random House, 1965), p. 155.

9. A statement of the economic grounds for U.S. opposition to the project was made before the U.S. Congress, Senate Committee on Foreign Relations, Subcommittee on International Organization Affairs, *Hearings, United Nations Special Fund,* 88th Cong., 1st sess., 1963, pp. 25–28. This statement is summarized in Stoessinger, *United Nations,* p. 156.

10. Ibid. (*Hearings, United Nations Special Fund*), p. 2.

11. U.S., Congress, Senate, Committee on Foreign Relations, *Legislation on Foreign Relations,* 90th Cong., 2d sess., 1968, p. 25.

12. The discussion of SUNFED to this point has been taken primarily from Rubinstein, *The Soviets in International Organizations,* pp. 91–102. See also Jacobson, *The USSR and the UN,* pp. 256–59; and John Hadwen and Johan Kaufmann, *How United Nations Decisions are Made* (New York: Oceana Publications, 1962) pp. 85–114.

13. UN document E/3393, Annex, p. 5.

14. Ibid., p. 3.

15. UN document A/4648.

16. Harold K. Jacobson, "Economic and Social Matters," in *The United States and the United Nations,* ed. Franz B. Gross (Norman, Oklahoma: University of Oklahoma Press, 1964), p. 259.

17. *Yearbook of the United Nations,* 1962, pp. 244–45.

18. UN document E/3790, p. 16.

19. *UN Monthly Chronicle* 4, no. 1 (January 1967): 108–09.

20. UN document A/C.2/SR 1083, p. 354. It is interesting to note the difference between the stand of the United States on this budgetary issue and its earlier stand regarding contributions to the Suez and Congo operations during the financial crisis of the United Nations culminating in 1964.

21. UN document A/C.2/SR. 1085, pp. 366–67.

22. UN document A/Conf. 37/SR.1 and 2. The second pledging conference, held on November 18, 1968, yielded similar results. Thirty-one governments made pledges totaling the equivalent of $1.4 million and the developed countries continued their opposition to the program. See *UN Monthly Chronicle* 5, no. 11 (December 1968): 99–100; and UN document A/Conf.41/2.

23. *UN Monthly Chronicle* 5, no. 1 (January 1968): 88–89.

24. For a Western diplomat's view on this point, see Rubinstein, *The Soviets in International Organizations,* p. 101.

25. Sidney Weintraub, "After the UN Trade Conference: Lessons and Portents," *Foreign Affairs* 43, no. 1 (October 1964): 37.

26. *New York Times,* March 22, 1964, III, p. 10.

27. John Pincus, *Trade, Aid and Development,* (New York: McGraw-Hill Book Co., 1967), p. 84.

28. J. C. Mills, "Canada at UNCTAD," *International Journal* 20 (Spring 1965): 214, cited in Harry G. Johnson, *Economic Policies Toward Less Developed Countries* (Washington, D.C.: Brookings Institution, 1967), p. 7.

29. See Johnson, *Economic Policies,* Appendix B, pp. 251–54.

30. See Jacobson, *The USSR and the UN,* pp. 208–12.

31. M. Lavrichenko, "Barometer of Interstate Relations," *International Affairs* (Moscow), no. 1 (1964), p. 62.

32. See Johnson, *Economic Policies,* Appendix B, pp. 251–54. The USSR abstained on the votes for the other two principles.

33. UN document E/Conf. 46/P.C./SR. 27, pp. 5–6.

34. UN document E/Conf. 46/C.1/SR. 14, p. 10.

35. UN document E/Conf. 46/C.1/SR. 7, p. 3.

36. UN document E/Conf. 46/C.1/SR. 41, p. 8.

37. For a description and evaluation of the GATT Action Program, see Johnson, *Economic Policies,* pp. 19–21; and Pincus, *Trade, Aid, and Development,* pp. 258–60.

38. UN document E/Conf. 46/C.2/SR. 27, p. 8 and E/Conf. 46/C.2/SR. 8, p. 9.

39. UN document E/Conf. 46/C.2/SR. 24, pp. 4–5.

40. UN document E/Conf. 46/C.2/SR. 25, pp. 5–6.

41. UN document E/Conf. 46/C.1/SR. 21, p. 5.

42. UN document E/Conf. 46/C.4/SR. 16, p. 5. Emphasis mine.

43. UN document E/Conf. 46/P.C./SR. 32, p. 7.

44. UN document E/Conf. 46/C.3/SR. 8, pp. 12–13.

45. UN document E/Conf. 46/C.3/SR. 19, p. 8.

46. UN document E/Conf. 46/C.3/SR. 40, p. 8.

47. UN document E/Conf. 46/C. 1/SR. 34, p. 3.

48. UN document E/Conf. 46/C.4/SR. 22, pp. 4–5.

49. UN document E/Conf. 46/51.

50. Johnson, *Economic Policies,* pp. 3–4.

51. Richard N. Gardner, *In Pursuit of World Order,* rev. ed. (New York: Frederick A. Praeger, 1966), pp. 164–65.

52. Ibid. See also UN document E/Conf. 46/C.3/SR. 32, p. 8.

53. S. Amjad Ali, "United Nations Conference on Trade and Development," *Pakistan Horizon* 13, no. 3 (1964): 265.

54. For a vigorous attack on East-West polemics at UNCTAD-I, see the statement by Ceylon in UN document E/Conf. 46/C.5/SR. 21, p. 7.

55. I. Shantalov, "In a Single Revolutionary Torrent," *International Affairs* (Moscow), no. 9 (1967), p. 22.

56. UN document TD/5/Add. 1, pt. II, p. 34.

57. Eugene Rostow, "From Aid to Cooperation: Development Strategy in the Next Decade," in U.S., Department of State, *Bulletin* 58, no. 1498 (March 11, 1968): 364.

58. John W. Evans, "The General Agreement on Tariffs and Trade," *International Organization* 22, no. 1 (Winter 1968): 84–88.

59. Richard Gardner, "The United Nations Conference on Trade and Development," *International Organization* 22, no. 1 (Winter 1968): 109.

60. UN document TD/56.

61. Gardner, "The United Nations Conference on Trade and Development," p. 109; and Roy Blough, "The World Bank Group," *International Organization* 22, no. 1 (Winter 1968): 159–60.

62. *Pravda,* March 5, 1967; trans. in *Current Digest of the Soviet Press* 19, no. 9 (March 22, 1967): 21.

63. UN document TD/60, p. 24.

64. A. Zakharov and L. Lobanov, "The UN and the Urgent Problems of the Developing Countries," *International Affairs* (Moscow), no. 5, (1968), p. 31.

65. *New York Times,* March 4, 1968, p. 52.

66. Ibid., March 31, 1968, III, p. 1. See also *UN Monthly Chronicle* 5, no. 4 (April 1968): 74–81; and UN document TD/L. 37, Annex I.

67. See *New York Times,* March 31, 1968, III, p. 1.

68. *UN Monthly Chronicle* 5, no. 4 (April 1968): 78.

69. L. Stepanov, "Summing Up," *New Times,* no. 15 (1968), p. 10.

Notes to Chapter 10

1. Leo Tansky, *U.S. and U.S.S.R. Aid to Developing Countries: A Comparative Study of India, Turkey, and the U.A.R.* (New York: Frederick A. Praeger, 1967), p. 171.

2. See Paul F. Sigmund, Jr., *The Ideologies of the Developing Nations* (New York: Frederick A. Praeger, 1963), pp. 103 and 133–34.

3. Henry Aubrey, *Coexistence: Economic Challenge and Response* (Washington, D.C.: National Planning Association, 1961), p. 257.

4. For an elaboration of this theme, see ibid., pp. 256–58.

5. Ibid., p. 256.

6. Ibid.

7. Harry G. Johnson, *Economic Policies Toward Less Developed Countries* (Washington, D.C.: Brookings Institution, 1967), p. 3.

8. Aubrey, *Coexistence,* p. 200.

9. U.S., Congress, House, Committee on Foreign Affairs, *Hearings, Mutual Security Act of 1955,* 84th Cong., 1st sess., 1955, p. 538.

10. D. S. Carlisle, "The Changing Soviet Perception of the Development Process in the Afro-Asian World," *Midwest Journal of Political Science* 8, no. 4 (November 1964): 406.

11. See V. Rimalov, *Economic Cooperation Between the USSR and Underdeveloped Countries* (Moscow: Foreign Language Publishing House, 1961), p. 13.

12. See *Pravda,* August 7, 1963, trans. in *Current Digest of the Soviet Press* (cited hereafter as *CDSP*) 15, no. 32 (September 4, 1963): 5.

13. *New York Times,* June 15, 1968, p. 5.

14. Klaus Billerbeck, *Soviet Bloc Foreign Aid to the Underdeveloped Countries* (Hamburg, Germany: Verlag Weltarchiv GMBH, 1960), p. 14.

15. Joseph S. Berliner, *Soviet Economic Aid* (New York: Frederick A. Praeger, 1958), p. 159.

16. Ibid.

17. Robert L. Allen, *Soviet Economic Warfare* (Washington, D.C.: Public Affairs Press, 1960), p. 236.

18. Ibid., p. 195.

19. U.S., Congress, Senate, Committee on Foreign Relations, *Hearings, Foreign Assistance Act of 1962,* 87th Cong., 2d sess., 1962, p. 266.

20. Carole A. Sawyer, *Communist Trade with Developing Countries 1955–1965* (New York: Frederick A. Praeger, 1966), p. 46.

21. See Allen, *Soviet Economic Warfare,* pp. 236–37; and Aubrey, *Coexistence,* p. 211.

22. Marshall I. Goldman, *Soviet Foreign Aid* (New York: Frederick A. Praeger, 1967), p. 128.

23. Ibid., p. 170.

24. Ibid.

25. U.S., Congress, Senate, Committee on Foreign Relations, *Hearings, Foreign Assistance Act of 1962,* 87th Cong., 2d sess., 1962, p. 268.

26. Ibid., p. 367.

27. *Ekonomicheskaya gazeta,* March 1, 1961, pp. 3–4, trans. in *CDSP* 8, no. 12 (April 19, 1961): 25–26.

28. Billerbeck, *Soviet Bloc Foreign Aid,* p. 15.

29. Sawyer, *Communist Trade,* p. 65.

30. Ibid.

31. Organization for Economic Cooperation and Development, Development Assistance Committee, *Development Assistance, 1968 Review,* 1968, p. 134 (cited hereafter as OECD, *Development Assistance, 1968*).

32. Ibid.

33. George Woods, "The Development Decade in the Balance," *Foreign Affairs* 44, no. 2 (January 1966): 212.

34. U.S., Library of Congress, Legislative Reference Service, *Some Important Issues in Foreign Aid,* August 4, 1966, p. 69 (cited hereafter as Legislative Reference Service, *Issues in Foreign Aid*).

35. U.S., Congress, House, Committee on Foreign Affairs, *Hearings, Foreign Assistance Act of 1969,* 91st Cong., 1st sess., 1969, p. 797.

36. Ibid. Also, in 1958 the United States and other Western aid donors agreed to revise India's payment schedule because of India's exchange crisis. Tansky, *U.S. and U.S.S.R. Aid,* p. 109.

37. In 1966 the United States and six other Western countries agreed to give Indonesia up to 12 more years to repay $357 million owed to them. *Washington Post,* December 21, 1966, p. A1.

38. In 1967 the United States agreed to let Poland use $9.5 million for a joint program of training English language teachers in lieu of repayment to the United States, *New York Times,* April 12, 1967, p. 16.

39. U.S., Congress, House, Committee of Foreign Affairs, *Hearings, Foreign Assistance Act of 1966,* 89th Cong., 2d sess., 1966, p. 522.

40. Legislative Reference Service, *Issues in Foreign Aid,* p. 69.

41. Kapranov, "The USSR and Industrial Development in the Newly Free States," *International Affairs* (Moscow), no. 6 (1966): 35.

42. Leo Tansky, "Soviet Foreign Aid to the Less Developed Countries," in U.S., Congress, Joint Economic Committee, *New Directions in the Soviet Economy,* 89th Cong., 2d sess., 1966, pt. 4, p. 957 (cited hereafter as Joint Economic Committee, *New Directions*).

43. Goldman, *Soviet Foreign Aid,* p. 111. Also, see table of Indian schedule for debt repayments to the United States and USSR, ibid., pp. 112–13.

44. Appendix B.

45. Goldman, *Soviet Foreign Aid,* p. 195.

46. Ibid., p. 72.

47. Ibid., p. 175.

48. *New York Times,* December 30, 1965, p. 5.

49. Ibid., November 24, 1966, p. 11

50. *Washington Post,* December 21, 1966, p. 1

51. *The Meaning of Multilateral Surveillance* (Paper delivered at the Seventh World Congress of the International Political Science Association, Brussels, Belgium, September 1967), p. 1.

52. Ibid., p. 20.

53. John K. Galbraith, "A Positive Approach to Economic Aid," *Foreign Affairs* 39, no. 3 (April 1961): 446.

54. Tansky, "Soviet Foreign Aid to the Less Developed Countries," p. 953.

55. Ibid., pp. 953–54.

56. Ibid., p. 970.

57. Kapranov, "The USSR and Industrial Development in the Newly Free States," p. 38.

58. These figures were derived from U.S., Agency for International Development, *Gross National Product, Growth Rates and Trend Data,* RC-W-138, March 31, 1967(cited hereafter as AID, RC-W-138); and Organization for Economic Cooperation and Development, Development Assistance Committee, *Development Assistance Efforts and Policies, 1966 Review,* 1966, p. 148.

59. Baldwin, *Foreign Aid and American Foreign Policy* (New York: Frederick A. Praeger, 1966), p. 26.

60. Ibid.

61. Efforts by John Pincus to calculate the real cost of foreign aid to the donor can be found in "The Cost of Foreign Aid," *Review of Economics and Statistics* 65, no. 4 (November 1963): 360–67; see also Goran Ohlin, *Foreign Aid Policies Reconsidered* (Paris: Organization for Economic Cooperation and Development, 1966), pp. 71–76. Compared to these approaches, the data presented in our discussion overstate the costs or burden of aid to the United States.

62. U.S., Congress, Senate, Committee on Foreign Relations, *Hearings, Foreign Assistance Act of 1968,* 90th Cong., 2d sess., 1968, p. 4.

63. Ibid., House Committee on Appropriations, *Hearings, Foreign Assistance and Related Agencies, Appropriations for 1969,* 90th Cong., 2d sess., pt. 2, 1968, pp. 381–82.

64. Jacob Kaplan, *The Challenge of Foreign Aid* (New York: Frederick A. Praeger, 1967), p. 193.

65. U.S., Congress, Senate Committee on Foreign Relations, *Hearings, Foreign Assistance, 1965,* 89th Cong., 1st sess., 1965, pp. 145–46.

66. Kaplan, *The Challenge of Foreign Aid,* p. 388.

67. Hans Heymann, "Soviet Foreign Aid as a Problem for U.S. Foreign Policy," *World Politics* 12, no. 4 (July 1960), p. 527.

68. See Harry G. Johnson, *Economic Policies Toward Less Developed Countries* (Washington, D.C.: Brookings Institution, 1967), pp. 84–94.

69. For precise data on nominal U.S. tariff rates vs. the effective rate of protection on various goods and categories of goods of importance to the LDCs, see ibid., pp. 98–102.

70. Ibid., p. 96.

71. *New York Times,* November 11, 1969, p. 1.

72. Frank M. Coffin, *Witness for Aid* (Boston: Houghton Mifflin Co., 1964), p. 48.

73. *New York Times,* August 26, 1967, p. 13.

74. U.S., Congress, House, Committee on Appropriations, *Hearings, Foreign Assistance and Related Agencies, Appropriations for 1966,* 89th Cong., 1st sess., 1965, p. 541. This 20 percent figure covers military and economic assistance. The average reduction in economic assistance over this period was 18 percent, while that for military aid was 22 percent.

75. David Truman, "The Domestic Politics of Foreign Aid," in "The New Look in Foreign Aid," ed. Thomas Peardon, *Proceedings of the Academy of Political Science* 27, no. 2 (January 1962): 64.

76. USSR GNP figures are taken from Stanley Cohn, "Soviet Growth Retardation: Trends in Resource Availability and Efficiency," in Joint Economic Committee, *New Directions,* 1966, p. 109. Category 16 exports to LDCs are from Appendix B. For a description of the method by which these calculations were made, see Appendix C.

77. Tansky, "Soviet Foreign Aid to the Less Developed Countries," p. 951.

78. See Appendix C.

79. The USSR population in 1964 was taken as 226 million for purposes of these calculations. U.S., Congress, Joint Economic Committee, *Annual Economic Indicators for the USSR,* 88th Cong., 2d sess., 1964, p. 218. Aid commitments and deliveries in 1964 from Appendix B. Data for 1964 are used in this analysis because it was the record year for Soviet aid commitments and affords the most generous estimates possible for assessing the Soviet aid burden.

80. U.S., Department of State, Bureau of Intelligence and Research, *The Communist Economic Offensive Through 1963,* RSB-43, 1954, p. 4.

81. Ibid.

82. For a typical article on aid as found in the Soviet press, see the piece by Arkhipov, First Vice-Chairman of the State Committee for Foreign Economic Relations, in *Pravda,* July 28, 1965, p. 5, trans. in *CDSP* 17, no. 30 (August 18, 1965): 22–23.

83. Nadia Derkach, *The Differences in Soviet Portrayal of Their Aid to Underdeveloped Countries in English and in Russian,* RAND, P-2853, January 1964, pp. 6–7. The Russian and English texts respectively are SSSR *i ekonomicheski slaborazvitye strany. Ekonomicheskoe sotrudnichestvo i pomoshch* [USSR

and Economically Underdeveloped Countries. Economic Cooperation and Assistance] (Moscow: Izdatelstvo sotsialno-ekonomicheskoi lituratury, 1963); and *Economic Cooperation Between the USSR and Underdeveloped Countries* (Moscow: Foreign Languages Publishing House, n.d.)

84. A. Smirnov, "Soviet Technical Assistance in the Construction of Plants Abroad," *Vneshnyaya torgovlya,* no. 9, 1959, trans. in *Problems of Economics* 2, no. 9 (January 1960): 56.

85. See G. Shabalina, "Druzhestvennoye sotrudnichestvo" [Friendly Cooperation], *Azia i Afrika segodnya,* no. 9, 1964, pp. 48–49; and Derkach, *Differences in Soviet Portrayal,* p. 8.

86. Milton Kovner, "Soviet Aid Strategy in the Developing Countries," *Orbis* 8, no. 3 (Fall 1964), p. 634.

87. Ibid., p. 633.

88. *Vneocherednoy XXI s'ezd KPSS* (Moscow, 1959), pt. 2, p. 240, cited by Kovner, ibid.

89. OECD, *Development Assistance* 1968, p. 266.

90. GNP figures derived from AID, RC-W-138. Aid shares from U.S., Congress, House, Committee on Foreign Affairs, *Hearings, Foreign Assistance Act of 1969,* 91st Cong., 1st sess., 1969, p. 99.

91. U.S., Congress, House, ibid.

92. Ibid. For a more thorough analysis of the problem of burden-sharing, see John Pincus, *Economic Aid and International Cost Sharing* (Baltimore: Johns Hopkins Press, 1965).

93. For example, see Frank M. Coffin, *Witness for Aid* (Boston: Houghton Mifflin Co., 1964), p. 194.

94. Edward S. Mason, *Foreign Aid and Foreign Policy* (New York: Harper & Row, 1964), p. 6.

95. U.S., Congress, Senate, Committee on Foreign Relations, *Hearings, Foreign Assistance, 1965,* 89th Cong., 1st sess., 1965, p. 584.

96. Eastern Europe, for purposes of this analysis, includes Bulgaria, Czechoslovakia, East Germany, Hungary, Poland, and Rumania.

97. The GNP of these six countries in 1964 was calculated to be $101.3 billion, in Maurice Ernst, "Postwar Economic Growth in Eastern Europe," in Joint Economic Committee, *New Directions,* p. 877. The GNP of the USSR in 1964 was calculated to be $293 billion, in Cohn, "Soviet Growth Retardation, p. 109.

98. U.S., Department of State, Bureau of Intelligence and Research, *The Communist Economic Offensive Through 1964,* RSB-65, 1965, p. ii. Soviet aid commitments for 1964 were $998 million.

99. Kovner, "Soviet Aid Strategy," p. 635.

100. Table 3, above.

101. Milton Kovner, "Communist China's Foreign Aid to Less Developed Countries," in U.S., Congress, Joint Economic Committee, *An Economic Profile of Mainland China,* 90th Cong., 1st sess., 1967, p. 613.

102. U.S., Department of State, Bureau of Intelligence and Research, *Communist Governments and Developing Nations: Aid and Trade in 1968,* RSE-65, 1969, pp. 2–3.

103. Goldman, *Soviet Foreign Aid,* p. 190.

104. Kovner, "Communist China's Foreign Aid," p. 614.

105. Dudley Seers, *Cuba: The Economic and Social Revolution* (Chapel Hill: University of North Carolina Press, 1964), p. 296.

106. Goldman, *Soviet Foreign Aid*, p. 139.

107. Ibid., p. 146.

108. Robert A. Scalapino, "Sino-Soviet Competition in Africa," *Foreign Affairs* 42, no. 4 (July 1964): 652.

109. *Peking Review*, no. 34, August 21, 1964, p. 16.

110. Kovner, "Communist China's Foreign Aid," p. 617.

111. The stance of the Chinese at this meeting as presented here is described by Kovner, "Soviet Aid Strategy," p. 637.

112. *Izvestia*, July 12, 1964, trans. in *CDSP* 16, no. 28 (August 5, 1964): 7–8.

113. Scalapino, "Sino-Soviet Competition," p. 642.

114. Ibid., pp. 650–51.

115. William T. Shinn, Jr., "The 'National Democratic State', A Communist Program for Less Developed Areas," *World Politics* 15, no. 3 (April 1963): 396.

116. Richard Lowenthal, "On 'National Democracy': Its Function in Communist Policy," *Survey*, no. 47 (April 1963), pp. 128–29.

117. The discussion which follows is based on a discussion of V. Kudryavtsev, "Dangerous Instigators," *Izvestia*, April 13, 1968, p. 5, trans. in *CDSP* 20, no. 15 (May 1, 1968): 27–28.

118. Thomas Schelling noted the role of Congress in enhancing U.S. bargaining positions vis-à-vis the LDCs in *The Strategy of Conflict* (New York: Oxford University Press, 1963), pp. 27–28.

Notes to Chapter 11

1. U.S., Congress, House, Committee on Foreign Affairs, *Hearings, Foreign Assistance Act of 1966*, 89th Cong., 2d sess., 1966, pp. 33–34.

2. U.S., Agency for International Development, *Proposed Economic Assistance Programs, FY 1967*, 1966, p. 106.

3. U.S., Congress, House, Committee on Foreign Affairs, *Hearings, Foreign Assistance Act of 1966*, 89th Cong., 2d sess., 1966, p. 123. For subsequent aid to these ends, see ibid., *Foreign Assistance Act of 1968*, 90th Cong., 2d sess., 1968, pp. 51 and 215.

4. See Marshall I. Goldman, *Soviet Foreign Aid* (New York: Frederick A. Praeger, 1967), pp. 168–71.

5. Ernst B. Haas, *Tangle of Hopes* (Englewood Cliffs, N.J.: Prentice-Hall, 1969), p. 252.

6. Philip Mosely, "Communist Policy and the Third World," *Review of Politics* 28, no. 2 (April 1966): 234.

7. *New York Times*, May 28, 1967, p. 12.

8. Ibid.

9. *New York Times*, June 14, 1968, p. 17.

10. Ibid.

11. *New York Times*, June 7, 1968, p. 2.

12. David Morison, "Soviet Policy Towards Africa," in *The Soviet Bloc, China, and Africa,* ed. S. Hamrell and C. Widstrand (London: Pall Mall Press, 1964), p. 34.

13. Herbert S. Dinerstein, "Moscow and the Third World," *Problems of Communism* 17, no. 1 (January–February 1968): 53.

14. Leo Tansky, *U.S. and U.S.S.R. Aid to Developing Countries: A Comparative Study of India, Turkey, and the U.A.R.* (New York: Frederick A. Praeger, 1967), p. 167.

15. Kenneth N. Waltz, *Foreign Policy and Democratic Politics* (Boston: Little, Brown and Co., 1967), p. 195.

Notes to Epilogue

1. *A Study of the Capacity of the United Nations Development System* [the Jackson Report] UN doc. DP/5, 1969; *Partners in Development* [the Pearson Report] (New York: Frederick A. Praeger, 1970); *U.S. Foreign Assistance in the 1970's: A New Approach* [the Peterson Report], Report to the President from the Task Force on International Development (Washington, D.C.: U.S. Government Printing Office, 1970).

2. *U.S. Foreign Assistance in the 1970's,* p. 4.

3. Ibid., p. 4 and pp. 26–28.

4. Ibid., p. 4 and pp. 29–30.

5. Ibid., p. 5 and pp. 34–36.

6. See *New York Times,* March 15, 1970, IV, p. 5.

7. *U.S. Foreign Assistance in the 1970's,* pp. 8–10.

8. Above, Chapters 5, 9, and 10.

Bibliographical Essay

‡ Two sets of literature have developed around Soviet and American aid efforts, with few attempts to build bridges between them. The major exceptions to this tendency of dealing with the two programs in isolation from one another is the excellent study by Leo Tansky, *U.S. and U.S.S.R. Aid to Developing Countries: A Comparative Study of India, Turkey and the U.A.R.* (New York, 1967). Tansky's work is essentially an economic analysis of Soviet and American aid to three countries—India, Turkey, and the UAR (Egypt). Henry Aubrey's *Coexistence: Economic Challenge and Response* (Washington, D.C., 1961) and Lucian Pye's article "Soviet and American Styles in Foreign Aid" (*Orbis* 4, no. 2: 159–73) should also be mentioned as useful comparative treatments of the two programs.

There are several useful sources for obtaining basic data on American economic assistance. The most comprehensive data for U.S. aid commitments by country, program, and year since 1946 are found in the series of special reports prepared annually by the Agency for International Development for the House Foreign Affairs Committee under the title *U.S. Overseas Loans and Grants and Assistance from International Organizations*. Data on actual deliveries of various types of aid can be obtained from the U.S. Department of Commerce series entitled *Foreign Grants and Credits by the United States Government*. More detailed data on the use of funds by AID are issued quarterly by that agency in its *Operations Reports*.

For more detailed information on various aspects of the American program, there are several invaluable sources. Among the publications of AID the most interesting, short discussion of its programming emphases is probably *Principles of Foreign Economic Assistance* (1963 and revised, 1965). Until fiscal year 1969 much useful information on aid program priorities could be found in AID's annual summary presentation to the

Congress, *Proposed Foreign Aid Program, FY——*. Since 1969, however, the format of this document has been changed and it is of relatively little use.

Two general purpose surveys of aid produced by the Legislative Reference Service of the Library of Congress are also informative—*U. S. Foreign Aid: The Purposes, Scope, Administration and Related Information* (1959) and *Some Important Issues in Foreign Aid* (1966).

The most interesting answers to the questions one would like to address to AID usually have to be dug out of congressional hearings on the aid program. As inefficient and as time-consuming as the process may be, one can obtain rich rewards if he is willing to go through the hearings on aid held each year by the Senate Committee on Foreign Relations, the Senate Appropriations Committee, the House Committee on Foreign Affairs, and the House Appropriations Committee. In 1957 an informative set of documents was produced by the Senate's Special Committee to Study the Foreign Aid Program entitled *The Foreign Aid Program: Compilation of Studies and Surveys*. This legislative evaluation of aid programs was paralleled by several major executive branch studies, the latest of which is the *Report to the President of the United States from the Committee to Strengthen the Security of the Free World* (the "Clay Report"), March 20, 1963.

The Development Assistance Committee of the Organization for Economic Cooperation and Development publishes an annual account of Western aid efforts under the title *Development Assistance Efforts and Policies*, in which the American program can be readily compared with those of other Western aid donors. Much useful information on aid trends, problems, and priorities can be found here.

There are numerous books on the subject of American aid, but only a few of the more important ones can be mentioned here. In terms of the nuts and bolts of the mechanisms through which financial resources are transferred from donor to recipient, Robert Asher's *Grants, Loans, and Local Currencies* (Washington, D.C., 1961) is unparalleled. The study by William Brown and Redvers Opie, *American Foreign Assistance* (Washington, D.C., 1953), still stands as the best history of early U.S. aid efforts.

The view of economic assistance by an AID official can be found in Jacob Kaplan's *The Challenge of Foreign Aid* (New York, 1967). David Baldwin has collected a series of selections in which the views of various U.S. officials in Congress and throughout the executive branch are given on an array of aid issues in *Foreign Aid and American Foreign Policy: A Documentary Analysis* (New York, 1966).

U.S. aid as an instrument of foreign policy has received much attention. Among the better volumes on this complex subject are George Liska's *The New Statecraft* (Chicago, 1960) and *Foreign Aid and Foreign Policy* (New York, 1964) by Edward S. Mason. The only book-length study confined to the domestic politics (really, domestic public opinion) of foreign aid is *The Politics of American Foreign Aid* (New York, 1967) by Michael Kent O'Leary. Several other volumes which offer penetrating analyses of the domestic and foreign politics of American economic assistance are David Baldwin's *Economic Development and American Foreign Policy, 1943–1962* (Chicago, 1966), John Montgomery's *The Politics of Foreign Aid* (New York, 1962), and Joan Nelson's *Aid, Influence, and Foreign Policy* (New York, 1968).

Two excellent studies of general U.S. foreign economic policies in terms of their efficacy in meeting the development needs of the less developed countries have been produced recently. Harry Johnson's *Economic Policies Toward Less Developed Countries* (Washington, D.C., 1967) and John Pincus' *Trade, Aid and Development* (New York, 1967) deal with the reluctance of the United States and the West to engage in meaningful trade reforms which would supplement developmental aid goals.

In addition to these and other books on the subject of American economic assistance to less developed countries, there are a host of articles too numerous to deal with here. A list of articles relevant to American aid efforts can be found in the bibliography of my doctoral dissertation, *American and Soviet Aid to Less Developed Countries: A Comparative Analysis* (University of Michigan, 1967).

The best data on Soviet economic assistance are available in Western and United Nations sources. I know of no Soviet source which offers meaningful comprehensive figures for aid commitments by country and/or by year. To compile a picture of Soviet aid from Soviet presentations, bits and pieces from various articles, books, and newspaper stories must be spliced together —but, due to gaps and ambiguities as to whether an announced credit is new or is part of a credit line negotiated in previous years, this approach is very unsatisfactory. Announcements of new aid agreements are frequently made in the Soviet press, but they do not regularly include information on the size of the package. Soviet aid deliveries, on the other hand, can be estimated from Category 16 exports (material and equipment for complete plants) to less developed countries. These figures are found in the series of annual trade statistics published by the USSR Ministry of Foreign Trade under the title *Vneshnyaya torgovlya Soyuza SSR za —— god* (Moscow, 1958–1968).

Data on Soviet aid commitments are given in a series of documents published by the Department of Economic and Social Affairs of the United Nations under the title *International Flow of Long-Term Capital and Official Donations*. But the most comprehensive figures and detailed information on Soviet economic assistance are found in U.S. government documents.

The best single source of data on Soviet aid is the series of research memoranda published each year by the U.S. Department of State's Bureau of Intelligence and Research. In recent years this document has been entitled *Communist Governments and Developing Nations: Aid and Trade in 196—*. Data are presented on new aid commitments by the USSR, East Europe, and China to all less developed countries. In addition, cumulative aid commitments are given for each recipient and there is a discussion of new thrusts in Soviet aid efforts from year to year.

Very informative pieces on Soviet aid are also found in several publications of the Joint Economic Committee of the U.S. Congress. See especially *Dimensions of Soviet Economic Power*, 1962; *New Directions in the Soviet Economy*, 1966; and the series of documents entitled *Annual Economic Indicators for the USSR*.

While not very large in comparison to the number of serious volumes on American aid efforts, there are quite a few book-length studies on Soviet economic assistance. The best single work is still Joseph Berliner's pace-setter in the field, *Soviet Economic Aid* (New York, 1958). Even though the book is dated and the conclusions are largely speculative because of the lack of data available at the time, the author addresses most of the interesting questions for which all of us have been seeking answers during the sixties. Other works of interest which give the Soviet aid picture as it was viewed by Western scholars in the late fifties are *Soviet Economic Warfare* (Washington, D.C., 1960) by Robert L. Allen, *Soviet Bloc Foreign Aid to the Underdeveloped Countries* (Hamburg, Germany, 1960) by Klaus Billerbeck, and Milton Kovner's *The Challenge of Coexistence* (Washington, D.C, 1961).

Two books have been published recently on Soviet economic assistance —B. R. Stokke's *Soviet and East European Trade and Aid in Africa* (New York, 1967) and *Soviet Foreign Aid* (New York, 1967) by Marshall Goldman. Goldman's book is particularly interesting because he has visited Soviet aid projects around the world. It is most valuable as an up-to-date data source which can be utilized to speak to the questions raised earlier by Berliner. Goldman also provides a bibliography of book-length Soviet works relating to USSR–LDC relations. Interesting translated Soviet books dealing with aid are *Economic Cooperation Between the USSR and Underdeveloped Countries* (Moscow, 1961) by V. Rimalov, A. M. Smirnov's *Mezhdunarodnye valyutnye i kreditnye otnosheniye SSSR* (Moscow, 1960) translated by the Joint Publications Research Service in October 1960, and *The USSR and Developing Countries* (about 1965).

The best single source on Soviet trade relationships with the less developed countries is *Communist Trade With Developing Countries: 1955–1965* (New York, 1966) by Carole Sawyer.

Space does not allow a comprehensive listing of articles by Soviet and Western scholars dealing with USSR economic assistance to the less developed countries. Such a list can be found in the bibliography of my dissertation cited above. It might be helpful to make a few general observations about Soviet sources of this nature, however. Most of the articles on aid in Russian for the domestic Soviet audience appear in the following journals: *Mirovaya ekonomika i mezhdunarodnye otnoshenia, Azia i Afrika segodnya, Voprosi ekonomiki, Ekonomicheskaya gazeta, Vneshnyaya torgovlya, Pravda,* and *Izvestia.* Several Western sources are available which provide English translations of many of the articles published in the journals listed above. These include the Joint Publications Research Service of the United States government, the *Current Digest of the Soviet Press, Problems of Economics,* the *American Review of Soviet and East European Foreign Trade,* and *MIZAN* which carefully follows internal Soviet debate on the evolution of policy toward less developed countries.

In addition to these translated materials, there are several periodicals published in English by the USSR which are useful—*International Affairs* (Moscow), *New Times, The World Marxist Review,* and *Foreign Trade.*

This essay has been confined to some of the data sources and interpretive works on Soviet and American economic assistance to less developed countries. No attempt has been made here to present studies dealing with closely related problems such as military assistance, general foreign policy orientations of the donors, economic and political development processes in recipient nations, or theories of political and economic development generated in the Soviet Union and America.

Index